Culture, Developmer ¬d Petroleum

The discovery, just forty years ago, of vast oil and gas reserves in the southwestern part of Norway, and more recently in the Arctic High North region, created an economic titan and posed a vast array of challenges for both the Norwegian government and the residents of this area. How to extract and transport all that oil and gas without despoiling the pristine environment? How to use this wealth in a socially responsible and sustainable way? How to prepare the rural High North citizens – traditionally fishermen and farmers – for a global, high-tech economy?

Adopting an original narrative approach to qualitative research, this book tells the stories of twenty-one individuals either living or having a genuine interest in the High North, from mayors and entrepreneurs to farmers and fishermen. Through these first-hand meetings, it constructs an ethnographic study that reveals how petroleum and development have impacted on the regional economy and culture.

This book will be of interest to all stakeholders in the oil-and-gas industry, and for students and scholars of organization studies, cultural and communication studies, environmental anthropology, natural resource management, and sustainable development.

Jan-Oddvar Sørnes is Associate Professor of Organizational Communication at the University of Nordland, Norway.

Larry D. Browning is Professor of Organizational Communication at the University of Texas and Adjunct Professor of Management at the University of Nordland, Norway.

Jan Terje Henriksen is Managing Director for Research and Patient Safety at Nordland Hospital Trust and Adjunct Professor at the University of Nordland, Norway.

Culture, Development and Petroleum

An ethnography of the High North

Jan-Oddvar Sørnes, Larry D. Browning
and Jan Terje Henriksen

Routledge
Taylor & Francis Group

LONDON AND NEW YORK

First published 2015 by Routledge

2 Park Square, Milton Park, Abingdon, Oxon OX14 4RN
711 Third Avenue, New York, NY 10017, USA

Routledge is an imprint of the Taylor & Francis Group, an informa business

First issued in paperback 2016

British Library Cataloguing-in-Publication Data
A catalogue record for this book is available from the British Library

Library of Congress Cataloging-in-Publication Data
Culture, development and petroleum : an ethnography of the high north / edited by Jan-Oddvar Sørnes, Larry D. Browning, Jan Terje Henriksen.
pages cm. -- (Routledge studies in environmental communication and media)
ISBN 978-1-138-77989-1 (hardback) -- ISBN 978-1-315-77097-0 (ebook)
1. Petroleum industry and trade--Social aspects--Norway, Northern. 2. Petroleum industry and trade--Environmental aspects--Norway, Northern. 3. Norway, Northern--Social conditions.
4. Norway, Northern--Environmental conditions. 5. Ethnology--Norway, Northern. I. Sørnes, Jan-Oddvar, editor of compilation. II. Browning, Larry D., editor of compilation. III. Henriksen, Jan Terje, editor of compilation.
HD9575.N62C85 2014
338.2'728094843--dc23
2014010960

ISBN 978-1-138-77989-1 (hbk)
ISBN 978-1-138-21027-1 (pbk)

Typeset in 10/12 Goudy by
Ocrvia Filmsetting Ltd, Stockport, Cheshire

Contents

PART VI
Mayors by surprise

Acknowledgments

This book grew out of four weeklong graduate seminars on High North culture, narrative, and data collection that were held in the Lofoten Islands and sponsored by the University of Nordland's Bodø Graduate School of Business. Three of its professors – Frank Lindberg, Frode Fjelldal-Soelberg, and Dorthe Eide – co-directed many of these workshops; they also helped select some of the stories for this book after coaching the students on how to focus them. These three professors proved indispensable, and we thank them for their unstinting support. We also thank Monica Brobakk, Head of the International Office at the University of Nordland, for administrating the fellowships, a job more demanding than it might sound. For two of our programs, we had the pleasure of staying at the lovely Nyvågar Robuhotell. Our special thanks go to Roger and Liv Tømmerås in the village of Henningsvær for hosting us at another lovely waterfront hotel, the Henningsvær Brygge.

Gaining access to sites for data collection is crucial for cultural fieldwork. Our very first project in the summer of 2009 had Brittany Peterson traveling from Bodø to southern Norway to conduct interviews with officials in Norway's prison system. Laila Lindberg kindly arranged those interviews and hosted Brittany as a weeklong houseguest while she collected data. We thank her for her hospitality. Thanks, also, to Ingunn H. Lysø, at the Royal Norwegian Air Force Academy, for hosting some of our fellows while on data collection in Trondheim. The twenty-one stories that followed that first project also enjoyed the help of several people offering to link researchers to noteworthy Norwegians. One such helper was Hege Christin Stenhammer, who provided contact information and acted as a liaison for more than one chapter in this book. Many thanks for that service, Hege.

Of course, the most indispensable of all were the nearly two dozen Norwegian individuals showcased in our stories who generously allowed us into their private and professional lives and who took the risk of having some stranger characterize them for public consumption. Thank you, one and all! We're sure our readers will enjoy meeting you as much as we enjoyed showcasing you.

John Trimble, Distinguished Teaching Professor Emeritus at the University of Texas, masterfully edited the entire manuscript, for which we are hugely grateful. He was ably assisted by Elizabeth Goins, who did double duty by also writing one of the chapters. This book would be much the poorer without their expert wordsmithing and sharpening skills.

In addition to the instrumental High North Fellowship Programme at Studies in the High North (SIU), which is funded by Norway's Ministry of Foreign Affairs, we enjoyed substantial funding support from Sparebank 1-Nord-Norge, Norway's eminent savings bank. We also received partial funding from The PETROSAM Project (Norwegian Research Council), Total E&P, BP Norway, Det Norske, North Energy, Statoil, Shell, Norwegian Oil and Gas Association, Nordland County Administration, and, last but certainly not least, the Bodø Graduate School of Business at the University of Nordland. Thank you, thank you for your generosity!

Our wives, Wencke, Victoria, and Hanne lovingly supported our work throughout the project. We can hardly thank them enough for bearing with us during the many, many months that were required for it.

Contributors

Arne O. Holm is special adviser at the High North Center of Business and Governance, University of Nordland, where he is editor in chief of HighNorthNews.com.

Ashley Barrett is an instructor at Baylor and a PhD candidate in Organizational Communication and Technology at the University of Texas at Austin. Her research focuses on how new technologies are being incorporated into, and utilized in, contemporary workplaces.

Brittany L. Peterson is an Assistant Professor in the School of Communication Studies at Ohio University. She conducts her research in prisons and in high-stakes volunteer organizations such as volunteer fire departments.

Caroline Sinclair is a PhD candidate in Organizational Communication in Communication Studies at the University of Texas at Austin. Her research focuses on the use of communication technology in global and distributed organizations.

Dawna Ballard (PhD, University of California, Santa Barbara, 2002) is an Associate Professor of Organizational Communication and Technology in the Department of Communication Studies at the University of Texas at Austin. She is interested in how our working lives shape our experience of time in multiple ways, both personally and professionally.

Elizabeth Goins (PhD, University of Texas at Austin, 2013) is a lecturer in the Department of Management in the McCombs School of Business and a post-doctoral fellow in the Department of Computer and Electrical Engineering, both at the University of Texas at Austin.

Frode Fjelldal-Soelberg (PhD, University of Nordland, 2010) is an Associate Professor in Marketing at Bodø Graduate School of Business at the University of Nordland. His research focus is on entrepreneurial marketing, tourism, and methodology.

Hindertje Hoarau-Heemstra is a PhD candidate at Bodø Graduate School of Business at the University of Nordland. Her research focuses on innovation and sustainable development of Nordic tourism businesses.

Jacob Ford is a PhD candidate in Organizational Communication and Technology in Communication Studies at the University of Texas at Austin. His research focuses on the social interaction of individuals in organizations with a particular interest in leader–member relationships.

Joseph Brentlinger is a PhD candidate in Communication Studies with a focus on Rhetoric and Language at the University of Texas at Austin. His research focuses on the public sphere, public memory, and the rhetoric of style.

Joseph McGlynn III is a PhD candidate in Communication Studies at the University of Texas at Austin. He researches the intersection of message design and persuasion in interpersonal and health communication contexts, focusing on the influence of linguistic cues on behavioral and cognitive processes.

Keri K. Stephens (PhD, University of Texas at Austin, 2005) is an Associate Professor in Organizational Communication and Technology at the University of Texas. Her research focuses on using redundancy and multiple communication technologies to examine multicommunicating in organizational meetings, health communication, crisis messages, emergency communication, and overload.

Krister Salamonsen is a PhD candidate at Bodø Graduate School of Business at the University of Nordland in the area of innovation and entrepreneurship. His research focuses on entrepreneurship and regional development, particularly related to oil-and- gas developments in the High North.

Leah LeFebvre is an Assistant Professor in the Department of Communication and Journalism at the University of Wyoming. Her research focuses on conflict in interpersonal communication among dating and marital relationships. In particular, she studies relationship turbulence, dissolution, and narratives using a variety of methodological approaches.

Madeline Maxwell (PhD, University of Arizona, 1980) is a Professor in the Department of Communication Studies in the College of Communication at the University of Texas at Austin, and is also Director of the UT Project on Conflict Resolution. Her research focuses on aspects of language and community.

Maegan Stephens is a PhD candidate at the University of Texas at Austin. Her research interests include political communication, news-gathering, and evolving communication technologies.

Matthew S. McGlone (PhD, Princeton University, 1994) is an Associate Professor of Communication Studies at the University of Texas at Austin. His research studies the role of social stereotypes in interpersonal interaction.

Matthew B. Morris is a PhD candidate in Communication Studies at the University of Texas at Austin. His research focuses on populist rhetoric, social movements, and the relationship between politics and the media.

Melissa Murphy is a PhD candidate in Organizational Communication and Technology at the University of Texas at Austin. Her research focuses on the move from offline to online communication, particularly as it relates to online communities and students.

Nadezda Nazarova (PhD, University of Nordland, 2013) is a researcher at The High North Center for Business and Governance at the University of Nordland and studies the logistical challenges related to oil-and-gas development in the Russian High North, particularly in the Barents region.

Nadina Ramcharitar is a PhD candidate in Organizational Communication and Technology at the University of Texas at Austin. Her research interests include action and agency, Health, Safety, and Environment (HSE) governance, compliance, and sustainable organizational practices.

Nicholas Merola (PhD, University of Texas at Austin, 2013) is a researcher who investigates the interplay between cognitive, social, and technological factors in computer-mediated communication with the goal of better understanding how computers can support human interaction. He has research published in books, journals, and conferences.

Preeti Mudliar (PhD, University of Texas at Austin, 2013) is a Research Scientist with Xerox Research Centre, India. Her research agenda centers on how technology access and use get embedded in the everyday life of underserved populations.

Ragnhild Johnson (PhD, University of Nordland, 2014) is a PhD candidate at Bodø Graduate School of Business at University of Nordland. Her research focuses on organizational structures related to project management in the context of oil-and-gas companies.

Stephanie Dailey (PhD, University of Texas at Austin, 2014) is an Assistant Professor in Communication Studies at Texas State University. She studies the processes of organizational identification and socialization, particularly through the use of technology and narratives in organizations.

Tom McVey is a PhD candidate in Organizational Communication in the Department of Communication Studies at the University of Texas at Austin. His research interests include the use of design thinking and design theory as a framework for examining organizational communication.

Editors

Jan-Oddvar Sørnes is an Associate Professor in Organizational Communication at Bodø Graduate School of Business at the University of Nordland. His research studies organizational communication and energy management with a particular focus on the High North and cross-cultural communication.

Larry Browning is the William P. Hobby Centennial Professor of Communication in the Department of Communication Studies at the University of Texas at Austin and an Adjunct Professor of Management at Bodø Graduate School of Business at the University of Nordland. His research areas include the role of lists and stories in organizations, information-communication technology, and narratives.

Jan Terje Henriksen is currently the Manager for Research and Patient Safety at Nordland Hospital Trust, and an Adjunct Professor at Bodø Graduate School of Business at the University of Nordland. His research focuses on applying structuration theories, communication theories, and innovation theories to the development of local industry when introduced to large-scale industrial development.

Prologue

People in the High North

Arne O. Holm, Bodø Graduate School of Business

From my living-room window in Bodø – every day, if I'm not traveling – I can watch tourists from around the world exploring my northern Norwegian coastal town. Day after day, they wander past with full bellies after enjoying the sumptuous lunch on the Hurtigruten coastal steamer. It's one of many cruise and freight ships docked not a ten-minute walk from my home; the Hurtigruten travels through Bodø on its journey from the southwest city of Bergen to the northeasterly Kirkenes, close to the Russian border.

In their eagerness to set foot on solid ground after a few turbulent hours on the open seas, the passengers are unsuspectingly hit by the Arctic chill and ice-cold winds threatening to tear apart their expensive handbags and coats. This arrival is not unusual for tourists visiting our region; the land invites experiences both brutally hostile and intensely beautiful.

The visitors negotiate their footing and stride during brief windows of reprieve from the weather, feeling a certain sense of robust satisfaction from mastering the harsh conditions in northern Norway's second largest city. Marching forward with purpose, they wander toward the city center in search of shelter, but their hopes will be dashed. On days like this, in a city sitting above the Arctic Circle, not even the rows of homes, shops, and offices can offer refuge.

The wind keeps the tourists' eyes firmly affixed on the asphalt like some kind of cruel joke by the weather gods; the very nature they have come so far to experience keeps them from seeing their beautiful surroundings. Or perhaps it is that winter storms come at a time of the year in the North when the light is at its weakest.

Many who visit my city share this experience. But unlike the hungry industrial investors looking for petroleum or minerals, tourists are more unassuming about how little they know about the people who call this place home, this place called the "High North."

Eight countries border the Arctic Ocean in a geopolitical area that has attracted formidable international attention over the past decade. Eight countries share the High North region and, with it, share a climatic fate.

At first, this region was symbolic of full-alert national security, East meets West. During the Cold War, the High North was ruled by diplomatic agreements and military truces. Now, economic interests and energy security policies, especially those of Norway, Russia, and Canada, rule this resource-rich region.

These new negotiations and processes are different from the Cold War, but no less complex. Where previous military alliances focused on the finer points of defense, today's investment strategies are based on international capital. This draws new nations into the developments, and the distance between those who extract the resources and those who live where resources will be extracted increases.

Let it be known to the readers of this book: the resources of the North are rich and abundant.

In a resource-starved world, the Northern seas are the world's breadbasket. The seafood industry is economically sustainable, the result of circumspect and diligent international management. The energy industry provides a potential solution to the puzzle of depleting global hydrocarbon resources. The mineral industry has grown from fueling crude manufacturing to fueling our cell phones and tablets.

These resources are harvested far away from the fuel tanks and dinner tables where they eventually end up.

Adding more complexity to this scenario, Arctic Ocean shipping traffic is increasing, the Northern aerospace technology industry is growing, tourism is becoming a realistic income source, and the crisis-preparedness industry – though still nascent – is promising.

Not only will most of these resources be transported and used somewhere else, but they are available in other places in the world. And thus we come closer to the core of this anthology.

The High North is an international project, a diverse organization of people with shared common interests and geography. Without knowledge of these people – their history, livelihoods, politics, and painstakingly built knowledge-based institutions – the High North could go horribly wrong.

This collection explores those who live in this region and the potential for the High North as a gateway toward new understandings, as a declaration of solidarity across national boundaries. But as in the rest of the world, the High North, despite its economic importance, has a limited common public sphere.

It's proof of how little we know about each other, and how others know even less about us.

But how can we learn more about the people when international media coverage focuses on initial public offerings and earning surpluses? Where the High North is defined by profits disappearing into giant corporate bellies, visible only in last year's earnings statements?

The real story is not about a mine eating its way into the rocks of the Stjernøy fjord in Finnmark, one of 250 owned by an international company operating in more than forty countries. No, the real story is about the Finnmark people who live and work in the mine.

When increased oil activity brings doubling or tripling housing prices in northern Norwegian communities, the costs don't mean much to companies exporting those resources to southern Europe. But these costs mean the world to the people who survive by working on the fringes of civilization.

Similarly, weakening Chinese economic growth not only has implications for Chinese workers in Chinese factories, but also for **High North** industries.

A breakthrough in climate talks, or a financial breakthrough for energy conservation, will instantly create geopolitical consequences, as well as the consequences for the societies slowly moving from a fish- to an oil-based economy.

The High North is like an industrial boom town; investments in the region invite both substantial profits and substantial risks, creating an international melting pot of modern adventurers. These investments depend on developing advanced-level technologies capable of operating under often-extreme weather conditions. In this way, the High North is financing both independent states and global future generations.

The High North is also a research hub, with an endless variety of seminars, conferences, and giant projects. There are projects on Arctic ice, projects on Arctic waters, projects on Arctic animals, and projects on Arctic lands. Knowledge acquisition from these projects will be crucial to the world's understanding of climate change. In this way, the High North is a meeting place for satisfying scientific ambitions and national interests.

But first and foremost, the High North is about its people, something we tend to forget.

I spend a lot of time at conferences, seminars, and meetings discussing the challenges of the High North for many countries – conversations with Canada, Russia, Iceland, the Faroe Islands, Greenland, Sweden, Finland, and, of course, Norway. Except that many of these conversations are monologues by men, monologues by industrialists and politicians.

I have also heard from many scientists at these conferences – experts on the weather, or geologists discussing the wealth lying deep within the mountains or underneath the seabed. But rarely have I heard from experts on regional business communities and democratic political systems. This knowledge – of the people living and working here, of the commercial and political implications of High North development for them – is lacking.

Often people confuse Antarctica with the Arctic, as if the systems were comparable on any level. Their amazement upon learning that humans – not penguins – live in the High North is a caricatured form of such confusion. But there are serious consequences when political institutions or international corporations try to transfer Antarctic agreements to the Arctic.

In this complex picture of northern resurgence, the research and science of communication play a crucial role. And in this book, different people with different positions and perspectives are given a chance to tell their stories. Individually and collectively, these stories help create a more accurate picture of the High North. Between the two covers of this anthology, we read of the High North we cannot ignore: the people.

Together these people, no matter how different, face similar challenges and uncertainties about the future. Just a few years ago, no self-respecting scientist would have predicted development on a scale of what is now happening in the High North. Recent chapters of northern Norway's history told stories of struggling urbanization and declining populations. But today the situation is quite different. The population is actually growing in the three northernmost counties. And many people actually commute into the region daily. People from all over the world flock to the Arctic, to feed a growing need for diverse industrial expertise and manpower.

The population growth in the region's larger cities is especially consistent, and with it come technological modernization and infrastructure improvement to surrounding areas. In turn, regional political systems become more complex and demanding. Regional universities expand the diversity of both research efforts and student bodies. Regional culture becomes more cosmopolitan. And all together, more people are working, commuting, and reproducing in the North.

But as the pace of Northern development accelerates, fresh challenges arise.

Indigenous industries compete with new industries. Labor and ownership conflicts sharpen. Sea traffic and pollution increase. Safety and preparedness requirements intensify.

The battle to reduce greenhouse gas emissions collides with the needs for expansion. Most of the headquarters of companies operating in the North are far, far away and still contribute only modestly to the local value creation, while cultural differences between existing businesses and "outsider" ones have a long way to go before they can be perceived as equals.

As you begin to read the book, keep this thought in mind: Norway's national goal – a nobly democratic one – is to combine energy companies, local communities, and policy officials in a cooperative communication group that makes room for each other's voices. The places of potential conflict where integration proves especially challenging are many – present–future, job–family, ecology–petroleum production, efficiency–fairness, and freedom–security, to name a few. Such joint consideration of these issues that could easily cause proponents into polar-opposite positions assumes, and indeed proves, that having information from all the points of view tends to moderate the views of decision-makers and causes them to be more considerate of the others on a given issue. These twenty-one book chapters show that Norwegians face the same problem the rest of us do: how to have one's own preferences met while acknowledging those of others.

The way forward depends on people; only dialogue can pave the path toward future High North development. By giving voice to different people – with different perspectives and first-hand knowledge of what Arctic life is really like – this book takes a step in the right direction, a step toward dialogue between the High North and the rest of the world.

1 Introduction

*Jan-Oddvar Sørnes, Larry D. Browning,
and Jan Terje Henriksen*

In 2006, the Norwegian government called for strengthening the knowledge infrastructure of the High North, a region it designated as the nation's top strategic priority. "Knowledge is at the core of our High North policy," it said, and is closely linked to environmental management, utilization of resources, and value creation (Ministry of Foreign Affairs, Norway, *The High North – Visions and Strategies*, 2011, p. 14).

This book aims to help answer that call.

Before explaining how, though, let us take a moment to define and situate the area.

The "High North," an elastic term adopted into popular Norwegian usage during the last decade or so as an English synonym for *nordområdene*,[1] refers somewhat vaguely to the huge land-and-sea area above the Arctic Circle that is shared by Norway and its eight neighbors: Sweden, Denmark (Greenland), Finland, Russia, Iceland, Canada, and the U.S. (Skagestad, 2010) According to the Convention on the Law of the Sea, all coastal States automatically have a continental shelf that extends 200 nautical miles from the coastline. But many countries, including Norway, have continental shelves that extend even further. So while Norway ranks as only the 70th largest country (323,779 km²) in total main land mass (excluding the islands of Svalbard and Jan Mayen), its exclusive economic zone (EEZ), including the islands of Svalbard and Jan Mayen, together with the continental shelf, totals 2,039,951 km² (Statistics Norway, 2013), making it equal in total area to the 15th largest country in the world. And a good chunk of Norway's mainland (Nordland, Troms, and Finnmark counties) – nearly one-third – lies in its High North region, populated with less than 10 percent of the country's 5 million people.

Despite its size, until recently the region was largely a forgotten backwater. But with the discovery of its apparently vast oil-and-gas reserves in the late 1960s, it suddenly became vitally important, both economically and politically. Its prospects were confirmed, in 2009, by a United States Geological Survey, which concluded that about 25 percent of the world's undiscovered gas and 13 percent of the world's undiscovered oil may be found in the High North, mostly offshore under less than 500 meters of water (Gautier et al., 2009).

Norway has been remarkably forward-thinking since the advent of the oil boom in managing the nation's resources. Much of its program has involved saving, not spending. For example, as of February 10, 2014, its Government Pension Fund was valued at NOK 5038 trillion ($825 billion), making it the world's largest fund. Thus, petroleum activity has been crucial for Norway's financial growth and its welfare state, representing about 25 percent of the nation's total value creation. The High North is vital to maintaining production and income for Norway (Ministry of Petroleum and Energy and the Norwegian Petroleum Directorate, *Facts 2012 – The Norwegian petroleum sector*).

When these forecasts for petroleum resources are coupled with the world's ever-growing thirst for energy, it's easy to see why the High North is Norway's top foreign-policy priority. The government's High North strategy reflects this and lays out priorities such as:

- To be at the forefront of international efforts to develop knowledge in and about the High North. "Knowledge creation is the center of the government's High North policy," said Jens Stoltenberg, former prime minister of Norway. The current prime minster, Erna Solberg, has reiterated this goal.
- To be the best steward of the environment and natural resources in the High North.
- To provide a suitable framework for further development of petroleum activities in the Barents Sea, and to seek to ensure that these activities boost competence in Norway in general and in North Norway in particular, and to foster local and regional business development.
- To further develop people-to-people cooperation in the High North.

Its bountiful oil-and-gas resources have allowed Norway to direct its strategy toward a number of important issues. It has allowed the country to ask, for example: What is our role in the world? How can we be a good global citizen? How do we educate our people for future generations? The answers to these questions are organized around Norway's four foreign policy priorities.

This book promotes these priorities. It is a research initiative fostering fresh knowledge; it employs academic partnerships; it features international cooperation (scholars from six countries); and two of the three editors of the book are Norwegian university faculty versed in Norwegian traditional values.

The emphasis on knowledge is at the core here, as it is a prerequisite for maintaining Norway's wealth and welfare system. The national goal is an aggressive one: it aims for Norway to be the leading knowledge source in the region, doing so by fraternally partnering with other progressive countries and exploiting their expertise. It is also only natural that those who live and work in the High North take the lead in building and communicating this expertise.

The present book is a collection of twenty-one ethnographic, real-life stories that help illuminate the social, economic, and cultural climate of Norway's High North in the first decade of the twenty-first century. They primarily focus on the problems and opportunities that exist there stemming from the oil-and-gas boom, now in its fifth decade. Our aim is to cast a human light on this time of change by telling stories of individuals who personify what is taking place in the region.

The opportunity to write this book arose from a program supported by the Norwegian government. A special feature of the book is the involvement of visiting scholars from the Department of Communication Studies at the University of Texas. They contributed sixteen of its twenty-one chapters. Their extensive participation in the project was made possible by a series of Ethnographic Research Fellowships offered during 2009–2013 by the Norwegian Government's Ministry of Foreign Affairs and the University of Nordland to University of Texas faculty and graduate students.

These Texas scholars joined forces with others from the Bodø Graduate School of Business at the University of Nordland. All of them got to choose their own topics in consultation with faculty from Bodø at an annual week-long workshop on qualitative research in Norway – locally known as "Qualitative Camp."™

Though all of our authors are in either the Business or Communication programs of their respective universities, they hail from six countries (Norway, Russia, the U.S., the Netherlands, India, Trinidad) and boast equally diverse educational backgrounds (psychology, marketing, tourism, management, communication, rhetoric, sustainability, energy), which adds to the book's rich perspective. With this mix of Business and Communication students and faculty as contributors, we address an array of cultural and developmental issues in the High North, focusing on topics such as economic development, environmental concerns, personal and professional growth, family relations, work–life balance, and other quality-of-life topics relevant to the region.

What is the theme of this book?

This research project arose from a comment made by Norway's former Minister of Foreign Affairs, Jonas Gahr Støre, when he spoke at the University of Nordland in March 2008. He said, "Bodø University College (now the University of Nordland) represents the philosophical center of the High North Strategy, with its focus on knowledge generation in collaboration with other nations." We took that to mean that the development of the High North represents an educational challenge as well as an economic opportunity. Stated another way, while the opportunity is fueled by financial gains derived from nonrenewable resources, a proper valuation of the High North necessarily includes a wider consideration of that area, and the larger country of Norway, in a time of change. We intend for these ethnographies to enhance that consideration.

The historical background

Norwegian society has changed profoundly since petroleum was found in the harsh environment off the southwestern coast of Norway in 1969. Norway is now considered a world-class example for resource use, which sets it apart from many petroleum-producing nations. Thus far, it has successfully avoided many of the political and economic problems common to nations blessed with abundant, nonrenewable resources. One such problem is having the rewards swept up by a few elites, while the average citizens not only lose their traditional way of life, but fail to develop the new skills that a modern petroleum economy requires.

How, then, has Norway avoided such problems? Chiefly, by investing democratically in its people.

We contend that Norway's successful petroleum evolution is no accident. While all of our stories portray individuals in contemporary Norway, the foundation for their stories and their lives is actually centuries old. Distinct from many other western countries, Norway has never had a significant aristocracy. From 1536 to 1905, Norway was essentially a territory of either Demark or Sweden. It did not become an independent country until 1905, and even then it was a rural country that depended on farming and fishing, especially in the High North where the winters are long and dark and even summer days can be chilly. Given those circumstances, the coming of independence in 1905 was hardly noticed. Life's challenges remained the same: men were the breadwinners and women lived a domestic, subordinate life. In the High North, farming and fishing remained the chief sources of income, and until the advent of closed-deck fishing vessels in the early 1900s, nearly half of all the fishermen perished at work from falling overboard into the frigid seas (i.e., died on the job). Industry restructuring and declining resources have had a negative impact on both registered fishing vessels and men. Since 1950 the number of officially registered fishermen has dwindled from 60,000 to around 10,000 today. The stories that our ethnographers tell reflect this radical change from fishing and farming to a more modern work life. In fact, many of our stories are about professional and entrepreneurial women and men working in jobs that did not even exist fifty years ago.

Method

Our template for these essays is Jon Franklin's *Writing for Story* (1986), a book that promotes a specific method for locating, and then writing up, a story. Franklin's scheme calls for the author to (1) identify a significant problem or difficulty that the protagonist is facing, (2) explain why that problem is momentous, and (3) convey why the reader would be interested in it. This character-in-action formula is written into these ethnographies of the High North of Norway to give a sense of the environment and the time in which these stories take place.

Following Franklin's strategy, we challenged our writers to draw the reader into a compelling story instead of showing off their expertise on the subject with a slew of scholarly references. For example, Dr. Matthew McGlone, the author of chapter 19, does research at the University of Texas at Austin on the professional development of female scientists and engineers. He was eager to collect data in Norway because the country has focused on educating women in those fields and making work–home life commitments seamless for them. McGlone is steeped in the literature on why women do or do not become professionals and what their sense of satisfaction is in the workplace. Yet, in the story he tells, he simply relies on an extended – and very revealing – conversation he had with an immigrant professional woman. One can readily infer his expertise from his storytelling, so nothing is lost from his having dispensed with the typical academic formalities of accreditation.

It is not the goal of this research team to present a rational and linear success story. Nor do we draw conclusions about Norway and Norwegian culture based on a single actor's actions and/or perceptions. Even this collection of twenty-one stories doesn't automatically represent the whole of the High North; telling another twenty-one stories could have easily showcased different people and professions.

Focusing on cultural integration naturally creates a requirement to look at all the factors, large and small, that support or undermine the cooperation among stakeholders in the High North. As a result, we examine how both big things, such as safety procedures on drilling platforms (chapter 9), and little things, such as a discussion in a local pub (chapter 17), make themselves known. We undertake a weaving together of pieces of the local cultural story of the High North. Given that these are cultural interpretations, the conclusions that can be drawn from them are necessarily indirect. There is no measure, no metric, for a subjective quality. Our stories are a collection of individual representations; they are scattered rather than unitary.

We wanted our storytellers to show, not tell. We asked them to demonstrate their depth of knowledge indirectly and with some sense of writing nuance. Rather than showing their expertise on the topic, we wanted them to show *prima facie* – at the first glance – what each story is about and why the reader might pursue it.

We have consciously emphasized storytelling over traditional referencing techniques here. Barbara Czarniawska, in her book *A Narrative Approach to Organizational Studies* (1998), puts a sharp point on this topic: "Because all narratives are grounded in chronology, the sure way of killing a potential story is ahistorical referencing." Referencing is usually accomplished by citing, either in the text or in a footnote, the books and articles used to buttress any given data set. The focus, with such a procedure, is on the theory rather than the character, a practice justified by the supposed disciplinary value it carries – that is, to know the theories and their authors is to know a field, and to know a field merits one's membership in the scholarly community. But, in our case, we are less concerned with the academic community and more with the common reader.

A narrative is a collection of people involved in some action that is not only marked by a beginning, middle, and end but that also can be assessed for its moral effect (right vs. wrong) when the story has reached its close. The story can be as policy-driven and grand as Norway's goal of promoting an entrepreneurial culture (chapter 11), or as local as the demands of a boss bent on extracting the maximum administrative work from a subordinate (chapter 16). Or it can be as natural and familiar as the story of a single fisherman who makes his living on a fishing boat and longs for more shore leave (chapter 17). These individuals, and others of equal interest, are described below in the chapter headings for the book.

Organization of the book chapters

Introduction and prologue

Prior to chapter 1 is a Prologue offered by Arne O. Holm titled *People in the High North*.

Part I: Passion before cash

The stories in Part I are all examples of how some idea, and not the financial rewards that might come from the idea, explains the actions of the story's protagonist. And while the first story in this section, *A Daredevil's Passion*, chapter 2, is about a person's entrepreneurial achievement, even this tale can be explained by the excitement the person has for his zany idea. *The Daughter Takes a Farm* story, chapter 3, is intriguing because it upends a Norwegian rural tradition – the tradition where the eldest son inherits the family farm while his siblings are left to fend for themselves. In our story, the eldest son has moved off to Oslo and became a high-tech player; he has no interest in returning to the farm or even having much to do with it. His sister, in contrast, decides to curtail her urban life and take over the farm on her own. The passion in this story is her joy of living in a natural environment and her reason for returning home. The counseling story, *Reindeers and Teepees*, told in chapter 4, tells of two women moving to the country to begin a recovery program for special-needs children. At the heart of their program is a petting zoo designed to connect the children with a natural and welcoming environment. *First Came Love, Then Came Chocolate*, chapter 5, provides an easy path to passion. A woman visiting a fishing island stumbles onto two things that make her happy: a business and a man.

Part II: Pushing for change in a foreign business culture

Here our stories help to illustrate issues involving trade, communication, and ecology between Norway and its northern neighbors, especially Russia. Chapter 6, *A Captain and His Way through the Ice*, is about a Russian sea captain and his career on a nuclear ice-breaker on the Northern Sea Route. His story is political, including what happened in the High North of Russia during the breakup of the Soviet Union, and the bureaucratic, legal agreement on who has the rights to what portion of the Barents Sea, which intersects the Northern Sea Route. Chapter 7, *One Ocean*, details the efforts, first promoted by Canada, to get countries with strong fishing traditions to practice good ecology while exploring petroleum resources.

Part III: Risking it

The "Risking it" section contains two stories. In chapter 8, *A Local Fire Hero*, the risk is clear-cut: a person finds himself rushing out of a pub and running into a nearby burning building to rescue a family, including a six-month-old baby.

This story gives a glimpse into Norwegian culture because it illustrates how one Norwegian instinctively responded to an emergency and informs us about blame, risk, disruption, and how this person carefully avoided any interpretation of himself as a hero, seeing as it would violate the requirement for modesty toward such incidents. *Keeping Law and Order*, chapter 9, is more institutional and subtle. It takes us aboard a danger-ridden offshore oil platform and shows us a safety administrator trying to bring the risk-prone and risk-averse behavior of her co-workers toward a sensible middle ground.

Part IV: *Fighting for what you believe in*

Cultural interpretations of Norway usually emphasize how community concerns trump expressions of individualism (Sørnes, 2004). The five stories in Part IV offer fresh perspectives on this familiar topic. All the stories in this section tell of the independence that one could more easily imagine from a more individualistic culture, such as that of the United States. In all these stories, the protagonists have some issue or moment where they stand out, and where they don't identify with the group that made the achievement, and where they make themselves the prime actor in the story they tell. In chapter 10, *Renegade Hero*, the environmentalist is so individualistic that others worry he is acting in his own behalf rather than for the political issues he purportedly supports. The entrepreneur we meet in chapter 11, *Easy Money*, faces the risk of not making his payroll while advancing new business ventures. What could be more isolated and individualistic than the story of *The Whistle-Blower* in chapter 12? Here a man risks both his salary and his very career to stand up, alone, for what he thinks is right and just. The *Lo–Ve Is Complicated* for Steinar ethnography in chapter 13 shows the tension within a person who's trying to create a small tourism business while simultaneously working with environmental activists to protect the very natural culture he plans to commercialize. Chapter 14, *The Progress Party*, shows how members of a small conservative political party resist the welfare state that tends to focus on the greater good for the most people.

Part V: *The dark side of Norway*

These next five stories are evidence that our ethnographies do not sugarcoat or idealize our analysis of Northern Norway. In Norwegian culture, some people commit crimes and go to jail, even if the Norwegian penal system is more humanitarian than the United States (chapter 15, *Norwegian vs. U.S. Prisons*). One person has a super-demanding job that ensures that any time she frees up for herself is quickly uncovered by a boss and filled in with still more administrative assignments (chapter 16, *The Norwegian Workplace Hustle*). *It Is Hard to be Suave* (chapter 17) redirects any romantic image we might have about fishing for a living and reveals, through a conversation in a pub, the loneliness, job dissatisfaction, and doubt a young fisherman has for his life. *Norway Under Attack* (chapter 18) builds on the mere snippet of data its two authors obtained near the end of their research stay to reveal what one young man did on that horrendous day of July 22, 2011 at Utøya Island to protect himself from the terrorist's attacks and let his family know that he was okay – just by sending a text message via his cellphone. The final story in this section, *Doubly Disadvantaged* (chapter 19), shows that no matter how much government policy tries to achieve opportunity for both women and immigrants, they often can still be left on the outside looking in.

Part VI: *Mayors by surprise*

These last three stories tell how mayors of three Norwegian towns got their positions. In the first one, *The Indian Bride* (chapter 20), an immigrant from India who had lived for years on an island community in Norway and who had briefly left that community to revisit her homeland discovers that in her absence her peers have elected her to be their deputy mayor, much to her surprise and delight. The second story, *First Female Mayor* (chapter 21), introduces us to the mayor of Hammerfest, the northernmost sizable city in Norway, the site of much opportunity and drastic change over the last decade propelled by new petroleum projects. The author relates how that mayor found herself plopped into the job when her boss took another position and how she fared in office. The final story in this section, *The Petroleum Renaissance* (chapter 22), shows how a mayoral leader's sense of success in his position is affected by the fortunes of petroleum exploitation and how his community adjusts to these changes.

In the epilogue, *Characters Solve the Complication: Writing about Culture*, by Madeline Maxwell, an ethnographer completes an analysis of our book's effort by interviewing the authors of the twenty-one chapters and then compares their intent with the results.

Lessons learned from the book

The first lesson learned is about access. One of the early assumptions of organizational research is that you can tell a lot about a culture by how open it is to outsiders (Bowers, 1973). The ethnographers who wrote these stories studied a culture that, they soon happily discovered, was open to them. Norwegians were quick to schedule an interview, willing to make extra time, willing to talk openly about their jobs and their lives, and then willing to recommend still another person for us to interview. Vacation scheduling occasionally offset their availability, but people appeared happy to share their lives with us because they believed in what Norwegian society was doing and in the specific goals and tactics used in pursuit of societal goals. Some cynics might attribute their cooperation to the homogeneous nature of Norwegian society. Cynics might also say that the participants in our study may have agreed to observation and interviews by American students chiefly out of curiosity about Americans – *who are these people and what are they doing?* But, in general, we think our interviewees honestly do believe in the direction of their culture and welcomed the opportunity to say so.

The second lesson learned is about adaptability and improvisation – about adjusting to what the characters of our stories faced and how they worked out the details of their lives to do the work they wanted to do. This especially holds true for the Norwegian women portrayed here. While we didn't set out to have a gendered view, most of our stories are about women and indeed were also written by women.[2] While the actual number of managerial roles shows men to be primarily in charge in the High North, the number of women in leadership roles in the High North is increasing. (Which is not surprising, as Norway has the national policy goal of increasing the percentage of women in leadership roles in board positions to 40 percent.) In truth, though, we have probably "over sampled" women's stories in our representation of the High North culture. In these ethnographies, we tell not so much about how they lead – although there is some of that – but mainly about the lives they led prior to being in their present roles, especially how they "fell" into their present position by surprise, or not by their choice, or how they ultimately adjusted to the demands of the position they found themselves in. While we hesitate to call them "best practices," there is much to admire about these women's stories. They display a kind of personal adaptability – taking advantage of an opportunity when the time came – that we could all learn from.

The third lesson learned from these ethnographies is about the acceptance of public and private administrative society in Norway, especially as we compare it with American private companies and government. Because Norway has a national goal of transparency, which is represented primarily through a records-and-reporting system and public access to it, the people in these stories have a remarkable trust in, and respect for, bureaucracy and their leaders, and a larger presumption of agreement over Norway's national goals. If there is a governmental requirement to fill out a form or to adhere to a policy, Norwegians normally comply because they presume there is a good reason for it. These examples of consensus and acceptance are far rarer in the United States, where a majority of our chapter writers are in graduate school and where trust in institutions is at an all-time low.

References

Bowers, D. G. (1973). OD techniques and their results in 23 organizations: The Michigan ICL study. *Journal of Applied Behavioral Science*, 9, 21–43.

Czarniawska, B. (1998). *A narrative approach to organization studies*. Thousand Oaks, CA: Sage Publications.

Franklin, J. (1986). *Writing for story. Craft secrets of dramatic nonfiction by a two-time Pulitzer Prize winner*. New York: Atheneum.

Gautier, D. L., Bird, K. J., Charpentier, R. R., Grantz, A., Houseknecht, D. W., Klett, T. R., Moore, T. E., Wandrey, C. J. (2009). Assessment of undiscovered oil and gas in the Arctic. *Science*, 324(5931), 1175–1179.

Ministry of Petroleum and Energy and the Norwegian Petroleum Directorate (2012). *Facts 2012 – The Norwegian petroleum sector*. Available from: http://www.npd.no/en/Publications/Facts/Facts-2012/

Norwegian Ministry of Foreign Affairs (2006). *The Norwegian Government's High North Strategy.* Available from: http://www.regjeringen.no/upload/UD/Vedlegg/strategien.pdf

Norwegian Ministry of Foreign Affairs (2011). *The High North – visions and strategies.* White paper. Available from: http://www.regjeringen.no/en/dep/ud/campaigns/the-high-north/high_north_visions_strategies.html?id=663391

Skagestad, Odd. G. (2010). *The 'High North': An elastic concept in Norwegian Arctic policy.* FNI Report 10. Available from: http://www.geopoliticsnorth.org/index.php?option=com_content&view=article&id=1%3Aan&limitstart=1

Sørnes, J.-O. (2004). *Information and communication technologies in practice – a study of advanced users in Norway and the United States.* Doctoral dissertation, Norwegian University of Science and Technology.

Statistics Norway (2013). *Statistical yearbook of Norway 2013.* Oslo: Statistics Norway. Available from: http://www.ssb.no/en/befolkning/artikler-og-publikasjoner/_attachment/146776?_ts=143c3b051c8

Notes

1 "The High North is a broad concept both geographically and politically. In geographical terms, it covers the sea and land, including islands and archipelagos, stretching northwards from the southern boundary of Nordland County in Norway and eastwards from the Greenland Sea to the Barents Sea and the Pechora Sea. In political terms, it includes the administrative entities in Norway, Sweden, Finland, and Russia that are part of the Barents Cooperation. Furthermore, Norway's High North policy overlaps with the Nordic cooperation, our relations with the US and Canada through the Arctic Council, and our relations with the EU through the Northern Dimension" (*The Norwegian Government's High North Strategy*, 2006).

Northern Norway, consisting of three counties (Nordland, Troms, and Finnmark) represents 112,946 km2, or about 34.9 percent of Norway's mainland. The population is fairly low, and represents only 9.5 percent (479,000) of Norway's total population.

2 Statistics: Eleven of our twenty-one stories are about women, and thirteen were written by women.

Part I

Passion before cash

2   A daredevil's passion

An entrepreneur shares his secrets

Ragnhild Johnson, Bodø Graduate School of Business

Hans Nordgård
Photograph by Geir Are Jensen, BodøNu

In 2001, a distraught Hans Nordgård, then in his late 50s, urgently rang the doorbell at the emergency entrance of a Brussels hospital. He stood clutching a container loaded with Arctic king crabs he'd caught back home in northern Norway and had brought to Belgium to market to its upscale restaurants. But now his precious crabs were barely alive. The container, formerly well sealed to preserve its special life-supporting mix of oxygen and other gasses, had gotten prematurely opened.

Doctors and nurses, hearing him explain his emergency, stared at the rumpled Hans in disbelief. "This is a hospital!" one of them shouted.

But for Hans, it was indeed a life-or-death emergency. Some hours earlier, he had placed that sealed container in a hotel fridge for safekeeping – one of several containers just like it that he had placed there. Wouldn't you know, someone on the hotel's staff, presumably overcome with curiosity, had opened it to take a peek, and that, for Hans, was tantamount to a catastrophe.

Hans isn't your typical entrepreneur; he doesn't build companies or develop commercial projects to make his fortune. Instead, he's a compulsive innovator driven by something intangible, a restless vigor, a product of his cultural heritage that accounts for both his idealism and his thirst for adventure. These characteristics have put him in a slew of unlikely situations, sometimes desperate, sometimes failing, and other times leading to spectacular success.

Hans gives fresh relevance to Wordsworth's famous line, "The child is father of the man." When just 12, he made his first big financial score by collecting and shipping three tons – yes, *three tons* – of cod tongue, a Norwegian delicacy, to markets in southern Norway. Youngsters in cod-rich fishing villages in northern Norway traditionally make spending money by harvesting cod tongues, but Hans, already the entrepreneur, not only sold his own production but also acted as an agent for his young schoolmates by selling their harvest to buyers higher in the value chain. Hans proudly opens his tattered 50-year-old notebooks and shows me the net figures of his enterprise back then. He is now 63 but retains all his boyish enthusiasm and charm. He has an informal, engaging style, wears knitted woolen sweaters and a permanent grin, and always seems to have yet another amusing story at the ready. He gleefully tells me, for example, about the time when he managed to inveigle permission from the Federal Security Service of the Russian Federation (aka the KGB) to start salmon farming within restricted military areas in Arctic Russia. He follows that one with a story about how he started up a factory producing cases for shipping fish – a company today worth more than $20 million. But in these and his other tales of entrepreneurship, a common theme emerges: Hans has only marginal profits to show for all his efforts, for whenever he's launched a new enterprise, he has invariably soon sold his interest in it and turned to a fresh adventure. The fun, for him, is in the creating, not the profits.

Should I stay, or should I go?

For us people of the High North, winter brings a time of long darkness, blizzards, and freezing weather, sometimes leaving us wondering anew why we ever decided to make this rugged region our home. But it is indeed our home. As I chatted with Hans, we found ourselves speculating about the area's future. Hans, ever the optimist, has no doubts about what he sees as the limitless opportunities here. His current dream is developing a massive, sustainable infrastructure for transporting energy from the point of extraction in northern Norway to global markets. No, he's not thinking of an offshore pipeline, which is the conventional solution. Instead, he proposes a tunnel that zigzags through the mountains of northern Norway, combining a pipeline with a new railroad line that would both benefit many communities and generate new on-shore industries. Imagine that, he says, eyes gleaming!

With increasing global interest in the Arctic regions, global warming creates new opportunities for oil-and-gas extraction, shipping, and industrial development. At the same time, because maturing fields in the south of Norway are now reaching their peak oil production, the industry is exploring new methods of extraction in the Arctic. So the High North's prospects look ever brighter – at least in theory. Yet continual attention is necessary to develop business in the High North that keeps creative people in the area, else they'll succumb to the lures of Oslo and other large cities in the south. In fact, in order to capitalize on the estimated industrial activity in the region, businesses and organizations will absolutely depend on a migration of workers from the south – or even internationally.

The issue that Hans is currently addressing is an active part of the ongoing debate about Arctic oil-and-gas extraction. Where should the focus be – offshore or onshore? Hans points out that the Snøhvit LNG (Liquefied Natural Gas) plant in northern Norway, located in the municipality of Hammerfest, brought that community a big spike in both population and jobs. He's certain that such facilities benefit their communities more directly than offshore solutions, where the oil and gas are transported out to sea with limited local economic effect. Without new industry and development, young professionals typically move south for better opportunities, and the Arctic communities become depopulated. At the same time, other regions, such as Helgeland further south, show two things: the importance of local entrepreneurs, and, over time, more locals being employed simply through the influx of workers from outside the region. Whether the field is onshore or offshore is of less importance here. What's important is that locals are invited in by the established industry.

My own experience bears out some of these generalizations. Back when I was a master student in Business Management studying the oil-and-gas industry, only a fraction of the graduated students in my class stayed in northern Norway. The majority moved south where there are more opportunities in that industry.

Today there are no clear answers being advanced for how local communities in northern Norway might best profit from petroleum activity, especially with respect to regional value creation. But Hans's experience with king crabs typifies what he'd like to see: projects that significantly change the future for the Norwegian High North and the people who live here.

While his proposed long tunnel, incorporating both a pipeline and a railroad line, seems like an epic project, I ask Hans, "Isn't your project in the daredevil category?" His answer shows how his thinking has evolved. "This project is built on thoughts about value creation in the High North," he says. "My thoughts lie with future generations – providing enough challenges so they want to stay within the region. We are losing people and valuable competence to the south. We need something, something *big*, and something that will change the total scope of development for the future of the High North."

"Is this your gift to the High North?" I ask with a smile.

"Well, I just started it [the idea]. If it is useful is not up to me to decide."

Hans proposes a solution for the logistical requirements that would augment the already expanding oil-and-gas industry in northern Norway. The current national conversation is mostly focused on gas transportation, sub-sea pipelines, and onshore LNG processing plants for preparing the gas to be transported by ship. Hans dreams of a grand scheme based on expansive thoughts born of long flights of research and writing, all of which he intends to publish in a book explaining how best to transport the resources produced by the big industries in northern Norway. Oil-and-gas companies are understandably concerned with the financial prospects of energy transportation. Profitability has to be the main goal, as profits are their bottom line. Hans argues that if we broaden our views about energy transportation – if, that is, we tie together all the related industries – the economic prospects will look far brighter.

Cultural heritage

So where does Hans's motivation come from? Chiefly, it seems, from his child-hood experiences. He grew up on the small island of Værøy in northern Norway. His family has been involved with fisheries for many generations, following the local tradition of using small fishing boats to extract resources from the sea, and then selling those same resources to markets in the south, much as the oil-and-gas industry operates today. It was as though his family was an industry unto itself; fisheries, markets, technological developments, and logistics shaped their daily life. His family evolved from being simple fishermen to a family having a sophisti-cated, market-oriented view of the industry they were supplying. When Hans was growing up, the Norwegian fishing industry was witnessing a transformation from traditional methods to the modernized fishing industry of today, so he directly experienced how his surroundings adapted to new trends in the industry.

Hans explains how there was always a positivity associated with churning up the fish. His family never lived by the clock; instead, they lived on what might be called cod, herring, or salmon time. When the fish were there, so were they. But over the years, daily operations changed from standardized ones to brand-new ones where they had no prior experience to draw on, so they'd have to sit in the dock's lunchroom and mull things over until they had a solution. Hans remem-bers these brainstorming sessions sentimentally. "They constantly improvised," he says, "and my ears were big when I listened in on their discussions."

It's the *process*, he says, that produces the possibilities; at times it has to be a quick decision. An example of this is how Hans's dad saw *possibilities* instead of just challenges. On their home island of Værøy, Hans recalls, the main source of income for many generations had been cod fishing. But in the 1960s, big schools of herring suddenly began appearing off the Lofoten Islands, the main fishing region in northwest Norway. At the time, nobody there saw a market for herring, a fish mostly used as bait for catching bigger and more valuable species. But using herring as bait produced a byproduct of empty wooden bait boxes, and Hans's father saw an opportunity there: he began filling them with ice and fresh her-ring, and then discreetly shipping them to processing facilities in southwestern Norway, where they'd find a welcome market.

Hans emphasizes that this innovation carried its own set of challenges. For one thing, his father had to be very guarded about his new operation lest others try to horn in on it, so he had to devise some unconventional methods for communicating with those new markets. Phoning them from Værøy was too risky, for it meant going through a manual switchboard, and he knew the people operating it kept no secrets. "Mostly ladies worked here," Hans recalls, "and many of them were married to men involved in the fishing industry. They connected the phone line from caller to receiver, which means they'd know who was contacting who." Hans's father philosophically accepted the reality that "secrets are hard to keep," so he practiced exceptional care whenever communicating about his new venture.

To conceal his plans, he travelled to the bigger city of Bodø, where he got a hotel room and contacted possible buyers for the herring via a larger and distant phone central where local phone operator wives couldn't tell their husbands what he was up to. His business went on for two successful years before the schools of herring inexplicably moved back down south to their original waters.

Drawing the moral line for me, Hans is Zen-like in his sensemaking. "It is all about seeing possibilities when the resources are at hand," he says, "and not to linger in conventional thinking. You have to leave your own body and view yourself from the outside, and then realize what you can do." He likens it to learning by traveling: "It is generally the same as when Norwegian students go abroad to study, and they experience a new culture and catch the ability to view Norway and themselves from a different perspective."

Growing up in a milieu where problem-solving was fairly routine encouraged Hans to dare to dream big and to think the previously unthinkable. His adventure-seeking is rooted in his childhood where he learned that keeping a secret is as important as creating a market for a new product.

The crabs

Hans's ability to think creatively and unconventionally is exemplified by his crazy adventure with Arctic king crabs. After obtaining a degree in fisheries economics, he became the sole person farming king crabs in the world between 2000 and 2006. But becoming that person was anything but easy. At the outset he had tons to learn, for crab farming was basically unprecedented then. So, in search of best practices, he went to Russia to work alongside a Bulgarian woman who held a PhD in marine biology and who had specialized in shrimp farming – the closest thing to crab farming Hans could think of. Working together in the basement of an old Moscow monastery, the two of them learned, and documented, the stages of king crab farming. At some point during all this research, the Russian fisheries authorities gave Hans permission to capture 50,000 king crabs for further farming – provided, that is, he agreed to have the crabs captured by a Russian public company in Murmansk. Fine, he thought. But upon returning to the Arctic regions of Russia where he and his corporate partner were to capture the crabs, he discovered that something was terribly wrong. The public company he had agreed to partner with had updated its office with new windows, and expensive imported cars filled the parking lot. Not only that, but the director who met him sported a new suit! Public buildings in Russia are usually decrepit, and their parking lots are dominated by dated and cheap Russian Ladas. Hans knew immediately that all these were bad signs. All the crabs earmarked for farming, Hans learned, had been sold on the market, and some parvenu Russians were now enjoying a nice meal of Hans's succulent crabs. Russian business culture can be tough, and anybody not aware of its dangers will lose in the long run. In this case, it was Hans. He realized then that the Russian agency had double-crossed him, and going to court in Russia would be a waste of money and time. So it was goodbye Russia, goodbye Bulgarian shrimp lady, and goodbye cooperation with Norway's neighbors in the east. Hans later learned that the Russian company didn't continue with the crab business; it simply turned around and sold Hans's hunting license. What capitalists!

Feeling terrible about the failed Russian project, Hans walked the darkened streets of Murmansk with no clue as to what to do next. But then, serendipitously, he met a fellow Norwegian, Tor Robertsen, who turned out to be in charge of Finnmark County's cooperation with Russia. Finnmark is the northernmost county in Norway and borders on Russia. Tor invited Hans and his nascent business establishment to the county of Finnmark.

Hans returned to Norway with a hard lesson in Russian business, with knowledge of king crab farming, and with the persistent belief that this project could and would be successful. He found himself in the Mayor of Vardø's office, pitching his project but being met by indifference. Hans explains that it seemed like the mayor was thinking something like this: *There is just another mad man, presenting some borderline project they want the municipality to be a part of.* "And if you look at it from that perspective, he was right!" Hans adds with a big smile.

Undaunted, he elected to proceed on his own. He installed huge glass fish-tanks in an old fish-processing plant, raised them well off the floor, filled them with fifty king crabs, and observed the crustaceans from underneath while he lay sprawled at his ease in an old Barcalounger. He sat there, day and night, observing their habits; Hans explains it as back-to-basic research. "The people from Vardø, who knew how I spent my time, were sure that I was utterly and completely mad," he says. "They were right, I *am* kind of mad!" Yet, the madman's time with the crab observation was not wasted; through this detailed observation he learned the crabs' habits and behavior patterns. He studied how they dealt with captivity especially when it came to eating habits, how they interacted, and the appropriate amount of current needed in the tanks in order to keep them clean.

Breeding the crabs proved possible, he found. But there were still some obstacles, especially the cost of feeding the crabs the appropriate diet. This proved a huge challenge.

Hans initiated several research projects to solve the issue of low-cost food for his critters. For this project to be viable, it had to bring profits. After considerable enterprise, he managed to win the cooperation of both the College of Fishery Science at the University of Tromsø and the Research Council of Norway, and together they managed to develop food that was within cost limits. The project grew steadily. Still, not a single crab had yet been exported out of the country, which basically meant that Hans had no income, though plenty of expenses.

Troubled times

By August 2004, he was pretty much broke, and no one, save Hans himself, believed the project would proceed, since it really looked both unachievable and unprofitable. Throughout the development period, Hans had travelled around and presented the project to various prospective investors. Responses were mostly positive, but he needed to offer proof that his crab production scheme would work, and he didn't have it. Hans is not afraid to admit that this was a rough time. "I sat in Vardø for three months, with no money to travel home to my family," he recalls. "I was broke, and decided that if no money showed up by Christmas, my bags would be packed and the project would be over. I went from 83 to 62 kg [180 to 136 pounds]. I was suffering."

During these months, perhaps for moral support, Hans read the book *Hunger* by the Norwegian Nobel Prize-winning author Knut Hamsun. He had read it once before without really understanding it, but this time he felt a new connection to Hamsun and his autobiography wherein he describes a time where he, too, was dead poor and constantly hungry, indeed famished. Hans was not aware at the time that his luck was about to change.

Then, in early December, Hans received a call from a man who had heard about his project and was interested in investing in it. But first Hans had to give permission to have his personal finances virtually x-rayed by a legal firm. "I think they searched my financial history all the way back to when I was a teenager," he recalls. Happily, the audit results were positive, and the investor's money – 1.5 million NOK – soon followed. In fact, it arrived on Christmas Eve. Hans's goal of getting financial support or giving up was reached with just a day to spare.

But then new problems arose. The crabs used for farming were still living freely at the bottom of the sea, and the permission to capture them didn't come without demands from governmental decision-makers. While Hans had managed to get a government allotment for capturing a specific number of king crabs, it carried the proviso that the crabs be on the dock by the first of January – only a week later. In a frenzy, Hans hired fishermen to do the job, in highly challenging conditions, working day and night. Earlier, on Christmas Eve, Hans had travelled home to celebrate his good fortune with his family – only to turn around the next day and go back to Vardø. All the equipment and technical tools had to be in place before the crabs got there, in –17 °C, and what we in northern Norway refer to as "the weather of Satan." Hans recalls the nightmarish image of the dock: chaos, crabs, people, and insane weather. Nonetheless, they managed to finish the task and get the captured crabs into the farming facilities. It was an epochal moment, Hans recalls: "I paid the fishermen, sorted out the paper work and went home, fired off a rocket [it was New Year's Eve], and clenched my hands in anticipation."

The truth comes out

Part of Hans's learning from his childhood became an enduring trait: to keep things close to his vest. But now he's prepared to reveal something he has kept hidden from everyone all this time, his investor included. It was never Hans's intention to process the crabs before they were exported – which would mean they'd have been dead and frozen. His golden idea was to export *living* Arctic king crabs to the gourmet kitchens of the world. He kept this ambitious plan secret because the project would have seemed so outrageous that no investors would have put money into it.

To pursue this wild goal, Hans did what he learned to do from his family's fishing business: he got more information. For this he called on Eyvind Hellstrøm, one of Norway's renowned chefs and TV personalities known for both his extravagant food habits and his cocky personality. Eyvind was initially a skeptic. But Hans, undeterred, packed up the crabs and flew them south, where he submitted them to a crucial quality-control test by Eyvind, the hardest-to-please chef in Norway. One afternoon at Eyvind Hellstrøm's famed Oslo restaurant, Bagatelle, two Arctic king crabs appeared, airborne from above the Arctic Circle and very much alive. Late that night, in a call from Eyvind Hellstrøm, Hans heard the words he has been awaiting all these years: "Hans, this is the new flagship of Norwegian seafood export!"

But even with this endorsement, the challenges were still huge. Exporting live king crabs proved much harder than originally thought. In transport, the crabs became anemic when oxygenated. But partnering with a professor in anesthesiology, Hans developed a secret gas mixture that would keep the king crabs alive during transport. After all of his effort, he knew that the knowledge from his research was part of what he had to offer – his distinctive competence.

The word about the live king crabs spread quickly to Europe's finest restaurants, and the demand for the product skyrocketed almost immediately. In 2007 Hans had the privilege of providing live king crabs as the main ingredient for one of the entrées in the renowned world cooking contest *Bocuse d'Or*, in Lyon, France. After all of his trials and efforts, Hans's live crabs were selected for the culinary equivalent of the Olympic Games.

But before that contest in Lyon, Hans had been invited to Brussels to present his Arctic king crabs to 250 chefs and restaurant suppliers from Europe. It was a crucial marketing event for Hans's business – something, he felt, that could either make him or break him. He arrived at his Brussels hotel with his live Arctic king crabs all nicely sealed in boxes and kept healthy with his special blend of gases. Hans had these boxes temporarily placed in the hotel's fridge, with one important message to the employees: *Do not, under any circumstances, open these boxes!* Some idiot, for whatever reason, failed to comply…

Diffusing the daredevils

Hans's ideas about innovation and his crab story reflect his daredevil style and his talent for creativity. But where do these ideas come from? What is his motivation for maniacally working day and night, exhausting his own savings, and being willing to lose fifty pounds, too? Where does such persistence come from?

His answer? "It is *passion*," he says with a big smile.

In truth, passion seems part of Hans's motivation in everything he does, whether it's spending hours with me sharing his many stories or spending months in an old Moscow monastery studying crabs.

His crab story made me eager to approach the topic of innovation more broadly than just through his reflections on the subject. After all, students can obtain a degree in Business within the field of innovation and entrepreneurship. Can we somehow link Hans's passion to what students learn theoretically at universities?

As you might now imagine, Hans has his own ideas about this! He agrees that entrepreneurial education can be useful for many, even if some constraints do exist. Thousands of students acquire the same education, go to the same lectures, and begin at a similar starting point, but they come out of it all with varying results. Government programs like Innovation Norway provide start-up resources and set standards for how to apply innovative techniques by anyone, yet Hans worries that such programs, in their standard form, kill innovation instead of nourishing it. While government and organizations such as Innovation Norway have certain standards and processes that need to be in place in order to secure support funding or investors, they don't instill the passion that Hans has experienced in his projects. He worries about the effect of standards. Great companies rooted in innovation wouldn't exist today if they had followed standardized processes. So the question remains: where does innovation come from? Also, how best to nourish it?

Our word "innovation" comes from the Latin word *novus*, which mean to "renew or change." In the academic organizational literature, the incentives for innovating are improvements in efficiency, productivity, quality, competitiveness, and market share. This implies that there must be economic value to be gained from any of Hans's projects. Yet his attention is hardly ever on the profits. We touched on this irony during our conversation about his most recent project. He told me that he is not economically driven; in fact, he looks like he is thinking the question over before he replies, "I haven't really thought about it." He says, "This is not where my thoughts are. My thoughts lie on the future of our region. I am what you can call a positive patriot. My thoughts lie with new generations." In such a statement, Hans exemplifies Norwegian national policy: How does the country plan for the quality of life for future generations?

Such planning for the future is crucial. Depopulation in the High North is a reality, and Hans explains that, despite what some think, this has nothing to do with our climate or harsh living conditions. It has to do, instead, with our not knowing how to build the right social and professional environment that attracts people. Consider, he says, the photos of newborn babies in the local newspaper in northern Norway. They typically carry a caption like this: "Ola/Kari was born in Oslo, on such-and-such date. They send their regards to Grandma and Grandpa in Bodø [city in northern Norway]." This shows, he says, how young families whose parents are in northern Norway settle down in southern Norway, and you see this *every day* in our local newspaper. Hans wishes it were the other way around – new and existing families settling down in our region in order to secure the future of the High North. But these people need jobs and opportunities. And that is where Hans's passion, rather than profit, lies.

In addition to being an innovator, Hans is a pioneer thinker. He dares to push the boundaries of "normal," and his warning bells are unconventionally placed. He presents the demand for a "daredevil" educational program – a program that teaches, and demands, testing the boundaries of normal. Teaching should be done by using examples from daredevil companies that have succeeded and that have been analyzed for exactly how they have succeeded.

Hans wants to hear about daredevil projects and their success. He shares with me his contrarian take on innovation conferences and their pitiful examples: "All I hear about is someone who has opened a new gym or a barber shop. This is *so* plain, and in my head this is *not* innovation. Such projects get standing ovations, and it is collectively decided that this is fantastic. Well, I don't see *anything* fantastic in it."

I ask Hans why he takes such a contrarian position. He says that his free-spirited nature might explain it. He has never been interested in safety and standards, he says; instead, he has constantly searched for challenges that require a sense of solution-based approaches. He is open to these new solutions, open to thinking outside the box; it simply is who he is. But he acknowledges the risks inherent in such thinking. "Nineteen out of twenty projects that have been on my mind have not been realized," he confesses, "but some of them are very much alive today."

That comment shows us the multiplicity of ideas that can appear in a mind like Hans's, with most of them not panning out. But of course the more ideas one hatches, the greater one's chances of seeing at least a couple of them be golden. This is why Hans insists that we should be encouraged to believe that the next golden idea could be ours.

The grand infrastructure

Hans is serious about helping secure the future of northern Norway. He is proposing an enormously bold long-term solution, one that will tie together the big industries of northern Norway by means of tunnels. Consider his rationale: Norwegian geography is unique, with jagged fjords shaping our coast and making it so long that, if straightened out, it would reach 25,148 km – that's more than halfway around the world. Meanwhile, the mainland in between the fjords is narrow and interrupted by steep mountains. Hans's solution is to drill tunnels through these mountains from fjord to fjord, from the Norwegian Sea outside the town of Mosjøen all the way to Kirkenes, the town closest to the Barents Sea, and connect all of the High North with an epic transportation system. Such a tunnel system would significantly shorten the distance for transporting resources, as an offshore pipeline would have to cover a much longer distance due to the crazy irregularity of the Norwegian coastline. Several opportunities lie in developing these tunnels: railroads, gas pipelines, electricity, CO_2 etc. Hans believes that building these tunnels would benefit many sectors, not just the oil-and-gas industry. The new railroad could be used for transporting goods like fresh cod from Lofoten, and ore and minerals from the inland; and the tunnels could be connected to Finnish and Russian railroads, thereby creating new trade channels. But Hans's thoughts remain focused on Norway's core products, "There are no goods as eager to get out the country as dead salmon or cod," he says, grinning.

Back in Brussels, Arctic king crabs have been kept alive with a special blend of gases, supervised by the on-call anesthesiologist at Saint-Jean Hospital. Hans Nordgård has been massaging their central nerve; slowly the crabs show signs of life and regain their strength. The surrounding crowd of tense doctors and nurses breaks out in a collective smile of relief. They did it! They brought the crabs back to life! Later, in another part of Brussels, 250 prominent chefs and restaurant suppliers are eager to see the next big thing in seafood imports: living Arctic king crabs! As Hans presents his crabs to these gourmands, he tells them the drama that had unfolded earlier at the hospital. The chefs don't believe him until they later read this headline in one of Brussels' biggest newspapers: "*Crab royal de Norwege au Hospital.*" Translation: "Norwegian king crabs *hospitalized.*"

What will it take, finally, to secure the future of the High North? Though on a whole other scale of challenge, that's a little like asking, How does one person – and a foreigner, no less – get a Brussels hospital to help him save some Arctic king crabs from dying?

Hans would answer, "*Passion!*"

We might all do well to learn from his example.

3   The daughter takes a farm
Organic farming in the Arctic

Tom McVey, Bodø Graduate School of Business

Marita Olsen and her husband Jan
Photograph by Kjell Arne Skogheim

That sweet moment of satisfaction that comes from seeing a completed check-list at day's end is one that Marita Olsen rarely experiences, but she cheerfully accepts it. Marita both owns and solely manages her family's ancestral dairy farm in Steigen, an area in northern Norway. Now, after six years of tireless toil, that farm is about to be certified entirely organic, making it a rarity in Norway and absolutely unique in Steigen.

Eager to see it for ourselves, three of us made the drive north into the Norwegian countryside and spent the day visiting her. Two of us, both students from the University of Texas, were eager to meet this intrepid woman; happily, the third, our friend Ragnhild (the ethnographer for chapter two), a student at the University of Nordland in Bodø, offered to chauffeur us there and help translate whenever we or Marita had trouble communicating. After about a three-hour drive, we arrived at the farmhouse, where Marita greeted us warmly and promptly invited us inside. I grew up in Kansas, the agricultural heartland of the U.S., and Marita's farmhouse gave me a strong sense of nostalgia, especially the coat pegs by the front door, all of them draped with mud-splattered jackets and coveralls, with muddy work boots below.

Once we were inside, Marita's home proved warm and designed for both comfort and function.

Marita is a slender, strong woman with thin brown hair streaked with wisps of gray. She wears a perpetual smile blended with a touch of steel in her eyes that leaves no doubt that she is serious about her work. Marita chatted lightly with us as she quickly put together an assortment of Norwegian cookies and cheeses, made a pot of coffee, and led us outside to a round picnic table next to the house. From here, we had a view of a few small barns and an impressive two-story building that looked newer than the others. The picnic table also offers an impressive view of her sprawling farmland, which flows along both sides of the small rural highway we had just left. Bordering the property are mountainous hills on one side and forest on the other, while continuous green fields filled the spaces in between.

After the coffee was poured, we started asking Marita about her farm life. One of the first things she explained to us is the work ethic required. "On any farm," she said, "there is never a point at which you can say, 'I've done everything that needed to be done today. Now I can relax.'" No, she said, sounding like a rural philosopher: "A long-term survival skill for a farmer in Norway is to be at peace with saying, 'There is more that must be done, but I'm stopping for now. It's time to relax for a moment.'" And that moment had come, so we all settled in, and Marita's stories and the passion for her work began flowing.

Maintaining balance and flexibility is critical indeed. For besides the enormity of the workload, Marita never knows when the next surprise is going to come along and challenge her best-laid plans. One day last summer, for example, her 6-year-old daughter came running into the farmhouse exclaiming, "I think there is a bull outside!"

A bit incredulous, Marita replied, "You *think* there is a bull loose? You aren't sure?"

You see, the bulls on her farm are kept in a separate building, each with its own space to lie down or romp in, as desired. A device on each bull's neck supposedly ensures that they stay in their own area. But to her surprise, a bull known for its temper had somehow broken its restraint and wandered outside. Most things Marita handles on her own, it would seem, but no farmer is an island unto herself. Fortunately, the farming community around Steigen is a close network of helping hands, so Marita was able to call a neighbor used to dealing with tetchy bulls, and within minutes he drove up to help corral the huge bruiser. His cautious approach on foot proved futile, though; the bull was having none of it and charged him. As the man ran behind his car for protection, Marita leapt onto her tractor and drove it between the two of them, giving him time to jump in his car. Then, with the two of them using their vehicles to herd the bull in the direction of its pen, followed by nudges with long metal poles, they were able to coax it back in.

Marita is a trailblazer, charting a life quite singular in her part of Norway. Not only is she pioneering organic farming, she remains a full time farmer in the north at a time when many rural northern communities like hers are shrinking as people emigrate south in ever-greater numbers. This leaves the same amount of land to be worked by fewer and fewer farmers, many now unable to take on the stewardship of additional land should more farmers choose to move away. Marita remembers five years ago when there were sixty farms in the Steigen area. Today that number is closer to forty. She believes there will be fewer than twenty within the next ten years.

Although she grew up in a rural community and pursued a career related to agriculture, Marita didn't set out to single-handedly run the family farm. She lived on it until she was 17, when she left to continue her schooling for another two years. Then, after spending still another year working on a farm in northern Germany, she returned to Norway to study agriculture for five years. Upon earning her degree, she next spent two years helping her father run the family farm. But she gave that up to work first as a journalist, then as an agricultural advisor on organic farming methods, the latter while living further south in scenic Lofoten, a string of northern islands popular with tourists.

In 2005, during that advisor phase, Marita gave birth to her first child, a daughter, Marta. When the baby was barely a week old, Marita's life suddenly took yet another abrupt turn. Her father had gone out to work on the farm, just as he did daily, only this time he suffered an accident – a fatal one. His untimely death came with additional consequences, some of them owing to Norwegian law. To own a farm in Norway, you're required to live on, and maintain, it year-round; no absentee landlords allowed here. Why? Because the government knows that if farms could be bought without restrictions, people looking for summer homes would snap them up. Soon, the surrounding rural communities would become ghost towns, reviving only during the summer when owners returned for vacations. This, in turn, would shrink agricultural activity in the country to unacceptable levels.

But the need for a sustainable food supply isn't the only reason for the government's program of supporting communities and their infrastructure year-round, particularly in the rural north. Norwegian cultural heritage and tourism are strong in part because so much of the land is well maintained. For example, people who have farms along the fjords, where the Hurtigruten cruise ships travel, receive a modest government stipend for their farming to encourage the maintenance of the pastoral scenery so popular with tourists. This natural synergy between local food production and tourism can result in thriving rural communities – but only so long as farmers are willing to live on and work the land.

When Marita's father died that day in 2005, the family suddenly faced a host of challenges, the biggest being what to do with the farm. Of the family's three children, one brother had died earlier in a traffic accident, while the other brother resisted moving back north to take over things. Since their mother couldn't possibly begin to manage the farm alone, selling it seemed the only choice. After all, Marita had a new daughter, a thriving career, and a life with her fiancé, Jan, in Lofoten. Though she occasionally had idle thoughts of someday moving back to the farm, she never dreamed she would ever be given the choice of either assuming full responsibility for maintaining it or losing it forever. Now she was faced with that very choice, and it was one that had to be made soon.

Marita discussed the idea at length with Jan. Taking over the farm would require adapting to a long-distance relationship, with him still selling agricultural equipment and supplies in Lofoten while she moved with their new baby out to the farm in Steigen. In feeling the persistent tug of the land drawing her near, Marita came to realize that she wasn't simply reacting to the death of her father. She felt a deep connection to the farm. It was one that her grandfather had built, and where her parents had lived and worked, and where she herself was born and raised. She couldn't just sell it without even trying to maintain her family's legacy, which could in time become her daughter's inheritance. If she gave it her best shot and couldn't make a go of it, only then she could sell it with a clear conscience.

With that realization, her decision was made.

Even so, coming back wasn't easy for her. She had been away for so long, she now knew only the community's elders, farmers of 60-plus years. She didn't know anyone her own age because so many of them had moved south or elsewhere, just as she herself had, to pursue an education, a career, a family. Little did she realize just how important her relationships with those elders would be, or how fulfilling.

The Norwegian government has a novel program where it actually pays for a person to help maintain a farm when the farmer is sick or unable to work. Happily, one such substitute-farmer was assigned to assist at Marita's farm while she considered her options. She was quick to joke, "Although the program does indeed provide much-needed relief, you'd better not get sick or die on a weekend because substitute-farmers only work Monday through Friday!" Even so, she was blessed with an excellent helper who stayed through his full two-month assignment as Marita gradually assumed more and more of the responsibilities of managing the land. After his term had been served, she hired a full-time assistant who would work ten days on, four days off. Marita could then stay in Lofoten for a ten-day stretch, returning to the farm to fill the four-day hiatus. Meanwhile, her mother continued to live on the farm, and was happy to look after her granddaughter while Marita worked.

After ten months, this pattern came to an end when Marita's helper left for a new position elsewhere. After a fruitless search for a replacement, she moved up to Steigen and took over the farm full-time. Though a daunting prospect at first, she soon found that in some ways it was easier to do the job herself. With an employee, she had put a lot of effort into fitting the work that needed to be done into ten seven-hour days. Now, as both owner and resident, she could work as long as she had to when she needed to. Of course, that had its own challenges. When could she possibly schedule time to rest?

The first year on her own proved enormously taxing for her. She survived, and thrived, if only through sheer force of will, but even that, she concedes, wouldn't have been enough without the steadfast support of her neighbors. As a local paper recently reported, the population of every community in Nordland county except for Bodø has shrunk in recent years, and this has Marita greatly concerned for the future of such critical support structures in rural communities. She jokes with her neighbors that they have to stay farming for at least as long as she does!

Marita's spirit is nonetheless unquenchable, and she laughs merrily when she thinks back on her first year. There were so many things she didn't know, so many basics that she struggled with alone. She resisted calling on her neighbors at first, wanting so much to be as independent as possible. So, instead, she made many calls to her brother and Jan in those early days, learning the basics that her father could no longer teach her and sparing her neighbors elementary questions.

Fortunately, those same neighbors understood her situation and always found a way to share their experiences in times of need. A favorite story Marita likes to tell is about her barn, where she stores the harvested grains used to feed the animals during the winter months. Some grain is kept at ground level, but there are also two large loft-like areas on either side of the barn several feet above the ground. A narrow, flat wooden bridge spans the two lofts, while another bridge, connected to the first, leads outside. Each is just wide enough for her small tractor, which she drives up, across, and back down again to collect the grain and then convey it out to the cows for their feeding times. In her early days, Marita had trouble navigating the bridge between the lofts. One time, she started crossing at an angle, then realized she wasn't going to make it to the other side before falling off. The more she tried to adjust the tractor, the more angled her approach became and the closer she came to disaster. Eventually, she had to make herself stop, swallow her pride, and call for help. The neighbor who responded to her call laughed as he righted the tractor, sharing his memories of getting into exactly the same predicament in his own early days.

Marita's relationship with her neighbors has grown over the years despite the challenges of keeping in touch. While the farmers see each other often in the course of their work, lending each other a hand, there's little time for socializing. Recognizing the need for camaraderie as well as work, Marita and the guys have started a new tradition of going out for beer and pizza on the first Friday of every month. Along with the socializing and beer comes a greater sharing of ideas and coordinating of work that seems to flow more easily and productively in this time of relaxation, which Marita and the others have come to cherish.

Today, Marita has a mid-sized farm with about eighty head of cattle producing milk and meat; with six years' experience under her belt, Marita is now unfazed by even the most complex aspects of managing cattle, particularly breeding and calving. She has twenty-four breeding cows, all artificially inseminated, so she can schedule the pregnancies to ensure that they're not all calving at once, and she can even predict the births quite precisely. Still, no amount of planning can prevent an awkward birth in the wee hours of the morning or predict to the minute when a cow is ready. Constant vigilance is key. For example, the last time Marita dropped by to check in on her pregnant cows she noticed that one in particular was nearly ready. Her udder was engorged, and she was acting aloof, a telling sign. Marita took her to a private stall reserved for calving, because as a cow approaches birthing, she typically wants to remove herself from the herd. If a cow isn't inside when the time draws near, or if it's feeding time and the others are gathering to devour the freshly delivered hay, she will break away from the others and head for the woods. Thus Marita has learned to be on full alert as calving time draws near. For example, when she lifts the gate in the morning and a cow rushes out with a focused purpose rather than with a casual stroll, she knows birth is imminent. Similarly, on hot days, when the cows typically prefer to wander back to the barn where it's cooler, any cow that wanders off in the heat is likely ready to birth. Getting away from the other cows isn't always easy, though. If they catch on that something interesting is about to happen, they'll want to stay where the action is. A pregnant cow might have four or five other cows following her around, agitating her. But even when dealing with a breech birth at 3 A.M., Marita enjoys the moment, relishing just how far she has come in her six years of running the show.

In addition to staying north while others are moving south, Marita Olsen is blazing other new trails as well. For one, it's uncommon for women to be managers of their own farms; Marita is one of only three such women in Steigen. Traditionally in Norway, boys take over the farm when the parents retire. In families with more than one son, the eldest will have the first chance to accept the inheritance, and there is typically some pressure on him to say yes. These days, while it's more common now for the oldest of the children, regardless of gender, to get first crack, it's still rare for a woman to assume the leadership role. A farmer typically doesn't make enough just from farming to support the whole family, so even if a woman inherits a farm, it's usually her husband who manages it, while she herself will hold down some traditional full-time job like teaching or nursing to supplement the family income. However, Marita knew from the start that this wouldn't be her path. It was her land, and she would manage it herself. Having Jan work the farm while she went somewhere else would have been unthinkable to her.

And Jan agrees. He has his own job, roughly four hours away. He has his own house there, too, and comes to work on the farm on the weekends with Marita and their daughter. His two sons from a previous relationship often come to visit too, pitching in while there. He enjoys his career as much as she hers, and they agree that their situation is just right for both of them. Marita jokes, "When he comes to visit he can do as much work as he wants, but I'm still the boss!" She also recognizes how lucky she is to have a dedicated partner who enjoys helping out. Marita believes she gets much more farm help from her husband than many male farmers get from their wives. He also understands that she can't leave the farm on a whim; traveling takes advance planning and arrangements. Taking off on a lark for a week in Bodø, Troms, or Paris simply doesn't fit the farming lifestyle.

Marita enjoys a surprising advantage that comes from being a female farmer. She jokes that because she's female, other farmers are more accepting when she decides to run her farm differently, especially when blazing another trail into the realm of organic farming. A firm believer in the organic way, she knew from the start that "going green" was a non-negotiable condition of her taking over the farm. Thanks to her previous position as an agricultural advisor specializing in organic farming, she was excited to have the chance to demonstrate her expertise to her community.

But actually doing so wasn't easy. Hers is the only organic farm in the area. Converting a traditional farm into an organic one takes years. Only now, six years out, is Marita close to being able to call her products "certified organic." One reason why that takes so long to achieve is that the cattle must be fed grass that hasn't been chemically fertilized. In typical pastureland, grasses become used to receiving nutrients from the top of the soil and therefore develop a shallow root structure, whereas in organic pastureland the roots must drive much deeper. As a result, switching to organic farming requires removing all of the shallow-root grass, turning the soil, spreading and working in manure, and finally reseeding. Tilling deep into the ground and flipping it over is especially hard work, for Norway is a land made up of fjords, mountains, and mountainous hills, and that means endless rocks and boulders. Marita jokes with her family that extracting rocks and spreading poop for 15 hours a day may not be her favorite job on the farm, but the reward of seeing reworked fields turning green and harvesting the organic grass for her cows makes the hard labor well worth it.

Marita lights up and leans into a conversation with a heartfelt passion when she talks about why she chose to farm organically, why it's something she has to do. She explains that she is deeply concerned about the toxins in the food we're eating – toxins we're destroying ourselves with. "For example," she notes, "if you eat five strawberries, four of them will have [toxins]." She jokes with a wink that the trick is to just eat every fifth strawberry. "But it's not just strawberries," she stresses, suddenly serious again. "It's everything. It's so easy to drive a tractor and spray the fields [with chemicals]. It's so easy to do it, and everything has to be done so fast and cheap. You don't have time to do it properly because people want to have cheap food." Marita is emphatic that farmers "should [be farming] in the good way and not the easy way because it is not good for us to eat all of these [toxins]." Even when we get just a small amount of toxins in every vegetable we consume, she says, they do add up.

But at least, she concedes, the farmers of northern Norway aren't using the same volume of toxic chemicals that are often used elsewhere. She notes, as an example, that farmers in the United States routinely spray their apples some twenty different times in a season, whereas in Norway it's typically just twice. Why just twice? Because it's colder in Norway, so Norwegian farmers don't face the usual insect problems. Yes, a cold climate can have its advantages.

Marita sums up her core values by explaining that she wants to know that the meat and milk she's producing is of the highest quality and is chemical-free. For her, it's all or nothing: if she can't farm to these standards, she won't farm at all.

Today, she enjoys a farm that has seen a remarkable evolution. Her latest accomplishment is the construction of a state-of-the-art cattle facility that she calls, simply, "the farmhouse." In the afternoons, when the hungry cows see Marita enter that facility, they know it's feeding time and start wandering in through the large open doors that connect to the pasture. One by one, each cow then comes to an opening just wide enough for a single cow. A computer reads the electronic chip in the cow's tag and either lets the cow through to the large open area to access fresh grass or, if the computer finds that the cow is due for milking, it opens a second gate accessing the milking stall. There, the robotic milking machine recognizes which cow is in the stall and automatically adjusts the milking sleeves to the exact size of that cow's udder before using a precise laser-guided system to attach them to the cow. The first time a new cow is milked, the robot must learn the form and shape of the cow's udder to ensure a perfect fit for future milking sessions. The design of this facility is such that being milked is one of the highlights in a cow's day here, for as the milking starts, especially tasty corn kernels begin pouring into a feeding dish. Often the corn is gone before the milking is done. When this happens, the cow will turn and look at Marita supervising things from her nearby office, then let out a plaintive moo. Marita's willpower usually melts at this point, and she'll key in the command that sends bonus corn pouring into the bowl.

Some days, when the cows don't see Marita enter the farmhouse, she'll step outside and call to them in a voice midway between talking and singing, saying (in Norwegian, of course), "Come! Come over here! I have some nice food for you! Come over now. I'm waiting for you. Please come." Marita then begins calling her cows by name and laughs as many of them recognize their names and come when called. Although others may cringe at the pun, Marita loves to point out that she is far from alone on the farm because she is constantly surrounded by her cow-leagues.

Marita once knew a family farmer who also used to name his calves when his daughters were little, and it was a terrible day for the girls when he had to send the cows to slaughter. Marita knows that a similar day is coming for her own daughter, Marta – maybe an even worse one, for the child insisted on naming her favorite cow after herself. Marita doesn't want to think about the day when she will have to send that particular cow to slaughter, but she knows this is a lesson all children must learn someday, especially farm kids. Little Marta will learn the circle of life as she herself did, and while it's hard to lose an animal you've come to care for as a pet, it's precisely because slaughter is the end result that it behooves us to treat the animals with love, care, and respect for their service to us.

After a tour of the farm and hours of chatting, Marita brought lunch out. Jan and his oldest son were there that day, too, and were glad to join in the festive meal after a hard morning's work. Following a delicious chow-down of sausages, assorted cheeses, and bread, Marita brought out dessert. And what was it? Leftover wedding cake! Bursting with happiness, Marita explained that she and Jan, partners for more than ten years, had just gotten married that very Friday. We exploded with surprise and congratulations when we realized that the two were celebrating their four-day anniversary. Leah, (the ethnographer for chapter five) one of the Texas students, incredulously kept saying, "Friday? Friday? Y'all said 'Friday' and I was like, oh, Friday. But you mean *Friday*! Oh my goodness!"

The wedding was a surprise for Marita's neighbors as well. Marita and Jan had invited their neighbors and relatives to come to a party celebrating the construction of the sleek new "farmhouse," which had been truly a community project. They expressed their immense gratitude for all of the time and effort that these people had poured into the many weekends spent constructing the building, but no one had even a clue that there was a second reason for the party. Marita had worked with the best man to arrange for the guests to be surprised. He informed them that the party would be in the new building, but first they would all be having lunch at a nearby community center. Once there, the best man then told them that before lunch, they were invited to attend a wedding in a nearby chapel. Feelings among the guests of being unprepared and underdressed were quickly put to rest when they discovered just who was getting married. Not surprisingly, the wedding was a huge success, and the reception following it, held in the farmhouse, was said to be the best the area had seen in recent memory. Word of the marriage even made it to some of Marita's neighbors who were then vacationing in Sweden. As soon as they heard it wasn't just a celebration of the new farmhouse, but a wedding for their dear friends, they cut short their trip and came right back, eager to congratulate the couple in person. Given all that love, when asked about the seeming loneliness and isolation of farming life, Marita can't help but grin.

Looking back over the past six years, Marita rests easy knowing that her decision to take over the farm was the right one. She laughs to herself as she remembers the uncertainty and doubt that plagued her at the beginning of this adventure. At the time she felt it was an enormous sacrifice to give up the luxury of free weekends and spontaneous outings with co-workers. Even though she now has to manage her free time to the minute, she enjoys a sense of peace and a rich satisfaction that comes from charting her own course, a peace she had never known in the city. On some winter evenings, she will douse the lights in her home and just gaze out dreamily at the lovely moonlit fields and the road running through them. Sometimes she'll see herds of elk meandering by, and on clear nights the stars sparkle with an intensity unseen in the city. One person's hardship is another's triumph, and Marita Olsen is content beyond words with her life as a farmer in the north.

4 Reindeers and teepees

Restoring young minds through the power of nature

Jacob Ford, Bodø Graduate School of Business

Hege Stenhammer and Maria Berntzen
Photograph by Maria Berntzen/Hege Stenhammer

The unprecedented wealth that stems from recently discovered oil fields in the Norwegian Sea has transformed Norway into a country bursting with new opportunities. In 1990, Norway established the Government Pension Fund Global to manage the new financial wealth from the oil. In only twenty years, the fund has become the largest sovereign wealth fund in the world. By investing the oil wealth into international financial markets and, more recently, real estate, Norway seeks to establish a long-term financial stability that is not dependent upon oil. Every fiscal year, Norway uses only 4 percent (more than $32 billion in 2013) of the Government Pension Fund Global as part of the budget. This means that oil money is poured back into Norway through grants, government programs, and subsidies. While none of the money goes directly into the pockets of the Norwegians (unless they are on some form of government aid), the massive influx of money into government programs, and the Scandinavian model of social democracy, makes it easier for individuals to leave a career in the private sector and pursue career opportunities with organizations supported by government funds. Two Norwegian women in Northern Norway have chosen to use this opportunity to leave their careers, one part-time, to start a nature-based camp for children who have emotional or developmental disabilities. Focusing the children's camp around the native Scandinavian Sami culture, the women temporarily remove the children from the classroom and relocate them into a historical, cultural, and outdoor experience. Their story reveals how a past world may serve to heal present troubles.

Karita

"My. Name. Is. KARITA!" The 11-year-old girl with Down syndrome paused thoughtfully between each word and ended her statement with a burst of exclamatory laughter.

She continued, in the same energetic fashion, to tell me that she knew more English words. Though she would barely make eye contact with me through her thick glasses, she seemed to enjoy meeting me, a visitor from a far-away world. Her round face lit up with excitement when I told her my name, Jacob. She then stood up and announced that she could sing in English, too. Karita's disability didn't stop her from seizing the moment, and the stage, to execute an excellent children's song in English. After her brief performance, she spoke again and carefully selected each word to maintain the proper translation.

"These. Are. My. Friends," she said, gazing at the ground.

Sensing my confusion, Maria, her teacher, gently clarified, "She has some imaginary friends with her today." Smiling, I looked down at the four non-existent friends to her left and introduced myself. More giggles flowed from Karita. As the memorable day was coming to a close and as Karita lost herself with her friends, I finally understood why two Norwegian women left their comfortable, conventional lives to embrace the challenge of helping children with emotional and cognitive disabilities.

Getting started

The day had begun with a jolt. I'd expected a phone call, sure, but not before my alarm clock went off. Worse still, my sore frame was still recovering from its maiden adventure in Norwegian rock climbing the previous day, so even reaching for the phone now proved a challenge.

"Hello?" I mumbled.

"Hi, it's Hege. How are you?"

"I'm great, Hege," I replied with faux cheer, hoping to convince her that her hospitality wasn't being squandered on someone who couldn't get up before 7:30 A.M. "Are we still going to Maria's today?"

"Why yes! I can meet you at the university in 45 minutes. Is that OK?"

"Yes, that should be fine. I'll see you there."

Hege was taking me to a camp for kids where, come fall, she would be working full-time as the pedagogical manager. Hege's dear friend, and soon-to-be coworker, Maria, started the camp, called *Ersvika Sami Siida*, in the acreage behind her rural house. The camp is located in Ersvika, a farming and forested area situated between the northern Norwegian cities of Bodø and Fauske in Nordland County. The purpose of the camp is to provide troubled children with a restorative outdoor experience that also exposes them to elements of the native Scandinavian Sami culture. Depending on the day, the Ersvika Sami Siida receives 30–40 students from schools in Fauske and Bodø. The Ersvika Sami Siida is not only a field trip destination for elementary-aged students, but also a place where children with emotional and developmental disabilities can come and learn alongside other children. The name of the camp is based upon the Sami who are the native inhabitants of Northern Scandinavia whose culture is nature-based and known for herding reindeer. *Siida* is a Sami term with a dual meaning. In one sense, it refers to the physical area where the semi-nomadic Sami share knowledge, resources, and housing. The Sami gather to learn from one another and to help each other in a community. Its other meaning refers to the cultural values of working together, sharing resources, and interacting with nature.

Hege told me that Maria, over time, saw as a teacher and following in the schooling of her own children a negative change in Norway's education system. She decided that children were too physically confined in their schools and so weren't receiving a well-rounded educational experience. According to Maria, nature offered a better education for children. Instead of reading about certain plants or animals, Maria wanted the children to be able to see, touch, feel, and experience the *flora* and *fauna*. Maria was inspired to provide something that removed children from the classroom for a whole day and gave them a true taste of nature. Maria strongly believes in the power of nature to heal and comfort children, and she has decided to devote her career to this purpose.

After a quick shower, I walked briskly to the nearby University of Nordland, in Bodø, Norway, to meet Hege and her son, but I still arrived ten minutes late. Nonetheless, she greeted me with a warm hello and a hug, clearly harboring no ill feelings toward me for my tardiness. Hege's son, Sigurd, six years old, sat in the back of the car and remained fairly quiet as Hege and I conversed. We buckled our seatbelts and set off for Ersvika Sami Siida.

Hege exuded vivacity and good cheer. A middle-aged woman with light, blonde hair neatly pulled back, she's beautifully fair-skinned, a gift of her Scandinavian heritage. So are her clear, blue eyes, the perfect complement to her blithe spirit. After spending a short time with her in prior social settings, I saw how she soaked up every moment of life and was committed to sharing her *joie de vivre* with others. Although my main goal of the day was to see the camp and meet Maria, I was excited to learn more about Hege as the day progressed.

The drive

The half-hour drive to the camp gave me a chance to learn more about the journey that had led Hege to be a part of Maria's camp. Hege was a well-educated Norwegian who grew up in the small northern town of Fauske, about 60 kilometers east of Bodø, where she has now lived for almost twenty years. She came from a successful and adventurous family. Her mother served different city council positions in Norway, but had since moved to New Delhi, India, to work as a Director for UN Women in South Asia. Hege's love of other cultures began at a young age when she spent three weeks in England at the age of fourteen, and it only deepened after a series of trips to visit her mother in India. By now, Hege has sampled more than forty countries. In the meantime, she had worked for various organizations in Bodø. Hege turned forty this past year. Together with her husband, Tom, she has four other children besides Sigurd, who is her second youngest.

While driving us, Hege told me how she came to be involved with the camp: "I asked myself, 'If I could do anything, what would I do?' When I really thought about it, I decided that I wanted to be with Maria. This work is important and it makes a difference."

Hege had achieved her undergraduate degree at the Norwegian University of Science and Technology (NTNU) in Trondheim, Norway, and pursued advanced degrees at the same university. But feeling burned out after nearly finishing her PhD, she decided to take a sabbatical from academe in hopes of re-finding her "passion for learning." She spoke with joy as she explained her decision to leave the security and financial stability of an established career path. When Hege described her new work at the Ersvika Sami Siida, her face lit up in excitement.

Hege described the Siida as a place where kids could get away from the classroom. "But it's not just an occasion for yet another field trip," she explained. Rather, it intends to holistically nourish youngsters who have cognitive, emotional, and developmental disabilities. According to Hege, the healing occurs through the children's group interaction with plants, animals, trees, fire, and a past culture. Instead of looking to new technologies or advances in medicine to help address some of the problems with children, Hege considers a child's natural environment to be the most important contributor to recovery and healing. She said it's essential to move the children into a singularly peaceful setting where they can be closer to nature and experience a life style that's utterly new to them.

The Sami people

Maria's camp is based on the culture of the Sami people, who are indigenous to Northern Scandinavia – Norway, Sweden, Finland, and Russia. Having lived there as nomads and reindeer herders for centuries, they developed well-established customs and ways of living. Even today, the Sami people have their own style of government, their own religious beliefs, and their own way of using things. Hege and Maria set up the camp like a Sami community because of the

Sami people's long-standing relationship with nature. In the past, these people relied absolutely on nature for their basic survival, so they learned to make use of every part of nature to sustain themselves. Literally nothing went to waste. If they slaughtered an animal, the skin and even every organ would be used for some purpose. In the same way, they maximized what nature gave to them. They were experts in sustainability. They had to be.

Maria and Hege

After Hege gave me a quick history of the camp, I asked about Maria. Hege described Maria glowingly as her "first love." The phrase sent my curiosity into overdrive. Why would she describe her best friend as a "first love"? What is the nature of their relationship? What does Maria look like? What is her connection to the Sami people, and why did she choose to work with children now?

After another minute of driving, I noticed a heightened anticipation on Hege's face. We were clearly getting closer. In due course we turned left off of the main road, and, with a fjord immediately to our right, we continued half a kilometer down a gravel road. Up ahead I spotted a house and barn off to the left, and, opposite them on the right side of the road, another house and barn. The latter house, Hege said, was Maria's. It resembled your traditional two-story Norwegian farmhouse, complete with a welcoming porch. Less traditional was the trampoline in the front yard. What visiting child would not be delighted at that sight!

The arrival

When we stepped out of the car, we were immediately greeted by a young boy, one of Maria's six children, who had been eagerly awaiting the arrival of Sigurd. A small, gray goat had trailed him to the car and now followed the two boys to the trampoline, which Sigurd was eager to play on again. The goat, as I learned later, was essentially a domesticated orphan. The kids got to pet it, pick it up, and enjoy it loyally following them around the yard like a puppy.

Hege walked past the house and showed me the barn around the corner, where I got my first glimpse of the Sami Siida. I also quickly encountered four chickens, two roosters, and a white goose that, Hege warned me, "can be kind of aggressive." She advised that I "go for its throat if it gets too close." I watched it warily while Hege introduced me to another of Maria's sons and to one of the teachers who worked at the Siida.

Next, Maria approached us.

Her long, wavy black hair was tangled and rough looking, framing an attractive face whose skin carried not even a hint of Norwegian DNA. Instead of being fair, she was dark, presumably thanks to her many years spent working outside, and that darkness was emphasized by the black liner she had traced around her light, grey-blue eyes. I was instantly drawn to them, but something in me didn't want to gaze into them too long, for they were piercing. But Maria dispelled my unease by brightly smiling at me and extending her hand, then even coming in for a hug.

She had a slight but strong frame, her shoulders bare but for the single strap of her shirt, which, like her work pants and boots, was workaday black. Around her neck hung a bear claw, a couple of sharks' teeth, and a string of multi-colored beads, all of which created a massive array of bursting color in stark contrast with her black attire.

Unlike Hege, Maria had some difficulty speaking English, and would unconsciously switch over to Norwegian, forgetting that I then had no idea what she was saying.

The siida and lavvu

One of the first things we did was to tour the "community area," or siida, which Maria had skillfully recreated. The siida, a collection of teepees arranged in a fairly tight circle, represented how the Sami worked and banded close together. Though nomadic, they would often stop and establish a siida wherever they expected to stay awhile. At its very center, out in the open was a fire pit over which was suspended a handmade rack where pots and food could hang to be cooked. Maria explained that the position of the fire pit in the middle of the siida was quite intentional. The Sami worshipped sources of energy, such as fire and the sun, which they considered prime sources of life and health.

A few tables surrounded the fire pit, at one of which a couple of children sat coloring. Next, the two women led me closer to the forest toward a skin-covered teepee, called a "lavvu." Because lavvus could be packed up and moved whenever the Samis decamped for fresh food sources, they were very practical temporary homes for these nomadic people. Each family had its own lavvu, and a collection of lavvus made up the siida. The Sami people constructed lavvus out of sturdy wooden posts that were covered by large, virtually indestructible reindeer hides. About twenty feet tall, each circular lavvu had sleeping room for six to eight people.

Inside the lavvu, in the center, two parallel wooden strips on the ground created a long rectangle reaching from the entrance to the rear wall. The area between these strips held the fire where dinner was cooked, plus any offerings made to the Sami gods. This space was considered sacred for both religious and practical reasons, since it featured the fire, so walking within or across that rectangle was forbidden. Pine needles covered the floor of the lavvu, creating a soft place to sit. Hege informed me that normally the Sami would sit on reindeer pelts to stay warm.

Each family in the siida had a lavvu, and each family member had a prescribed place within it. Except for infants and toddlers, all the children, for example, would sit on the left side. There they would sleep, play, and eat while the parents, who sat only on the right side, prepared dinner or slept. The mother would always sit near the back of the lavvu – on the right side, of course – where she kept her pot and other cooking utensils. She was in charge of preparing all the family's food. The father stayed closest to the entrance, near his stack of firewood. His job was to keep the fire freshened and at the right temperature for cooking.

Infants and toddlers sat between the mother and father so that they could receive assistance with meals. The small opening at the very top of the lavvu vented the smoke and also helped ventilate the entire structure.

Maria used the lavvu to show her students how the Sami people lived – how they would eat and how each person had an assigned role in the family ecology. It provided some perspective for the kids, who were otherwise trapped in the bubble of their current worldview and existence. Maria emphasized that it's next to impossible for children to understand the Sami culture simply by reading about it in a book. The best way is for them to get out of the classroom and into a reconstructed siida.

In the winter, a lavvu can stay comfortably warm thanks to its own fire pit. Maria said that it's valuable for her young charges to see how the Sami people used nature and energy sources for everyday needs. Instead of telling children about these things, Maria wanted to *show* them how they did it. She believed that opening the minds of children through nature and the Sami people would give them a far broader worldview and a renewed relationship with nature.

The reindeer

Next to the lavvu was an empty, two-stall stable. I assumed it was for donkeys or mules, but no, it was actually for two reindeer. Maria, with Hege's translation, told me that the Sami were traditionally reindeer herders, and many still are. In fact, the only people allowed by law to own and breed reindeer in Norway are Sami people or those able to show Sami descent. Reindeer management has caused quite a conflict between the Sami and the Norwegian government over the last eighty years. The government has made many attempts to regulate reindeer herding in Norway, but the early laws oppressed the Sami by privileging non-Sami agricultural settlers in the mid-1900s. A new agreement, reached in the late 1970s, focused on the industrial production of reindeer to create profits and economic stability for the Sami (Riseth, 2003). But that created still more tension with the government because it disregarded the cultural aspects of reindeer herding. Possessing reindeer allows the Sami to promote their culture, whereas those Sami who don't own reindeer are limited in their ability to share their cultural history with the modern world.

The Sami have also been at odds with the Norwegian government in educational considerations. At one time, Sami children were forced to go to Norwegian schools and weren't even allowed to speak their native language. They were required to learn and speak only Norwegian. As a result, many Sami today are unable to speak the same language as their extended family members. While the government has tried to work with the Sami, there have been significant conflicts between the two entities.

Maria reached out to an older man, Annfinn, who is of Sami descent, to work at the camp. He owns its two reindeer and has an important role in the work at Ersvika Sami Siida. Besides providing the reindeer for the kids to pet and observe, Annfinn has also helped Maria develop the content of the camp and promote the Sami culture. His extensive personal knowledge of that culture helped shape Maria's vision for the camp. Much like the two reindeer and the nature of the Sami, everything at Maria's camp has one overriding purpose: to help these youngsters experience, in a natural setting, something completely new and fun, and thereby experience positive feelings for a change.

The purpose

After our short tour of the siida, Maria, Hege, and I sat down for some pre-lunch coffee. It gave me a chance to ask Maria, directly, some questions about the siida. She said that she started her camp in order to help heal young people, especially those struggling with depression, social anxiety, and other emotional and developmental problems. She believed that placing the children in a siida allowed them to learn, first hand, about nature, the energy of fire, and the Sami culture. They would then leave with a new perspective on their troubles and with a new sense of peace.

Maria said that the central focus of the traditional siida was energy. She explained that the Sami needed the sun and heat to survive, so these were both privileged at the siida. Thus, in her own siida, most mornings include a time of meditation for the children to connect with this energy. Even as we were talking, Maria, a devout sun lover herself, shifted to the right a couple of feet because the sun had temporarily hidden behind a tree branch and had cast her in shade.

"We have to soak it up while we can," she said through a big smile and thick Norwegian accent.

Maria also believed that the siida and the sun would "feed your soul." Besides providing energy, the place was very much about feeding the spiritual side of a life.

While we were enjoying our coffee, Maria began to explain some details of nature immediately around us – ones that we probably would never notice. For example, she picked up the leaf of a weed growing right next to me and explained that this is what the Sami use in painkillers. She then found me another edible leaf and proceeded to discuss the two leaves in detail, explaining how the Sami would use them with great effectiveness. Then she picked up yet another plant – this one a flowering plant – and explained how a drop of dew would settle in the middle of its petals every morning, and as the day went on, the flower would absorb the water for nourishment. Maria believed that there are many such aspects of nature that we typically overlook. Even as she spoke about leaves and dewdrops, I could see the depth of her belief. She was not only giving me a botany lesson, she was also showing me some of the significant meaning she found in nature.

Then, without warning, she stood up in one quick motion, said something to Hege in Norwegian, and left us. Hege explained that Maria was ready to work, but she didn't have anything for lunch quite yet, so she had gone to get more food. Given all her emphasis on nature, I half-expected her to go capture one of the goats and slaughter it before my eyes, then use the bladder as a canteen for the day. Instead, she went to the closest grocery store and came back with a baguette. After munching our lunch, it was time to work.

The work day

Work was important to Maria, and you could tell that she expected to work all day, every day. That particular day's assignment, which we offered to help her with, was to move her fourteen sheep and twelve goats from one pasture, now grazed down, into another pasture that had grass up to our elbows. That involved herding the animals into a temporary pen before moving her entire electric fence over to the new pasture. Oh, and one other thing: she said she also wanted the fence to include the small creek that ran through the property so that the animals had ready access to fresh water.

But first Maria needed to get them out of the old pasture and corral them into the holding pen. So she put some feed into a metal bin, started banging on it, and watched as the animals burst out of the fence and ran toward her. But some saw greener grass in a different area and bolted for it, while a few of the smaller animals escaped through a hole in the temporary fence.

While Hege and Maria continued to corral the herd, I busied myself with disassembling the electric fence and moving it over to the new pasture.

Meanwhile, watching Maria and Hege talk and work taught me the yin–yang relationship they have. While Maria tried to move the animals into the new pasture, Hege, without prompting from Maria, already located a long rod to help direct them. It brought home something that Hege had said about her friend.

"Maria loves to start things," she said. "She will have an incredible idea and start it out without a plan and without any thought to how much it will cost."

The project for the day, moving the sheep and goats to a new pasture, was a great example of how Maria made decisions. The new pasture wasn't even close to being ready for fencing yet. The grass there was way too high, and it would have to be mowed before any new fence was put up. But Maria proceeded undaunted.

Hege, on the other hand, was a finisher. She wouldn't start a project unless she knew that it could be successfully completed. Maria needed Hege to finish her projects while Hege needed Maria to start ones that she never would've begun in the first place. Hege asked Maria some specific questions about where she wanted the new fence and how she wanted it to look in the end. Without these questions, Maria probably wouldn't have even planned out where the new fence was going. The combination of the two differing personalities and work styles showed me how differences can be complementary. The relationship maintained a delicate balance and rarely reached either of the extremes. The deep-rooted, symbiotic friendship would be crucial, I thought, to the success of the siida and its work.

Hege came and told me that we needed to user her power trimmer and trim the grass so that we could place the fence into the ground. Maria's young son had tried, but the trimmer proved too heavy for him, so the job fell to me. Which was fine. I had used a trimmer countless times back home, so I was comfortable with it. I fired it up with ease and began cutting the wet, wispy grass.

Everything was going well and I had the first main part of the perimeter marked out along the road. Hege had already started to come behind me with the fence. At one point, though, I stopped when the trimmer got clogged from excess grass. It was then that I noticed that the bottoms of my jeans were covered in tiny grass clippings. I hadn't planned on field work that day, but it was a nice day and I really couldn't complain. The sun was out and I was strengthened by the idea that I was contributing – in a small way – to the siida.

All of a sudden, the trimmer's motor revved and I saw a bright orange piece of something go flying. Ah, the darn line had run out. I told Hege and then went off to the small shop next to the barn in search of fresh line. But I didn't find any there, so I returned to the pasture for instructions only to find Hege trimming with an old wooden scythe. It required the user to swing it horizontally. The blade was surprisingly sharp, and Hege had to make sure she kept her feet out of harm's way. After watching her for a bit to learn the proper technique, I took over. Soon, I felt like I was finally becoming part of the place. There I was, using an archaic tool, working the land. Imagine that! In the background, I could hear the babbling brook that had previously been muted by the trimmer's motor. It was very soulful. Meanwhile, the repetitive motion and sweaty work felt both therapeutic and productive.

Well, not totally productive. I managed to clip the electrical fence twice with the scythe, even after Hege had warned me to be careful. But we eventually crossed the creek and finished the fencing operation. By now it was about 3:30 in the afternoon. Maria came by and pronounced herself very impressed with our work. I think this little project was a great example of the complementary talents of Maria and Hege. While Hege and I were working on the fence, Maria had already moved on to a new project.

Our final task involved moving the animals from the temporary pasture into the newly fenced one. Maria grabbed the same metal feeding bin that she had used earlier and headed to the pen. She opened the door and the twenty-six animals came streaming out, bleating and baaing. Maria led them out at a brisk pace in a sort of triumphal procession. The sheep and goats definitely knew who was boss. The animals were almost tripping over each other to get closest to their shepherd and her metal bin. The flock was so close to Maria and each other that they moved, seemingly, as one unit. With the sun beating on her smiling face, and all her animals behaving perfectly, Maria truly looked in her element, happily leading the animals into a greener pasture where more food and a refreshing creek awaited.

The departure

Before saying my goodbyes, I was able to meet the children who happened to be at the siida that day: Karita and Christopher. These two children were around ten years old, and both had developmental disabilities. Even though the day was not scheduled to be a day with kids, Maria and Hege always keep the door open in case anyone needed to come.

Karita and I had a fun interaction, and the siida seemed to have a positive effect on her. She was bright and smiled and sang a beautiful song. Christopher, on the other hand, must have been one of the children suffering from depression.

He bore scars on his head, either from an injury or surgery, and I felt a deep compassion for him. Unsuccessfully trying for a moment of eye contact with him brought home to me the difficulty of the women's job. I have worked with youth before, but never with children carrying disabilities. Sometimes, I decided, maybe the best thing you can do is to just *be* there with them.

But for me it was now time to go. I thanked Maria for letting me come out and asked her if I might come again. Sure, she said, and recommended I return in a couple of weeks when there would be more kids around. I agreed, and told her to save any more trimming for me. Just then, Hege suggested our going back into the lavvu one more time, saying she really wanted me to *feel* the energy of the place. I have to confess that I never did feel it the same way she did, but there was no denying the belief written on her face that this primitive structure could somehow help children struggling with depression, divorced parents, or other difficulties.

Still, at that moment, sitting in the lavvu, I finally got it. It wasn't about the pasture for the sheep. It wasn't about the domesticated goat or the aggressive goose. It wasn't even necessarily about the Sami people. It was about two women who saw a problem in their culture and cared enough about young people to find a way to help. I suspected that any ability of Maria's siida to help lift young people out of depression wouldn't come primarily from the peaceful setting or the explanation of Sami culture, but rather from the generous souls of the two women who had committed their lives to helping struggling youngsters find a place of peace.

Reference

Riseth, J. A. (2003). Sami reindeer management in Norway: Modernization challenges and conflicting strategies. Reflections upon the co-management alternative. In Jentoft, S., Minde, H., & Nilsen, R. (Eds.), *Indigenous peoples: resource management and global rights* (pp. 229–246). Netherlands: Eburon Academic Publishers.

5   First came love, then came chocolate
Pioneering a new Værøy tradition

Leah LeFebvre, Bodø Graduate School of Business

Jeanette Johansen
Photograph by Lofoten Sjokolade

In 2005, Jeanette Johansen was working as a hairdresser in the northern Norwegian town of *Skrolsvik*, living a busy but mundane life. One weekend at the Codstock music festival in Henningsvær, Lofoten, while taking a breather at the local pub with some girlfriends, she chanced to meet an attractive man named Remi, who introduced himself as a graphic designer from Værøy, a village out in the remote Lofoten Islands. He, too, was attending the festival, and he took an immediate fancy to her.

Jeanette, a bit wary and not looking for love, rejected his advances that night, but Remi, not the least dissuaded, later tracked down her home phone number and started patiently courting her long-distance. Two years of phone calls and text messages later, Jeanette finally surrendered and moved to Værøy to give their budding relationship an honest try. It proved a visit that would revolutionize her life.

Today, Jeanette is the proud owner of Lofoten Sjokolade (http://www.lofoten-sjokolade.no/), a chocolate business that grew and flourished despite the skepticism of everyone but her now-husband Remi and their children. Her chocolates are not only delicious; they're also distinctive and surprisingly healthy. Unlike conventional chocolatiers, Jeanette uses Konfektyrsjokolade – a pure quality chocolate with less sugar and real cocoa – to create her confections with no added sugar, no butter, and a bold taste. This has helped Jeanette brand Lofoten Sjokolade as unique from other Norwegian and European chocolates, and has helped her to grow her business in Værøy and beyond, with Web sales annually alone now totaling nearly 2 million NOK ($330,000).

When she first started her shop, back in 2008, Jeanette was quite the novice chocolatier. But today she can claim an experienced palate, ample expertise, and two employees who assist her ever-developing venture. Her success isn't just personal; it also extends into the local Værøy community, increasing sustainable job opportunities outside the historic stockfish industry of this village despite all odds and skepticism.

The locals never figured that a chocolate producer could be successful on an island of just 750 people and a struggling tourism industry. They all remembered the businesses that had failed before Lofoten Sjokolade – businesses that received financial support from the government but still couldn't turn a profit in Værøy. So, yes, this beautiful yet isolated location couldn't seem less promising for a chocolate shop, of all things. Little did they know.

A small fishing village

Though Værøy translates in English as "weather," locals like to call it "the island of bird catchers." And it's a fitting description, for Værøy is home to large, remarkably domesticated seabird colonies – so domesticated that inhabitants once used their bare hands to capture eagles. But besides its plentiful bird life (puffins, cormorants, terns, sea eagles, and guillemots, among others) that makes it a bird watcher's paradise, the island features some of Norway's most picturesque, craggy landscapes, with stunning midnight summer-sun vistas, uninhabited white sandy beaches, and, for the Arctic, a relatively mild Gulf Stream climate.

More than 80 percent of Værøy's 750 islanders work, live, and breathe the fishing industry. In the Lofoten Island region, that means fishing cod in the winter, Greenland halibut and saithe (polluck) in the summer, and herring in the autumn. Although the winds can be harsh on Værøy, the island weather conditions offer a perfect climate for hanging and drying fish. Summer provides temperatures ranging from 11 °C to 15 °C (52 °F to 59 °F) and a cool midnight sun, while winter offers long dark nights and temperatures from –2 °C to 2 °C (28 °F to 36 °F). Drying is the oldest known method of preserving fish, with a thousand-year-old history. Since the beginnings of the Viking era, dried fish, known as "stockfish," have been the cornerstone of northern Norwegian culture.

The village celebrates its age-old partnership with nature by depending on stockfish for its livelihood, but that livelihood comes with a price; stock fishing depends upon the natural environment to preserve the fish without additives. After making their catches, Værøy's fishermen sell living cod and other varieties to local companies who bleed the fish to ensure a quick demise and maximize freshness. After this critical gutting-and-cutting operation, the fish are hung from large wooden drying racks all over town throughout the winter. Besides depending on island weather, Værøy pays another price for this long-established process: the stench of drying fish is pervasive and hard to forget. But, in exchange, the odor fades away as the summer approaches and the fish are transformed into a pricey and culturally significant cuisine.

Although Værøy may appear a simple fishing village, the global impact of the stockfish industry – Norway's oldest industry – is significant. The combined value of harvesting, drying, sorting, and packing involved with its stockfish production translates to export values of nearly 1 million NOK annually (269,000 per capita) on Værøy. Norwegian stockfish is in demand all over the world, with Italy, Spain, Nigeria, Sweden, Croatia, and the U.S. being the largest export markets.

Based on this demand, Værøy decided in 1984 to build a regional airport at Nordlandet, on the island's northern side. No one lived in that area because of its tumultuous weather, but the Norwegian Meteorological Institute supported its construction, so it got the go-ahead. After two years and 15 million NOK, the airport, spanning 800 by 30 meters (2600 by 98 feet) and connected to the island by dirt road, officially opened on June 1, 1986.

Unfortunately, dangerous winds and low flight regularity constantly plagued the airport. Aircraft were not allowed to take off or land if winds exceeded 20 knots, which frequently blew in from the west. The airport had the highest number of flight cancellations in Norway during its four-year operation. Despite forewarnings and one close call, the planes kept flying.

But on April 12, 1990, an accident finally happened; just one minute after takeoff, a commercial plane crashed, killing all five people aboard (http:// aviation-safety.net/database/record.php?id=19900412-0). The Norwegian Ministry of Transport and Communications permanently closed the airport some two years later and put it up for sale. Since 1993, the only way to and from Værøy is by ferry or helicopter (http://www.avinor.no/en/airport/varoy/ frontpage).

New beginnings

Not long after the plane crash, Remi, who was working as a graphic designer and finishing his degree in Australia, returned to Værøy for a weeklong family visit and saw an ad for the airport sale. Despite the infamous tragedy, the offer intrigued Remi; he liked the idea of working from home in this beautiful, remote village. With a winning bid of roughly 1.5 million NOK ($250,000), Remi bought the airport, complete with tower, and moved back to his childhood community.

Today, that tower is not only home to Remi, Jeanette, and their four children, but also where Lofoten Sjokolade got its start. As her business has grown, Jeanette moved from the old pump garage where she started her business to the first floor of the tower, where she personally greets every customer that visits her shop. Few believed a chocolate producer could ever make it on this small island, but Jeanette's family encouraged her to pursue her dream, and she found the persistence and talent to make it happen.

To begin, she applied for start-up money with the local government, just as many hopeful Værøy entrepreneurs had in the past. Though she garnered minimal support at a community meeting, where skeptics were rife, Jeanette remained determined. Although she acknowledged the idea sounded a bit crazy, she argued that her business would bring success both to herself and to the Værøy community.

Eventually, local officials, wanting to be fair, agreed that she deserved the same opportunity for success or failure as other entrepreneurs had gotten, and awarded her the start-up money for Lofoten Sjokolade. She also applied for financial assistance from Innovation Norway, who rejected her initial proposal flat-out. But again, Jeanette was undeterred. After filing complaints, she received a new case and was eventually awarded the money, as well as an entrepreneurial mentor. This new partnership with Innovation Norway proved invaluable; the expertise and financial support helped turn Jeanette's dream into a reality.

Without the necessary training, equipment, or a business plan, she set about building her chocolate business one pot at a time. First, she bought some molds to represent the artistic and natural inspiration of her surroundings. But since she didn't know exactly what to do with those molds, her next step was researching novel combinations of chocolate instead of traditional recipes from Belgium and France, where most European chocolatiers are trained.

There were no premier schools in Norway, and especially not in her remote part of the world, so Jeanette, like a good inventor, taught herself, starting with only a few ingredients in the airport home's kitchen and using her children as test subjects. Her first efforts produced flops. Jeanette had to learn to temper the chocolate to get the right texture and appearance, and as she poured the batter into the molds, she didn't know whether to expect disaster or perfection. With the ding of a timer, she'd grab her hot pads and turned over the molds. Eventually, as the chocolates emerged from the oven, looking delicious and tasting even more delectable, Jeanette found herself swelling with pride and happiness. *This may just work*, she thought to herself.

One thirsty tourist

Then one day, without much time to digest either the candy or her potential success, she heard a knock at the door. It was a thirsty tourist asking to refill his canteen. Jeanette complied, offering the stranger both water and – why not? – a sample of her new creation. He happily accepted a small bag of chocolate and departed as abruptly as he appeared.

The next day, Jeanette continued her experimenting. Little did she know, though, her candy had become an overnight sensation. She looked up to find a group of Værøy visitors lined up outside her makeshift shop. Hard at work since early morning, Jeanette didn't even have the chance to taste her second batch before it all sold. That single passerby had triggered an avalanche of consumers, and Jeanette was stunned; she couldn't make the chocolate fast enough to meet the demand. Her adventurous spirit, persistence, and that serendipitous encounter with the wandering tourist had transformed the future of her chocolate business.

Today, demand still exceeds production, especially in the summer months during tourist season when her candy just flies off the shelves. Tourists hear of this strange little chocolate shop over in the old airport and are intrigued, or even suspicious, and come to see what's up. Jeanette explains that, on countless occasions, they'll arrive looking bewildered at the sight of her multi-colored cats sprawled across the picnic tables and a seemingly vacant tower on the windy shoreline. They cautiously open the white door, surprised to see brightly colored shelves lined with naturally flavored artistic creations, and are welcomed in by Jeanette's warm smile.

Any doubts are quickly replaced by appreciation for the exquisitely – and sometimes even erotically – shaped chocolates that taste even better than they look. The patrons' euphoria starts with the nose. They'll find themselves savoring the sweet, rich smells wafting throughout the shop. More often than not, they'll leave with full bags of chocolates in their hands and smiles on their faces.

In one case, Jeanette recalls two men who had traveled up from the southern region of Norway. Along the way, they had picked up a German tourist who was hiking the country. The German asked them whether they all might stop for a moment at some shop called Lofoten Sjokolade, for he had heard about its delicious treats and was eager to try one. The Norwegians agreed. When the three of them pulled up to the old airport tower, the German thought his companions were playing a joke on him. Surely this couldn't be a chocolate shop! But they assured him it was. Hesitantly he opened the door in hopes of meeting this mysterious chocolate maker. Overcome by the sights and smells that greeted him, the German sat silently in Jeanette's shop for a full hour, just absorbing the sensual pleasures. What better testimonial?

A family business for the community

Lofoten Sjokolade quickly outgrew Jeanette's kitchen in that airport tower. Now she is looking to build an even bigger shop. With more business came the need for more help, so Jeanette hired two local residents. Her shop has created jobs for the community, but it has also become a symbol of possibility in this small fishing village.

All over Northern Norway, populations are aging and declining; young people simply aren't staying in these communities to work in traditional industries or live off the mainland. And it's not just because of the region's remoteness and often harsh weather. The cultural traditions of rural locations don't exactly welcome entrepreneurs, as evidenced by the many skeptics who doubted this chocolate shop could actually be a Værøy success story.

But Jeanette and her chocolate production have established her business and her own place in the community. Local residents have come to respect not just her accomplishments but her economic contributions to their village. And now, tourists aren't the only ones supporting Jeanette's business; the villagers themselves buy her chocolates year-round as gifts that wrap Værøy culture in a delicious package.

All you need is love

When Jeanette first visited this small fishing village in 2007, she could not have known she would find three unexpected loves there – Remi, Værøy, and chocolate. She doesn't miss the hustle and bustle of her previous life. Now she lives a life that feels timeless. She's even discarded her wristwatch.

Immediate success could easily overwhelm a first-time chocolate maker, but Jeanette is fulfilling a lifelong dream of being an independent business woman, owning and running a chocolate shop. Jeanette experiences no stress because she has her beloved children, her cats, her supportive husband, and her chocolate. This intimacy has grown from the natural environment; less than a hundred meters from her home and business, the clear blue waters of the Arctic meet white sandy beaches. The remote island may be undesirable for many, but for Jeanette, it offers the harmony and serenity of a simpler, purer lifestyle.

Similarly, tourists are drawn to a clean environment literally a stone's throw from the ocean. Lofoten Sjokolade is also the only chocolate producer in all of Northern Norway, an attraction that draws tourists, showcases Værøy and its fishing traditions, and symbolizes new opportunities for local culture.

It was love that brought Jeanette to Værøy, and according to her, when you eat Lofoten Sjokolade, you should feel like you're in love, too!

Part II

Pushing for change in a foreign business culture

6 A captain and his way through the ice
A history of the Northern Sea Route

Nadezhda Nazarova, Bodø Graduate School of Business

Mikhail's view from the bridge of his icebreaker
Photograph by Mikhail

Some say that northern people are like birds of a feather that flock together. In Moscow in May 2010, the country's foremost conference on the Northern Sea Route (NSR) – "Northern Sea Route: Strategy of Renewal" – gave them a good nesting place. The list of participants, which included CEOs and ministers, was even more impressive than the venue, the imposing hall of the President Hotel. During coffee breaks people would disperse into small groups to chat about the various ways that the NSR would promote rapid Arctic development.

Feeling somewhat miscast in such a fancy assemblage, one noble-looking man stood alone at a round coffee table. Maybe early 40s, delicately tailored and sporting side whiskers on a weathered face, he looked not so much lost as utterly placeless there. His name was Mikhail; translated from the Hebrew it means "(one) who is like God." Like many of the guests, he was a native Muscovite, or at least from near Moscow. But unlike many of them he was hardly a stranger to the High North. In fact, for nearly half his life, twenty years, he had stood at the wheel of an icebreaker. Unlike these landlubbers, he was a mariner through and through.

Curiously, nobody in his family had shared his wanderlust and interest in seafaring. His father was the head of a food-industry enterprise; his mother worked in the laboratory of a large chemical plant. The wash of the waves he was always hearing had come not from them but solely from books. As a young lad, he had devoured plenty of books, mostly about sea adventures, and they could inspire and teach him about all imaginable twists and turns of his future profession. He started to read these books in elementary school. He soon lost himself in Hugo's *Ninety-Three* and *The Toilers of the Sea*, and Sabatini's *The Odyssey of Captain Blood*. But his favorite was Kaverin's extraordinarily popular Soviet novel from the early 1940s, *The Two Captains*, featuring two valiant men who devoted their lives to the development of the Russian Arctic. It took for its leitmotif the famous last line of "Ulysses," Lord Alfred Tennyson's nineteenth-century poem: "To strive, to seek, to find, and not to yield." This inspirational line has spoken to many adventurers and determined souls; indeed, it was inscribed on a commemorative cross in honor of the Antarctic explorer Robert Falcon Scott and his team, who died on their return trek to the South Pole in 1912. Together with his best playmate, Alexey, Mikhail dreamed about all the epic challenges described in the books they raced through. At that time, maritime navigation offered one of the few options for adventurous souls wanting to expand the borders of their huge country, which felt sealed off from the rest of the world. Perhaps the only other two professions that then allowed crossing the borders were the arts and politics. But only the sea would not constantly claim one's freedom. Instead, it promised even greater feelings of being untrammeled, even happily lost and forgotten. As Mikhail proved, one could fall in love with the sea through reading books. But to be smitten with the High North one needed to live it out.

At 17, Mikhail dreamed about doing something really heroic in his life, something entirely different from the stagnant and predefined life of a city dweller. So, hungry for adventure, he packed a small suitcase, bought himself a one-way train ticket, and went far, far north to Murmansk, Russia's largest port above the Arctic Circle. There he enrolled in the Murmansk High Engineering Marine Academy. Though he was allotted six years to prepare himself for Arctic waters, after just one year he became a deck trainee on the *Kruzenshtern*, a four-masted barque – a tall ship, originally built as a cargo vessel in 1926, but now a marine training ship that was capable of being operated by a small but skilled crew. After being surrendered by Germany to the USSR in 1946 as war reparation, the *Kruzenshtern* had achieved renown in many international regattas. And the one in 1978 was no exception: the barque won the regatta, beating ships from Oslo in Norway and Harwich in England. Isn't it any boy's dream to train for the sea on such a fast, gorgeous sailing ship? And not just fast, but the largest vessel in its class at that time! In the Oslo harbor the teams were met by the Royal family. A smile always touches Mikhail's face and his eyes gleam when remembering those magical days. And there was still more magic for him. Right before his graduation, he met a girl who agreed to wait for him on shore while he pursued his future adventures. She understood him, being from the family of the *toilers of the sea*. The boy's dream was likely to come true.

After graduation he spent twenty years with the Murmansk Shipping Agency, exploring every corner of the NSR. As the first chief officer of a nuclear ice-breaker, he prowled the Arctic far and wide, carving the ice channels in the Yenisei Bay and the Gulf of Ob, probably the toughest areas along the Russian Arctic coast. His assignment was to provide a safe, speedy passage for the vessels carrying cargo along the NSR destined for building up the Northern territories and supplying West Siberia's oil industry. It was part of the big Arctic plan to make the Russian north the shortest link in the global trade flows between East and West. Though that link also featured endless ice fields and subzero tempera-tures, it was worth it: the NSR provided one-third shorter delivery time from Rotterdam to Yokohama, Japan.

Mikhail's many years of fight, or maybe friendship, with the Arctic sea ice made him a perfect candidate for helping supervise the Varandey project located in the Nentsy Autonomous Area, the area to the north of Murmansk and Arkangelsk, bounded by the Ural mountain range from the east and by the waters of the three Arctic seas – Kara, Barents, and White – from the north. In the local, Nentsy language Varandey literally means "ends of the earth." Initially, it used to be the habitat of indigenous Nentsy folk – hunters, reindeer-herders, and fishermen. The habitation started a new life in 1974 when the first geologists arrived there. But by the end of the last century the entire population was resettled from the area, now deemed a Natural Disaster Zone. Due to enormous winds there, which for at least fifty days each year exceed 15 meters per second, the severe waters of the Barents Sea steadily reclaim new spaces from the land, washing away any signs of human presence. That is why the LUKOIL company decided to replace its temporary terminal there – a terminal with a low off-loading capacity that it had operated since 2000 – with a permanent, ice-resistant off-loading terminal for oil tankers. This would help secure its further delivery of oil to international markets throughout the year.

The terminal had special meaning for Naryanmarneftegaz (NMNG), the joint venture between Canadian ConocoPhillips and LUKOIL, created in 2005 to enable the development of resources in Russia's Timan-Pechora province. Via subsea pipelines, the produced oil is transferred to the terminal some 22 km away in the Barents Sea. While the area is ice-free much of the year, it's always under potential attack from drifting ice, a serious threat to any transloading operation and, therefore, the company's efficiency. So the project clearly needed an expert in ice management. In short, it needed Mikhail. And he, for his part, needed challenges and further development, so that employment seemed meant to be. He joined NMNG in 2008 as a senior engineer on safety of marine operations.

Though a rather small company relative to Russian oil-and-gas established traditions, NMNG has made a welcome contribution to the High North development, chiefly by ensuring oil deliveries despite the wildly unpredictable, hostile waters of the Barents Sea. Remarkably, the company also won a typical "oil vs. environment" debate when in 2010 it was named the "Best Russian Company with regard to industrial security, work safety and environmental control." It could have been considered one of few success stories from the High North in modern Russia.

But then, without warning, NMNG's rosy future dimmed when the draft of the new law on the NSR upended everything.

The new law

The prior rules of navigation governing the NSR lines had been approved by the USSR Ministry of Marine Fleet back in September 1990. While these rules certainly helped protect the fragile marine environment there from ships in areas covered with ice for more than six months a year, the exact borders of the areas delimiting the NSR had been left legislatively undefined. So once the new era of Arctic development had commenced, with its plan to open Russia's Arctic waters for year-round navigation, including by foreign vessels, the issue of the NSR's borders took on fresh urgency with the Russian Ministry of Transport. It eventually drafted a new federal law cumbersomely titled "On amending certain legislative acts of the Russian Federation in part of State regulation of commercial navigation by lines in the area of The Northern Sea Route." Besides its good intentions to protect the Russian Arctic waters from negative effects expected from knowing international navigation, the borders of the NSR were now to be defined so as to make navigation, it claimed, "more convenient from a practical point of view and will not cause unnecessary questions" – that is to say, the larger the area controlled by the Administration of the NSR, the safer the navigation for all the vessels will be.

Good intentions, yes, but there was a downside. At the planning stage, when the main logistics scheme was to be defined, it was thought that the tariffs on ice-breaking services would continue to grow, but at a rational and affordable pace. However, with respect to expanding the NSR's borders to the west, as it was suggested, oil transportation from the Varandey terminal would partially go by the NSR line. That may have led to the company's cost increase by 530 rubles per ton of oil. In which case, additional expenses for the company would amount to 4 billion rubles per year, something not considered when the cost–benefit analysis of the project had been prepared years earlier. The worst consequences, if the law were accepted unamended, could be that NMNG would search for a cheaper transportation option and choose another transportation mode, popularly known as "shifting to the pipe." In that case, an ice expert at the company wouldn't be needed anymore. The NSR would lose approximately 7.5 million tons of oil produced by NMNG, not to mention its potential reserves, which by 2015 were expected to reach 19 million tons. And this was also without includ-ing other projects that could leave the NSR – projects such as the Prirazlomnaya platform, intended to be the world's first Arctic-class ice-resistant oil platform, and Transnet's construction of an oil terminal at the port city of Indiga on the Pechora Sea. The latter was expected to contribute 12–24 million tons per year to be transported by sea.

Such a law has long been on its way – right from the disintegration of the Soviet Union. Expanding the borders was considered the easiest way to increase cargo volumes along the NSR, which were still four times lower than they were in 1980s. In those times the Russian High North with its tantalizing great NSR was privileged, growing, and promising.

Ice-breaking and the Northern Sea Route

It is difficult to say when the history of the Russian north began. Simply stated, while Europeans were exploring and colonizing America and Africa, Russians were moving north and east. But that Russian migration wasn't supported by the state; rather, it rested on popular and entrepreneurial initiative. The steady rec-lamation of northern territories led to the development of the NSR. And when the state finally turned its face to the north at the end of nineteenth century, northern expeditions and ice patrols became regular occurrences.

The exploration of the northern territories didn't stop even during World War I or the revolution of 1917. But, meanwhile, *planned* Arctic development got started in the 1920s and then expanded in 1932 when the NSR project got its own administrative unit: the Chief Directorate of the Northern Sea Route. Its goal was to finalize establishing the northern transport corridor, or "northern-eastern passage," and to make it fully functional by arranging regular cargo flows along the northern coast. As a transport artery it needed blood to function. With strong financial support from the government, the Directorate ambitiously – even audaciously – started a slew of projects. It launched several shipping agencies, polar aviation, a network of weather and scientific stations, and whole new port cities requiring huge human resources to establish and keep the whole system functioning for decades. Especially in retrospect, the Directorate made abundant sense as a centralized coordinating mechanism that could integrate and align the interests and needs of different units, and allow the Arctic system to be balanced and to function as one organism – one that could survive World War II, contrib-ute to the economic development of the Soviet state, and become a source of pride for Soviet citizens.

There had always been people who devoted their life to the North. Many of Russia's best graduates preferred the Arctic to all other available options. True, they'd find no oranges on the grocery shelves in the northern cities; even apples were available only occasionally. But they always had an ocean teeming with fish, and land full of tundra riches. On top of all that, they had a clearly defined navigation course, a course sometimes quite shaky in other parts of the country.

With surprising speed they were able to raise the economics of all Arctic zones and maximize cargo flows in all rivers and sea routes. Here, the icebreakers truly proved their worth. The first Arctic-class icebreaker was built in 1898, while the first nuclear icebreaker, the *Lenin*, was built in 1959. Even the development of Western Siberia's oil-and-gas fields in the 1970s–80s speaks to the invaluable work that the ice managers and other distinguished specialists had been performing in the Arctic for several decades. According to the "deal of the century," as it was immediately hailed, an agreement was signed between the USSR and the Federal Republic of Germany in 1970 with the latter promising to supply 1.2 million tons of big-diameter pipes for the construction of a gas pipeline to Western Europe. At the time, the only way to deliver such an oversized cargo was by sea navigation, and that remains the only option today. Without icebreakers, nature alone would dictate its rules of navigation with respect to both the duration of cruises and their routes.

Mikhail also contributed to that milestone history of Russian Arctic. In the 1980s he was the second officer on the diesel-electric icebreaker *Kiev*. The icebreakers of that type were able to extend the navigation period till October, or even November, and thus could annually pilot up to 300 additional vessels through the ice. Hence, timely technology development and its rapid implementation allowed the toilers of the Arctic sea to spend more time at the wheel and to win the fight with the capricious weather. The shipment time from Murmansk to the Far East even in October was reduced to ten days, while the icebreakers' teams used to watch astern the convoys of vessels delivering timber, pipes, and other products to areas of vital concern to the country. The annual cargo turnover at that time was around 6–8 million tons, and that was not even the limit. Due to the well-functioning navigation that was the main supply channel, geologists of the Nentsy Autonomous Area discovered, within the space of three decades, seventy-three oil-and-gas fields. The Arctic revived.

Not surprisingly, then, the idea of the essential and inevitable development of the High North went from one governor and government to another being absolutely supported and promoted by the state. The strategic importance of the Northern artery was unquestionable. In terms of weighty matters of state, the Soviet approach to the High North development definitely had something present-day leaders could learn from – in particular, those who came to power after 1991.

The new reality: stop the engine!

The commercialization reforms undertaken in Russia at the outset of the 1990s were, first of all, aimed at breaking up the old system. Free-market relationships inspired by the West were thought to be the end-all answer to the deeply centralized Soviet system, which by many was seen as restraining the country from normal, and faster, development. As a result, the country was set on market trail and allowed all previously state-owned, state-financed enterprises to enjoy what's called *free floatation*. But neither the country nor its citizens proved ready for such radical transformations of their functioning and living against the clock. For there to be market relationships, there must be a market. And it was not there. Poor incomes could not provide industries with their required and timely needs in Material Technical supply. Instead of a smooth and systematic conversion to the new system of management, the system just stopped and collapsed. Any assets that could be privatized were grabbed, lost, or sold in pieces. It was painful to see. People's salaries went unpaid for months or even years, yet most continued to do their work anyway. Teachers still had students to teach, and the sick still needed medical attention. Yes, there were no apples on the grocery shelves in northern cities. But they could hardly be found even in central regions during those hard times. Even bread and other essential products had to be distributed via a coupon system. The previously well-tuned system of product deliveries to remote northern areas by sea was occasionally disrupted. On average, in the period of 1993–1997 state financing was next lower order than the decade before. As a result, by 1997 probe boring fell by fourteen times and by seventeen times for seismic activities. The previously well-functioning polar system, consisting of many strongly integrated units for several decades, was pulled apart.

Mikhail and his family decided to stay in Murmansk. The certificate of shipping competency that he had received thanks to his many years in the North could still get him food and clothes. By that time he was a chief officer on the nuclear icebreaker *Vaigach*, a ship able to operate in temperatures down to –50 ° C and able to break ice 1.77 meters thick. *Vaigach's* main task was to carve a way through the ice for metal-loaded ships from Norilsk and timber- and ore-carrying vessels from the river port of Igarka to Port Dickson in Malaysia. As a wit once observed, without shipping one part of the globe will starve to death, while the other will freeze. In the North, fishery and cargo transportation will always be needed. But even if there was work for Mikhail to do during the 1990s, the country was going to ruin, and his old dream about the Arctic was icing up again.

Though the NSR was finally opened for foreign vessels, seafaring cargo volumes fell several times the amount typical for the NSR prosperity period. The nuclear icebreakers were assigned to the federal state unitary enterprise (FSUE) Atomflot (literally "nuclear fleet"). Atomflot belonged to the State Atomic Energy Corporation, an umbrella utility called "Rosatom," and was given the freedom – or rather the burden – of financing itself by charging companies a fee for any support services it provided. The icebreaker fleet absolutely depends on being worked to full capacity. At first, Atomflot was receiving governmental subsidies, and so was able to stay the course. But in 2003 all subsidies stopped. As a result, the financing of operating expenses for maintaining the expensive icebreaker fleet was entirely transferred to those companies requiring icebreaker services. And as long as no new "deals of the century" were forthcoming, the Russian nuclear fleet – the only one of its kind in the world – was left standing idle in the harbors. As a result, the tariffs for icebreaker services kept constantly growing, and fewer and fewer companies could afford those services. This also meant, of course, a reduction of Mikhail's time spent in the Arctic waters. In 2005 it was decided that the tariffs would now be charged per ton of freight and pegged solely to the type of cargo, not to the ice class of the vessel, the escort distance, and the navigation season. At the time, inflation and the growth of nuclear fuel prices could justify that. But not the whole thing. So while the Arctic was no longer locked by the ice, since modern nuclear icebreakers can break the multi-year ice, the NSR was locked by forbiddingly high tariffs.

In 2007 state subsidies were reactivated, but the tariffs weren't reduced – in fact, they remained at the maximum level. So Mikhail saw no hope for personal improvement if he stayed in his current position. While the tariffs were determined from the top, the average costs for ships going the northern route were 30 percent higher than by using the longer distance Suez option. At the same time, Mikhail realized that even if the Ministry of Transport reduced the tariffs to zero, absolutely nothing radical would happen. The companies would not line up anyway because the Arctic had not become less complicated, less risky, and less expensive to ship through. Pure economic gain is just the first step toward considering the north-eastern passage an alternative to the established Southern route; lack of return cargo capacity, inefficiencies of port logistics services, and navigation safety issues came attached. Therefore, he thought, if Mintrans and Atomflot continued to stand fast, they would end up, in Pushkin's words, as *an old wife back at the bottom of the ladder*. That just remained to be seen.

This comparison of Atomflot policy with an old woman from one of Pushkin's fairy tales seemed extremely poignant to Mikhail. In "The Tale of the Fisherman and the Fish" the main idea is that unlimited greedy demand for commodities leads to their disappearance. The old man had caught a magical golden fish that promised to fulfill any wish in exchange for its freedom. But the man's greedy wife first pined for a new washtub, which she duly received. Then for a new house. Then for a palace, a royal status, and still more unreality. Finally, the exasperated fish restores her original poverty and gives her back her old washtub. Unfortunately, there is no place for divorce in fairy tales. In fact, Mikhail did not want that to happen, as nobody would win from such an outcome. Those who had not used the icebreaker services before or had found another solution would not use them anyway. That gut feeling motivated him to complete the qualification course for captain in 2005 in St. Petersburg Makarov Marine Academy. After becoming a captain, he could choose for himself which ice to break. This led him to the NMNG company in 2008.

Even if such a unique and cost-intensive logistics solution as the construction of the northernmost off-loading terminal was imposed by conditions of those days, the project was considered one of the success stories. Southern oil transportation routes via Russia's pipeline system were overloaded; in addition, the quality of the oil transported via pipeline was much lower. Therefore, for the NMNG, on behalf of its owner, LUKOIL company, to have future growth opportunities and the necessary commercial flexibility to change the export markets, independence from the state-owned pipelines was the only option. This alternative solution – to have an independent petcock (i.e., a valve for controlling the flow of gas or oil) – provided the company with the right to sell the oil of better quality for a better price.

However, it was also a happy time for the newly born captain. Even though that part of the Barents Sea was covered with ice less than six months a year and characterized by fairly moderate ice conditions, he never sat without a job. For him, global warming was still a myth. Even nuclear icebreakers were sometimes inevitable in that relatively tolerable part of the sea. They were needed to provide diesel icebreakers with a necessary commercial speed in order for the company to keep its time agreements with partners. Also, there were periods of drifting ice, which is no less dangerous than the permanent ice, since it can easily damage a tanker or the terminal. That is why, as a captain during any loading operation, Mikhail received data from the scientific institutions and used all the experience and intuition he had to keep the tanker clear of ice. He had to suspend or restart the loading process depending on what he assessed as the safe time to do it. What precious minutes they were for him! That is why when the Ministry of Transport decided to shake the money tree and extract fees from the companies operating in the areas newly included in the NSR, he started to worry again. The system was no longer oriented toward the country's wealth; it was pure business for all sides involved. And therefore, each of the parties would do anything to get a piece of the pie.

Meeting the ice

Sometimes new policies create new opportunities. But that was not the case with this new policy. Mikhail gave that law the codename of *if-you-don't-want-to-play-let's-find-any-who-can-pay*. That is why he participated in the conference where I interviewed him – the one on the "renewal of the NSR" in the luxurious President Hotel. He yearned to speak out and be heard. Several months after that Moscow conference he gave a speech at The International Arctic Economic Forum in Murmansk. It was one of those pompous events where everybody was exclaiming the necessity of Arctic development while at the same time demonstrating an embarrassing ignorance of other opinions and even facts.

Mikhail was almost the last presenter at the Forum, and a good half of the participants had unfortunately already left the hall, including all the big actors in the Russian Arctic with their potentially huge volume numbers and even greater prognoses. While others' big volumes were only potentially big and therefore would be only potentially suffering in future, Mikhail's rather small company, NMNG, unofficially referred to as "the most western oil-and-gas Russian company," was doing its job quite well, and already had real numbers to lose. They just were not impressive enough.

In a very polite way Mikhail imparted the company's apprehensions in terms of the coming law on the NSR. He mentioned that despite the repeated recourse of the LUKOIL company to the Ministry of Transport regarding the inexpedience of moving the NSR's boundaries westward to Cape Kanin Nos, the Russian Ministry of Transport on 26 August 2010 informed the company that "the NSR's aquatorial borders are to be expanded due to the necessity of establishment of state regulation of maritime shipping in the areas covered with ice most of the year." From several years of successful operations in the area, Mikhail knew that the area near the Varandey project was covered with ice only from January till May; that was less than six months! What's more, in January the thickness of ice didn't exceed 30 cm, while by the end of May the ice was crashed enough. Clearly he was no stranger to the things he was talking about. So, the leased-out tankers were able to operate without icebreaker assistance with ice thickness up to 1.5 meters. But they still leased a diesel icebreaker and an icebreaking tug, knowing all too well the unpredictable weather and ice conditions there. Mikhail admitted that they agreed to pay for a nuclear icebreaker when one was really needed. Nobody wants to jeopardize a ship or the terminal and least of all people's lives. For him it was a betrayal from the Ministry of Transport that "just did not want to work hard for better management," so he complained. Clearly, he thought, "the new system is not working. People changed. Everybody just wants to make easy money for himself."

NMNG's lobbying efforts proved futile. The company was too small to be heard. "When bigger companies start to suffer and lose money," Mikhail predicted, "they will cut Atomflot down to size. Definitely, size does matter in this case but implies a lot of paperwork which steals time from the real job to be done. And I am against wasting time." So he believed that one day something, somehow, would start to function again. Observing how big state-linked companies enjoy favorable perks for project development – perks like tax remissions and abatement in fees – it was logical to expect that icebreaking issues for them will be negotiated as well. The status of a natural monopoly awarded to Atomflot suggests that for big volumes it will be easier to get a discount on tariffs. But time was running out. Deep inside, he expected that after the clear and direct message supported by calculations that he gave at the Forum, he would be heard. Or that at least it would prompt more discussion of that issue with participation of all involved parties. But a couple of months later Naryan-Mar hosted a visiting session of the Committee on Maritime Issues of the Federation Council. Various hot topics were discussed, even the one concerning the NSR's change of borders. Alas, for some reason, representatives of NMNG weren't invited. Mikhail regularly checked The Russian Ministry of Transport's webpage but still saw no progress, let alone any radical changes to the initial version of the law's text. One more official letter, this time also signed by ConocoPhillips, who outright started to worry about their investments in the project, was sent to the Ministry asking to withdraw from the extension of the NSR borders. But the *shifting-to-pipe* alternative was getting more and more realistic. With all that it implied.

That day Mikhail made the best of a bad job. After having left the office for home earlier than usual, he walked by a beautiful old small church. He thought it's always good to pass by the church if possible since it makes you think about your beliefs. New Year's Eve was approaching, and he needed to find a goose for a family dinner. The trick was to find a really good one. He went to the market early the next morning before work and bargained with the butcher to save a good one for him. The key now was to prepare a goose for the festive table. The rest was a sure thing, more or less.

Breaking the ice

Mikhail quit NMNG several months later. Due to power games, his work was getting more and more *dry*, farther and farther from the sea. Shuffling paper was not what he had trained for these many years. He was missing the *water noise*. Happily, an old friend and ex-teammate now working in the organization responsible for all marine infrastructure development recommended him for the position of deputy head of ports and fleet operations. There he could once again deal with icebreakers, tug-boats, and port infrastructure. He got the job and was instantly absorbed by a lot of new interesting work that he was well prepared for, given his expertise and years of experience. Again he started at 8 o'clock every morning and didn't leave earlier than 7:30 P.M. He liked it much more than doing nothing, than being useless, than feeling warm in a claustrophobic Moscow office. In fact, the draft of the new law was not enacted as the Mintrans wanted it to be. In July 2012 the draft was approved with major adjustments: the defined water zone remains unchanged while the amount of the ice escort fee depends on the amount of services actually rendered to the customers. Hence, it was a just winning of economic sense over the bureaucratic mind of certain institutions. However, Mikhail's *victory* came much earlier than the good news regarding the new law. Returning to the ranks of the *toilers of the sea*, he started to believe once again in a great future for the Russian Arctic. Once again it was at least partially in his arms, and he knew where to *turn the wheel*.

7   One Ocean
Sharing the sea in Newfoundland and Labrador

Keri K. Stephens, Bodø Graduate School of Business and Stephanie L. Dailey, Texas State University

Maureen Murphy Rustad
Photograph by Maureen Murphy

When traveling on the seas off the coast of Hammerfest, Stavanger, or Lofoten, outsiders would never know that they are actually traversing a grid. The water is divided into clearly defined sections that help people know how to find a lost ship or know where they hold a license to explore for oil and gas. This type of virtually invisible set of identifiers is also common in many other countries in the High North, like Alaska, Canada, and most recently Greenland.

While every country, and often province or state as well, has different people, laws, and specific concerns, they share some common history that often is linked to their extended reliance on the sea for food. They are fishers and hunters, and the sea forms the foundation for their cultural identity. People living in the Arctic and Pan Arctic also share some similarities in their climate. While the Gulf Stream helps countries like Norway by keeping their waters typically free from ice, other countries like Greenland and the Newfoundland area of Canada have icebergs that can complicate their existence in and around the sea.

In the past half a century, oil exploration in the High North has brought new opportunities to these sea communities, but it has also introduced several challenges. Some communities cling to their history and want to maintain the culture that has provided them their identity for so long. But the trends in these communities suggest that the population is declining, and the income achievable by living off the sea fluctuates significantly year to year. Yet the Newfoundland and Labrador areas of Canada have found creative ways to share the sea between two major stakeholders – the fishing and petroleum industries. These industry sectors work together to harvest resources from the sea, and an organization called One Ocean facilitates this collaboration.

One Ocean is a not-for-profit corporation that was created in 2002 as a liaison for the provincial fishing and petroleum sectors. Housed at the Fisheries and Marine Institute (Marine Institute) of the Memorial University of Newfoundland, One Ocean provides a forum for information exchange and facilitates communication between the two industries; often translating between oil and fisheries languages. The One Ocean model has enabled the fishing and oil industries to communicate and address concerns before they become problematic. The organization operates on the principle of equal stakeholder representation on its governing board. The One Ocean Board consists of equivalent industry representation; six directors from the fishing industry, six directors from the petroleum industry, and a Chairman. Director Maureen Murphy Rustad manages day to day operations and shared the story of One Ocean with us. In the narrative that follows we elaborate on issues of stakeholder communication and provide detailed examples of how One Ocean has managed to facilitate communication between these diverse stakeholders while still honoring the fishing culture of this community.

Living by the sea

"I love the fish harvesters," says Maureen. "Fishing is our culture, our politics, and our social system. Everything we know is based on it: the food we eat, the songs we sing, the colors we paint our houses – like jellybean row." Jellybean row is a nice descriptor of how brightly painted houses look as they sit close together facing the sea. The houses in Newfoundland and Labrador are all painted a different bright color and it is not uncommon to see a red, a green, a blue, and even a pink house, all right next to one another. Growing up, Maureen was always told that the different colored houses make it easier for fishers returning from the sea to locate their house even from quite a distance. That is a strong visual sign of the prominence of the fishing culture in Newfoundland.

Maureen Murphy Rustad, the Director for the One Ocean Corporation, grew up in Newfoundland. She is a "towny" but spent summers with friends who lived and fished on the sea. Those experiences had a profound impact on her respect for the ocean and the fishers. She even remembers hiding at the end of the summer as her father came to retrieve her and take her back to her town. She left Newfoundland and spent several years in Europe where she became interested in marine affairs. She returned to Canada to complete her degrees, spent time working in marine organizations and the oil-and-gas industry, and joined One Ocean in 2003. Now she is doing what she loves. Some days she dons a heavy black down jacket with reflectors on each shoulder, rubber boots above her knees, no makeup, and a hat that will keep her warm in the coldest Arctic winters. Other times she wears her business suit, a touch of makeup, and nicely styled hair to meet with government representatives or executives in the petroleum industry. Spending any time around her will clearly reveal that she has one foot in the world of business and the other firmly planted in the culture of the sea.

Maureen experienced the devastation to her community as the fishermen watched their cod leave the area and their livelihoods almost evaporate in the early 1990s. The industry was almost completely devastated as the fishers learned to cope with their changing waters. She admires their fisher spirit because they were able to shift their expertise from ground fish to shells and regain their livelihoods. This was not an easy transition because the required fishing gear is different and learning the patterns of how to profitably capture shellfish did not happen overnight. Living by the resources of the sea is hard and ever changing. In some years bad weather or economic conditions like the price of fuel can significantly diminish the fishers' catch and cut their profits to almost nothing, while other years they can make a nice living off the sea. She has a profound respect for these people and the strength of their culture.

But fishing is not necessarily a growing industry. There are annual quotas on fish and shell harvesting that can fluctuate year to year. Many people blame overfishing for the cod devastation and for other fishing and marine mammal supply concerns today; therefore, the industry has become much more regulated. Even the tourist fishing industry is regulated. When the price of fuel is high, almost 25 percent of everything a fisher makes goes to pay for fuel. Moreover, complex regulations restrict where fishers can cast and where they can travel by boat. Maureen explains, "They want to fish and they want their children to fish, but they are very pragmatic and they know the chances of their children fishing are slim." Fishing is the culture and highly valued, but fishing can be a hard way to earn a living.

Offshore oil arrives in Newfoundland

In the latter part of the twentieth century, the fishers began to notice that they were sharing their waters with new people and new technologies. Fishers were accustomed to being alone on the sea. As oil exploration began off the coast of Newfoundland, there was seismic activity that helped the geologists identify where to drill. Fishers found themselves having to share the sea with the petroleum industry. One day in the late 1990s, a call came into the Marine Institute inquiring about the new activities in the waters. When the University realized that no one had complete answers, they decided to convene a group representing fisher harvesters and the oil companies to provide a place where people could ask and answer questions.

The informal group evolved into a formal organization and it still operates on the founding principles that include providing a neutral forum for both sectors (i.e., fishing and petroleum); facilitating communication, information exchange, and shared opportunities; assisting the fishing and petroleum industries in understanding each other's operations and activities; and endorsing cooperation, transparency, and a proactive approach to the exploitation of marine resources. The group now meets face-to-face four times a year. One Ocean is not mandated by government; it is industry driven. One Ocean Board Directors participate on a voluntary basis and it is their commitment that has developed and maintained the level of trust and excellent working relationships.

We don't speak the same language

For the past few decades many organizations have recognized the importance of identifying their various stakeholders and the priorities and concerns of each group. Elaborate models have been constructed to help people pinpoint the power differences and the legitimacy of stakeholder concerns that organizations should address. One Ocean has realized there is much more to understanding stakeholders than simply identifying their concerns. This process of understanding begins by examining the language and jargon used by stakeholders.

"What the hell is an Orphan Basin?" a fisher called One Ocean to ask. All of a sudden Maureen realized that the terms used by the oil-and-gas industry for the offshore regions were very different from the number and letter identifying system – e.g., 3Ps – used by the fishers. The fishers know the waters very well and reference it using the North Atlantic Fishery Organization (NAFO) regions to communicate offshore sea areas. Yet the oil-and-gas companies call offshore oil regions "basins," and one of those basins is named the Orphan Basin. In the fisherman's situation, he had been inquiring about proposed offshore oil-and-gas activity in what was described as the Orphan Basin. Most likely, the petroleum stakeholder never knew that the fisher would use a different term for a basin and was not deliberately attempting to use language to alienate the fisher (even though many of us have seen people use jargon for this purpose). But the result was extreme frustration and a complete inability to communicate.

Both stakeholders were trying to determine where they were physically located in the offshore, but they used completely different language and identifiers. When Maureen realized that these groups were miscommunicating, she decided to create a single document that provided both industry-specific labels for the offshore. By using this tool, fishers and those in the petroleum industry clearly could see how the two offshore identification systems mapped onto one another. In retrospect, the solution was quite simple, but it took someone who understood both languages to translate, explain, and create a tool to clarify the communication issues.

Maureen had worked in both industries and realized that miscommunication often has an easily explainable root cause. Industries regularly create their own vocabularies to identify themselves, to simplify their intra-group communication, and to create their own subcultural bonds. Yet this commonly practiced behavior creates problems as people from other groups and subcultures try to communicate. The importance of translating between these industry subcultures is vital for accurate communication practices. The Orphan Basin is only one of many examples that illustrate how an organization capable of translating between industries can improve communication.

The One Ocean organization

There are many other ways that the One Ocean organization has worked to facilitate communication between the various stakeholders. Since 2002, this multi-stakeholder organization has worked hard to help different industries understand each other's work. Knowing the business needs of one another, along with actively putting a name with a face, has helped this group work through many difficult challenges.

As one would expect, there are differences of opinion on many issues concerning the petroleum and the fishing industries. An important component of the Board in this organization is the consensus-building approach. This guiding principle was introduced by One Ocean's first Chairman, the late Dr. Arthur May, and remains a fundamental premise for One Ocean members. "A voting system is easier and faster than consensus decision-making, but Dr. May realized the long-term resolution would be more effective," explains Maureen. The current Chairman, Mr. Bill Wells, continues the practice to ensure Board members have the opportunity to work through the issues and achieve a better understanding of concerns.

Knowledge of each other's business practices

This Board could not have these types of successful discussions if they didn't know about the business practices and concerns of each other. It's one thing to claim to understand the needs of a divergent stakeholder, but recognizing the details of what the other parties need to be successful in their businesses is a completely different thing. "There is not a single person on our Board who could not tell you where the fishermen will be fishing in May and the types of boats and gear they will be using," claims Maureen. Over time oil company representatives have come to understand the effort, risk, and expense involved in the fishing industry. Fish harvesters have explained and sometimes had to remind others that they invest a lot in their businesses. Up to a quarter of their earnings pay for fuel, and then on top of that they pay their crew, have equipment and maintenance costs, and they often risk their lives as part of their daily work. One day of lost work in peak fishing season can cost them a considerable percentage of their earnings. While the oil companies might use dollars to explain a financial loss, fishers use percentages because the dollars are not comparable.

The Board has also learned to trust one another over time. While trust can certainly fluctuate, the multiple-year relationships, formed over shared meals and an occasional beer, facilitate communication so that a fishing industry representative on the board can call an oil executive and talk directly if the situation warrants that action. They know one another on a first-name basis. Tom, the fisher who is on the water hundreds of days a year, knows Sam, the oil executive who spends most of his time in business meetings. When problems arise, they have relationships that keep their behavior in check. Maureen explains, "It is really difficult to be difficult to someone you know, even at the Board level."

In the beginning, Maureen remembers that there were some uncomfortable moments during consultation meetings between the fishing and petroleum industries. Thankfully, Maureen is really direct, and she is very good at taking virtually any critical comment without flinching. One-on-one, she can also dish it out if she needs to. These work-based language norms had to be understood, and when differences are that obvious, sometimes people need coaxing to share their views. It is easy for one stakeholder group to make assumptions about another. Maureen still remembers saying in an early seismic consultation meeting, "Perhaps the fisher harvesters should be asked when it would work best to do seismic surveys." Essentially this group realized that part of their goal was to negotiate with one another using a very principled type of negotiation strategy. Since they now knew about each other's business needs, they could anticipate ways to work together to meet both parties' objectives.

Talking it out has become a norm for One Ocean. The group operates on the same guiding principles it developed more than a decade ago. The oil-and-gas industry funds the group, and while that does occasionally raise some eyebrows, Maureen is very quick to say that it is in everyone's best interest that the funding happen this way because the oil-and-gas industry is in a position to contribute financially and it wanted to fund the organization. One Ocean works vigilantly to maintain neutrality, and disputes are handled with minimal government or media intervention. This group feels that they can successfully co-exist using a unique process deeply seated in trust.

Communication tools to simplify complex and inconsistent rules

Over time, new oil-and-gas fields have been developed, and new concerns have arisen. There are now three producing fields: Hibernia, Terra Nova, and White Rose. As one would expect, the fishers, the oil companies, and the government all want to maintain safety in the waters. Zones around production fields are allocated by Canadian and international regulations. The names and size of the zones are different for each field; Terra Nova has a 10 nautical mile (nm) Precautionary Zone and a 5 nm Safety Zone while Hibernia and White Rose have a 3 nm Safety

Zone. Every installation has a 500 meter zone area that prohibits any vessel other than its own from entering. The production fields are not far apart and fishers are familiar with this offshore region; however, as Maureen explains, "there are no lines or traffic lights out there, so it can be confusing for fish harvesters." Fishers are familiar with and observe the standard 3 nm safety zone, calling it the "radio" or "call-in zone." But when fishers were contacted by installations stating they were violating zones that were more than 3 nm out, it seemed wrong to fishers, who became frustrated and stopped answering their radios. Importantly, when fishers have to travel miles out of their way to avoid a safety zone, it costs them extra gas for their vessel and valuable time. This becomes a serious issue for the oil-and-gas industry. If communication cannot be made with a vessel entering a zone, the field goes into safety mode, where precautions vary. The oil company might send a supply ship to the unknown vessel; or, more drastically, it might even put its installation into shut-down.

When Maureen at One Ocean heard about the issues, it didn't take long to track down the source of the miscommunication. After several conversations with board members, she convened industry members to draft an Offshore Communication Protocol – a one-page map-like document that illustrates and identifies various safety-zone data for each field and contact numbers to reach one another. The document is bright blue with graphics depicting the safety zones demarcated with yellow and orange. There are details depicting the radio address to call when entering each area and the various safety protocols to follow. After board approval, she laminated these wheelhouse-friendly pieces and sent them to the stakeholders in early April of 2010. The Protocol piece also provides fishers the ability to radio ahead to the installation, and if it is safe to do so, they will be authorized to traverse the field (outside the 500 meter zone) and shorten their travel.

Building knowledge beyond Newfoundland

To keep One Ocean on the cutting edge of knowledge, technology, and successful practices, the organization sponsors and attends Study Tours and conferences. Study Tours can be described as a way to share information between industries and research organizations. They typically consist of face-to-face meetings where a diverse group of people exchange information on best practices, share research, interact informally, and learn as part of the event. One Ocean has sponsored their own Study Tours, and board members have learned a considerable amount by communicating ideas in this format.

Quite often these tours occur in a location conducive to learning about the topic. For example, Maureen participated in an Arctic Dialogue and Study Tour hosted by the Bodø Graduate School of Business in Bodø, Norway, for more than five years. This Study Tour was conducted in part on the Hurtigruten Coastal Steamer, a fleet of ships that still serve an important cargo-carrying function and also accommodate passengers in a rustic cruise ship format. During this dialogue, Statoil (an international predominantly Norwegian-owned oil company) gave presentations along with groups like the Norwegian Ministry of Fisheries, oil-spill-response research organizations, and the Hammerfest City Manager. In the middle of these discussions, the Hurtigruten would sound its horn and pull into ports of the cities perched on the northern coast of Norway. The tour participants got to visit the liquefied natural gas plant in Hammerfest and see the fishers hoist their nets on the docks in the same afternoon. As the Hurtigruten pulled away, the participants saw the towns disappear in the distance and all that remained were the towering snow-covered mountains and the small areas of land that break up the ocean off the coast of Northern Norway.

In 2010 there was representation on the Arctic Dialogue Tour from Greenland where a hunter's fishing tale was translated, and the audience sat transfixed as they learned about his way of life. Oil exploration off the coast of Greenland is fairly new, and because Newfoundland also experiences extreme marine ice conditions, there is a possibility that others' experiences can help Greenland. Representatives from Alaska spoke about offshore activity, and local entrepreneurs and indigenous people shared their ways of life.

When Maureen first attended the Arctic Dialogue and Study Tour, she was excited to share One Ocean's work with representatives from Norway, Russia, the US, and other countries. She was a bit surprised and honored that people found so much hope in the One Ocean story. It is not common for stakeholders with interests as diverse and controversial as fishing and petroleum to come together and talk on a regular basis without heavy governmental involvement. She was invited back repeatedly because the international audience was hopeful that the success of the One Ocean model could be experienced in their own countries. Through these experiences and conversations Maureen has grown to understand and respect the One Ocean model profoundly, but she is also keenly aware that this model will not necessarily work in the same form in other countries.

A model in stakeholder communication

One Ocean represents a group of divergent stakeholders that has learned how to successfully co-exist. This is an important distinction for One Ocean. They do not simply co-exist, they *successfully* co-exist. They are fortunate that their group began meeting and working together before conflicts prevented them from being willing to communicate. It is likely that other organizations wanting to look to One Ocean as a model will need to consider where the stakeholder relationships stand as the facilitating organizations and people try to encourage dialogue. This is not necessarily a model to simply copy and import to another country or industry. Maureen believes that other groups who want to form a One Ocean-like organization need to create their own model. They might be inspired by many of the principles and actions of One Ocean, but every situation is slightly different.

One of the major themes in the One Ocean story is the role that trust plays in this group. It takes time to develop trust and it can be broken with a single action. Maureen explains that trust must be continually re-developed because trust is not stable, even in a successful group. Others who want to use the One Ocean model should consider that these trusting relationships developed over many years, and it takes time and energy to understand the business practices of different stakeholders. People need to be willing to listen to others who are quite different from themselves and find ways to develop shared objectives.

Another unique aspect to One Ocean is the unification of the fishing industry in Newfoundland. Around the world there are many other fishing communities that share a similar history and set of concerns with the Newfoundland industry. Parts of this story are applicable to fishing communities in Norway and even the United States. Yet one major difference is that the fishers are all part of a single organization, so board representation can happen more easily. If the fishers were not centrally organized, deciding representational issues would be considerably more difficult.

In addition to the centralized fishing industry, the government intervention in the fishing/petroleum co-existence is much lower in Newfoundland than in most other offshore oil operations. There are certainly regulations, like safety and offshore licensing when the government is involved, but the government is not the communication liaison; One Ocean plays that role quite successfully. The One Ocean Board includes government regulators of the fishing and petroleum industries with Official Observer status. They are not directors, but it is important to have them in the room during discussions. Essentially, when the concerned parties are able to *successfully* co-exist, direct negotiations and communication can reduce the reliance on government intervention.

Future thought

Oil is regularly in the news today all around the world, but so are other global concerns. While this story clearly explains the successful co-existence of two industries, there are several additional things to consider that span beyond the oil and fishing community. The One Ocean story is actually a wonderful example of what happens when divergent stakeholders are willing to engage in a process of productive communication. This is not an easy process. Countless books provide advice and recommendations for how groups engage in dialogue and simply come to the table to talk. Yet despite the advice and detailed processes outlined in these books, groups often fail. One Ocean reminds us that communicating is hard work and involves a considerable investment in truly understanding what all stakeholders need. It takes mutual respect and time, but if stakeholders have people who can serve to help translate the technical differences, the group has a chance at learning to trust and work together.

Part III
Risking it

8 A local fire hero

The tension between community acceptance and risk-taking

Joseph Brentlinger, Bodø Graduate School of Business

Øystein Strømsnes
Photograph by Linda Storholm

Despite its remote location just north of the Arctic Circle, and despite its smallish population (47,000), Norway's seaport town of Bodø can prove remarkably cosmopolitan. The locals who populate the small town are outspokenly proud of their cultural heritage. *Those in Oslo are sub-arctic*, they'll tell you: *We are Arctic!* But there is also the bustling University of Nordland, which attracts some 6,000 students from all over the world, not to mention the sustained wealth from the town's oil and fishing industries, a lure to immigrants looking for a better life. And so while you hear Norwegian spoken about town – in the coffee shops, the stores, the *glasshuset* (the glass-enclosed shopping center in the middle of town) – you soon learn that Bodø has an underground, second spoken language: English. If you are Norwegian, you'll speak Norwegian and

English; if you are Russian, you'll speak Russian and English; if you are German, you'll speak German and English; and if you are from the U.S., well, you'll speak English and *American*. Bodø, then, just may be the smallest international hub in the world.

Øystein Strømsnes is Bodø, born and bred. A young man in his early 20s, with short sandy blond hair cropped on the sides and slight lines etched in, a permanent five o'clock shadow, and a kind yet resolute face, Øystein loves his home so much he chose to attend the University of Nordland. He says, "I was five when my father took me to my first Bodø/Glimt game," mentioning the local professional football club as proof of his love of home. *Glimt*, or a *glimpse* or *flash*, is perhaps meant to connote the team's quickness; but in the High North, where the sun *glimts* for the entire summer without setting, it's easy to read the name ironically. His favorite player this year is number 18, Christian Berg, the team captain. Øystein describes with pride the reason for his favorite: "He's a Bodø boy."

Pride through such a culturally and historically significant sport as football fosters regional rivalries. Bodø/Glimt's major rival is the team from Tromsø, a city even further north. But there is another, lesser rival in Bergen, a city to the south. Its team, Brann, or *Fire*, carries an equally ironic meaning. Bergen gets more rain than any other city in Europe.

With so many linguistic, cultural, and regional barriers to community cohesion, it might seem like there is little in the way of maintaining a sense of *Norwegianness* in the High North. But a cultural code prevalent throughout Scandinavia shapes its citizens' social behavior in this respect. The code – called *janteloven* – is a collection of ten rules, each of which reinforces the ideals of self-effacement, humility, and modesty. It says: *You are better than no one; don't stand out; don't call attention to yourself*.

Janteloven commands an undeniable influence over Norwegians. Aksel Sandemose coined the term in 1933, with the publication of his work *A Fugitive Crosses His Tracks*. As a cultural trope, the disparate feelings, cultural conditions, and constitutions that eventually fell under its heading might be centuries old, though the name itself is relatively new. People in Norway usually understand *janteloven* to mean the disparate acts by people that discourage community formation. In their desire not to appear uppity or call attention to themselves, Norwegians typically don't look at one another on the street. Nor do they say hello to one another as they walk by. Nor do they sit next to or speak with anyone on the bus. As a result, Norwegians, to outsiders (and at times, even themselves), seem introverted, suspicious of others, perhaps even rude. Also to an outsider, it may seem that *janteloven* inhibits one from doing great deeds. After all, to do a great deed inevitably invites publicity.

But at the same time, *janteloven* implies something insistently egalitarian. It's a reminder that everyone has a face. Everyone has a name. Everyone counts. Øystein's story, concerning the night the immigrant house caught fire, comprises many of these disparate elements that become understandable through the invocation of the term *janteloven*, both in their complimentary and pejorative connotations.

"It was pretty dramatic, at the time," Øystein recollects, the immigrant house just in the background. It was a Wednesday in Bodø the night the fire was started. It had to be a Wednesday, Øystein says, because that night he was working with one other person at *Sku Bare*, the local pub next door. In Norway, Wednesday is called "lille Lørdag," *little Saturday*, Norwegian Drinking Night. This lille Lørdag, they would need the extra help.

Everything began for Øystein with a word: *Brann!* At the time he was a student by day, a bartender by night. It had been a typical Wednesday until then, with lots of students drinking lustily, and a few locals, too, already anticipating the summer break when the students go home. *Min Dag* – "My Day" – played over the speakers. Everyone sang drunkenly to the tune. Women danced in the narrow aisle between the bar and the tables. A couple of soused men tried to dance with them. The next morning, some people would surely be late to work or to school, but now, there was, thankfully, only now.

Suddenly, someone who'd been outside smoking a cigarette ran in shouting "*Brann!*" Everything stopped – the dancing, the singing, even the drinking – and people peered out the front window. Sure enough, there was black smoke coming from the immigrant house next door.

There is little special about the immigrant house. It stands, L-shaped and four stories high, with white prefabbed panels above the shops that occupy its first floor. Atop those shops are small flats, about thirty in all, the second- and third-story flats having tiny green gates attached to their windows which act as balconies. It is these gated windows that attract one's attention. At their top, which is about waist-high, the gates might be able to accommodate one person snugly. But, though they remain as wide as the windows they protect, as their frames move down toward the bottom of the window they taper toward the building itself, so that at the bottom there is no room for proper footing. They are the only outlets for the flats other than their front doors. But they're so cramped that you can only stow your boots there to dry, or lean out on to smoke.

After seeing the rising smoke, the bar patrons rushed outside into the bitter night air and stood as one, watching the plume slowly swelling and trying to decide what to do about it.

"Has anyone called the fire department?" someone asked. "Does anyone know the people in there?" asked another. "Should we help?" asked a third.

But they were stymied. Drinking, in Norway, is considered a serious business. If you're drinking, then you should stick to *drinking*, not risk taking on dangerous tasks. And you don't allow others to either, for you assume responsibility for their welfare as well. Given this code, you rarely find drinking and driving in Norway. Have one beer? Then you walk home, or you are carried, or you call a taxi. Safety matters, and even a small amount of alcohol can be unsafe.

And so Øystein, the stone-sober bartender, took charge. Reminding everyone they had been drinking, and vowing to help, he sprang into action. First he called the emergency number. Then, after urging everyone to stay put, he went toward the building on his own.

The smoke was now pouring from the building. As he was debating what to do, the ground-floor door opened and occupants began running out. At the same time, a few of the building's many upstairs residents emerged onto their tiny terraces and shouted to one another in their native tongues, seemingly asking each other questions. Øystein thought, *Why are they heading for their windows? How many of them are trapped?* He looked up at those tiny, suddenly fragile gates and could see still more people leaning out, frantically shouting at each other and at the crowd below. Patrons, now also worried for their neighbors piled out of the bar. They shouted back at the people hanging out of their homes. For a moment, the world had frozen.

Then some of the upstairs residents ran back inside their flats, only to return, moments later, bearing sheets. They clearly intended to make ropes out of them, which they were going to tie to the gate railings to rappel down to the gathering crowd below.

But those flimsy railings were designed only for decoration. Øystein shouted at them to stop, pleading with them to wait for the fire department, which was sure to be arriving any moment. But, in their panic, they ignored him and kept assembling their makeshift ropes. So Øystein did the unthinkable. He ran into the immigrant house himself.

Inside, all was pandemonium, with people shouting and screaming at one another in the corridor. Such was their panic that their Norwegian was forgotten; their English, too. Only their native languages remained. Øystein understood nothing.

He began pushing people out, urging them to run, shouting in English so that people could understand him. Then he himself ran – upstairs. Once there, he grabbed anyone in the hall and directed them to the stairs. Then he knocked on what doors he could, getting more people out. Then he ran up another flight of stairs to the third floor. So dense was the smoke there that the long corridor was almost pitch black. He paused, feeling defeated.

But he heard people screaming further ahead, so he charged ahead anyway, despite the smoke's sting. After a couple more meters it became impossible to breathe. He reluctantly turned and ran back down the two flights of stairs to the safety door, and then to the outside.

But once outside, he saw, to his horror, some people above, still frantically screaming from their perches. Meanwhile, the patrons of *Sku Bare* looked on, still mindful of his warning. But Øystein wasn't finished. He went from one end of the building to the other, surveying, scouting, trying to determine the best rescue strategy. He saw some residents on the second and third floors, still standing on their small terraces, but he also was cheered to see still others – people who, moments before, had been shouting from within the building – now out on the street, shouting encouragement to their friends above. He looked down the road leading to Highway 80, where the fire engines would have to come from. They were still nowhere in sight. He couldn't even hear the scream of sirens. So he did what he thought was right: he went back into the burning building another time.

At each door he could reach, he knocked furiously and yelled "Get the hell out!" Some residents, now realizing that the window ledge wasn't their only option, opened the door and ran to safety. Then he braved the third floor once more. Once there, he spotted, to his surprise, a human form up ahead, moving deeper into the corridor. It turned out to be another man braving the smoke.

Øystein caught up to him, grabbed him with both arms, and yelled "Get the hell out!" But the man, frantic, refused to listen and struggled to break free. "My family!" he cried to Øystein, pointing toward the top floor. "My family is up there!".

But Øystein restrained him all the harder. "Fuck you!" he said to the man. "Don't think about that, think about yourself! Get the hell out! If you run up there, you can kill yourself as well." After a brief argument, and finally convinced by Øystein's assurances that the fire department would do what it could outside, the man ran with him back down the flights of stairs and out to the clean air below.

Outside, the chaos had only intensified. The people on the street were shouting more frantically than ever to those residents who had remained on their precarious ledges. They, too, were becoming increasingly panicked. They went again for their makeshift ropes. Øystein yelled up at them that the fire department had to be coming at any minute, and, as with the father only moments before, he began to quell their fears. But then, up on a third-floor terrace, he saw the reason for the father's desperation. A wide-eyed woman stood holding a bundle, bouncing it, comforting it. A 6-month-old child!

The residents who'd been preparing to rappel down from the building had seen the same thing! The woman saw what they were doing and improvised an idea of her own. She wrapped the child in a sheet, crafting a basinet while leaning on the bars of the terrace. Lifting the bundle beyond what little safety the terrace provided, she began lowering it to the second floor. There, a volunteer crawled up the railing, his feet stabilized by his companion, and with one hand gripping the iron bars, he reached with his other as far as he could and finally grasped the makeshift basinet. Tenderly, he lowered the child to the woman holding his feet. The couple then lowered the bassinet to the child's father, who could only watch the whole drama unfold from the street below. He reached. He grabbed. He held. Cradling the baby in his arms, he looked up and shouted something to his wife in his native tongue. She shouted something in return. They both smiled.

Øystein shouted as well. He told those on the terraces once again to remain calm, to wait for the fire department, and, most importantly, not to go back inside or open the doors to their flats. That is, unless they heard him knock. Whereupon he ran inside a third time and knocked on the few doors he could reach, but he could reach no one else. As he came back out into the world, he finally heard the sounds of sirens. Fire engines came screaming into view. The firefighters, like Øystein, did their duty. With their ladders they rescued those from above, with their hoses they put out the fire within, and with their training they treated the injuries of everyone below.

The night of the fire, there were some injuries. Some people had to go to the hospital. Others spent some time in temporary shock. But luckily the fire had been spotted soon enough, and there were people like Øystein on the scene, and of course the neighbors who helped lower the baby. Otherwise there might have been more people grievously injured, or some who perhaps may have died. But, miraculously, there were no fatalities that night.

A couple of days later a dramatic article appeared in the local paper describing the fire that night. Accompanying it was a photograph of Øystein himself, broadly smiling, with his dirty blonde hair, his kind face, his resolute eyes, standing in front of the building. The photo's headline read "*Brann Helt*" – *Fire Hero*.

His fellow Bodø boys would chide him for weeks, calling him a *Bergen Brann* fan.

Sku Bare is a cozy pub with a very *local* feeling. Because of *janteloven*, and the perceived introverted behavior of Norwegians in general, it can feel less than welcoming to the immigrants living in its little borough, known as Mørkved (*the dark wood*).

The name *Sku Bare* has an interesting etymology. The word *bare* is easy enough to understand – *bar*. But *sku* is another story altogether. When juxtaposed to *bare*, *sku* means "I was only planning to …," implying that one was simply planning to go to the bar for one drink, but ended up staying the entire night. On the night of the fire, that is in fact what most of the patrons did.

After the firefighters had finally finished extinguishing the blaze, most of the patrons trickled back into *Sku Bare*, where they rehashed the event and sought relief from the biting Bodø wind.

But not the immigrants. These unfortunates, who only hours before had had a home, now had nothing but their lives and the clothes on their backs. And so there they sat, shivering, in the cold Bodø night, not knowing what to do, where to go.

Their plight was not lost on Øystein and his fellow bartender, Ørjan. Seeing the cold, huddled people, they knew they had to do something for them. So they shared their concern with the patrons and explained to them what they now planned. The patrons almost unanimously concurred. They grabbed their *Bergans*, their *Norrøna*, and their *Canada Goose* jackets, pulled them on, and made their way outside. Øystein and Ørjan followed them out, to say their farewells to their customers, and to welcome their new ones in.

Slowly, unsurely, the men, women, and children entered the bar, a place still foreign to most of them. It simply felt Norwegian. *Janteloven*, it seems, affects everyone. They would not have felt at home there. That is, until they had no home of their own.

Øystein and Ørjan stowed their bar supplies – the bottles of beer, wine, and liquor; the pint glasses, wine glasses, and shot glasses – and turned on the coffee machine. Then they pulled out their plastic soda bottles and the milk normally reserved for making White Russians. They made drinks throughout the night, just as they'd planned, but for the rest of the night they poured drinks for families who suddenly found themselves refugees.

Every bar in Bodø, or at least those with an outside patio, stocks blankets tucked away in a corner, or an office, or behind the bar. In a windy town just above the Arctic Circle blankets are practically a necessity, just to keep a customer warm and in place. This night the blankets were used to keep the children warm. The kids were comforted with a little milk, a pink blanket, and an arm over the shoulder. Meanwhile, their parents sat wondering and waiting, anxious over what would happen to them and their children. By 3:30 A.M., the usual closing time for *lille Lørdag*, there was still no word from … Well, nobody knew from whom they were waiting for a word. And then, at about 5:00 A.M., a call came. The wider community, and not only *Sku Bare*, had come together. The fire department had found emergency housing for the next night.

Buses arrived at the bar. The immigrants gathered what few belongings they had, put down their glasses of milk, soda, and coffee, and headed toward the door. Little was said. Little could be said. The exhausting night had taken its toll.

In the days and weeks that followed, the immigrants were transported to different places. Some of them found new homes. But for most, the government had to find long-term housing in apartments. This meant uprooting children from their schools, and of course their parents got uprooted with them. It was all very sad, very dislocating. But at least the Bodø community had come together to provide, as best it could, some relief for these immigrant families.

The day after the fire, a Bodø newspaper reporter interviewed Øystein. The reporter hadn't asked for Ørjan. Nor had he asked for Linn, the bar's owner. Nobody knows if the victims were asked. But everyone would know about Øystein.

He met the reporter at *Sku Bare*. Happy to answer any questions, he matter-of-factly related what had happened and how it had happened. He mentioned how Tine, an off-duty employee hanging with some friends, had been the first to spot the smoke. He mentioned how he had dashed into the building three times. He mentioned how Ørjan had helped with the refugees. He talked about *Sku Bare*. He talked about the baby lowered to the ground by sheets.

Afterwards, Øystein went about his day. In his own eyes, he was simply someone who had found himself in a place where he could be helpful. He had only done what anyone else in the same position would have: he had helped, and then he had answered a reporter's questions. That was all. He went back to work, and also back to studying. The tranquility Bodø offers those who walk its streets returned as quickly as it had left.

Two weeks before, though, there had been another immigrant house fire. At that fire, there had been a man in a position similar to Øystein's. That man had been in the right place to help, and he did so openhandedly. That fire had gotten a small write-up, semi-buried in the middle of the paper. Øystein had read that article and thought nothing more of it.

But the second fire – Øystein's fire – had set off speculation. Was someone starting these fires? Was there a racist or nationalist sentiment that linked the two tragedies together? Or was it simply a freak coincidence? Questions needing answers demand attention.

Perhaps it was a slow news day. Or perhaps the fire investigators had picked up on a pattern that hadn't been immediately recognized. But for whatever reason, the second fire got front-page treatment. Øystein was a little embarrassed when he first saw the story – so much so, in fact, that he missed the *Fire Hero* pun altogether. But as the days after the publication of his story went on, things began to change, and the Bodø tranquility set in once more.

Øystein's buddies took delight in the publicity he had gotten. They were proud of his bravery, and unworried that he got so much recognition. But they did like to rib him. "So, you're changing sides?" they'd ask. "Are you a *Brann Fan* now?" They told him that if he ever found himself on the outs with someone, all he'd have to do is set a fire, then put it out! It was all said in good fun, and it was funny. Øystein laughed right along with the rest of them.

But still something ate at him. The inaccuracies, the omissions.

He had never told the reporter that it was he who had first seen the smoke. He was sure he'd said that Tine had run in and told everyone. And he was sure he had mentioned Ørjan, and also sure that he had talked about the baby. But the story seemed to focus on him as a hero, and on the arson question. It even seemed as though the immigrants themselves had been overshadowed, that the smoke of the story had subsumed them just like the smoke of the fire had threatened to do.

And then there was the fact that the story itself got bannered on the front page. Hadn't the earlier fire earned just a small story buried in the middle of the paper, not a two-page account unfolding from the front page? Hadn't this other man been an even bigger hero for having *put out* the fire? And what about all the others who probably helped that man too?

It was one thing to be gibed by his buddies: they could rib him good-naturedly. Nobody was upset that they weren't in the reported story. But the man who had saved so many a few weeks before was furious with Øystein's newfound notoriety. Øystein ran into the guy and his girlfriend not long after, and all the girlfriend wanted to know was why Øystein's story was front-page news, while her boyfriend's story had barely made the paper's middle section: "Did *you* put out the fire?" she asked. "*He* did." The jealousy and splitting that is so often attributed to *janteloven*, then, had reared its head through the simple act of publicity.

No single example can be comprehensive of a given culture. Culture – be it a small one that emerges in a bar, or an immense one that encompasses a society – is more than the sum of its parts. That being said, a single example can reveal quite a lot.

Janteloven's influence will inevitably affect all Norway's citizens in one way or another. If you feel too good about yourself – or if others think you do – people will bring you back down to earth. Being singled out, whether for a good deed or a bad one, has consequences. If some institution singles you out, the collective brings you back in. Or if the collective singles you out, then some institution will remind you that you, too, are just one of many. Cohesiveness, then, rather than humility, seems to be *janteloven*'s foundational characteristic. It is society that calls one into being, and whatever else it may do, *janteloven* helps to create and maintain community.

As it turns out, the fires were indeed arsons. And the arsonist was most likely an immigrant himself, who had been denied the right to remain in Norway, currently one of the richest countries in the world. Singled out, he retaliated, most people believe, turning on those who were just like him.

But now the immigrants have slowly trickled back into Bodø society. A year after the fire, Norwegian children finally got to see their friends come back from exile. "It was a sad day, the day my son's friend from school left," Linn, the bar owner says. "He was really sad. But she came back not too long ago." The immigrants, some of whom were temporarily housed on an island not long after the fire, are returning. Or many of them are. Their old residence next to the Sku Bare has been rebuilt, with a new outside staircase meant to help anyone escape the building should another fire befall it.

The immigrants speak Norwegian if they can. They speak English when they need to. And they speak their native language to one another. Just like everyone who lives in Bodø.

But *janteloven*, as a culturally cohesive concept, will inevitably change. Most often it is the most pejorative aspects of egalitarianism that are highlighted: the rudeness; an introversion that is world-famous; the jealousy. But with new faces, new means of communication, and new perspectives from native Norwegians, the more positive aspects of egalitarianism may seep into the cultural idiom that is *janteloven*. It is a strong sense of community that keeps Norwegians from drinking and driving, just like it was a sense of cohesion (in the form of survival) that simultaneously led Øystein into a burning building three times while at the same time keeping the patrons at his bar safe.

In many ways, Øystein's story exemplifies this possible change. *Janteloven* has the ability to influence people within its reach; but people also have the ability to influence the reach of *janteloven*. Standing up for oneself, accepting the universal ribbing from friends, the disdain of others, people are able to remind others that they are proud to have been brought up a certain way – in this case, a quintessentially Norwegian one. Øystein is just one of many, but always and forever himself. Øystein is a Glimt Fan, a Fire Hero, a Student Government Leader, and at the same time, just another Bodø boy. He's proud of it.

References

Birn, Randi. (1984). *Aksel Sandemose: exile in search of a home*. Westport, CT: Greenwood Press, p. 1.
Sandemose, Aksel. (1933). *A fugitive crosses his tracks*. Oslo: Tiden.

Appendix

The ten laws of janteloven

1. You shall not believe that you *are* something.
2. You shall not believe that you are as much as *we* are.

3. You shall not believe that you are wiser than *we* are.
4. You shall not imagine that you are better than *we* are.
5. You shall not believe that you know more than *we* do.
6. You shall not believe that you are more than *we* are.
7. You shall not believe that *you* are good for anything.
8. You shall not laugh at *us*.
9. You shall not believe that anybody cares for *you*.
10. You shall not believe that you can teach *us* anything.

9 Keeping law and order in the Norwegian oil-and-gas industry
The challenges of safety regulation

Nadina Ramcharitar, Bodø Graduate School of Business

With nearly twenty-five years' experience in Norway's oil-and-gas industry, Liv[1] has fair claim to being an expert on its culture – or at least that part of it dealing with its health, safety, and environmental concerns, otherwise known as "HSE." A Harstad native, she spent sixteen years working at the Petroleum Safety Authority (PSA). And before that, eight years as HSE manager of a local exploration company. And even before that, some years in the aviation and nuclear industries, two other high-risk domains. So Liv has plenty of stories to share about these industries, as who wouldn't, even after a brief tenure in management. But she really comes alive when discussing the responsibilities and challenges she faces in her current role as an HSE manager, which, one gathers, is sort of like being a cop. Or a judge. Or a psychologist. Or maybe a little of all three.

Her official job is to help keep people safe on the job. Given the daily hazards of the oil-and-gas industry, which has its share of fatalities and lesser accidents, this is no small matter.

But to keep people safe on the job, she must be a rules enforcer. That is, she must ensure what's called "compliance." Now this would be easier if all the rules she's obliged to enforce were totally reasonable, or reasonably flexible, which may be saying the same thing. But some of them seem a bit silly even to her, which often happens when bureaucrats or lawyers write them, since they tend to view the world from behind a desk rather than out in the field. For a person as commonsensical as Liv, this makes for headaches. How can one operate in the real world of nuances when the rules themselves don't recognize nuances?

Another problem she faces is that the employees she's charged with managing tend to fall into extremes: they're either over-compliant, mindless followers, whom she calls "sheep," or they're sneakily rebellious, independent-minded smarties, whom she calls "wolves." She's supposed to admire the first group and bridle at the second group, but it's not that easy, for the "sheep" make observing the rules occasionally seem dumb while the "wolves" make rebellion occasionally seem enlightened. In addition, the "sheep," while dutifully obedient, are rarely creative when it comes to performing tasks. They just go through the same familiar motions.

"But wouldn't you prefer that everyone follow the rules?" I ask her, feeling perhaps a bit sheepish myself.

"Yes, we want them to follow the rules," she allows. "Compliance *is* important. But it's the *way* they comply."

You want people really thinking on the job, using all their critical faculties, not blindly following a worn path, she says. The offshore petroleum environment is already risky enough, and ignorant compliance can be just as dangerous as not complying at all. Liv wishes the sheep would be more mindful, critical thinkers.

Which brings her again to the "wolves," whom she characterizes as "the goal-oriented, assertive, and clever ones." Her face lights up as she talks about them. Liv explains that these employees actually value safety just as much as the sheep, but being creative thinkers, they're always looking for better, more efficient ways to execute tasks. And this often leads to their taking short-cuts, which typically involves some noncompliance – though they'd probably term it *"reasonable* non-compliance." You can tell where Liv's affection lies as she brags about "wolves" being "the creative ones." I'm quickly getting the sense that she's more than a little wolfish herself.

"They say, 'Okay, I'll fix the problem and I'll do it like this.' And then we have the sheep. They follow the rules, but they aren't that goal-oriented." Nor are they innovative, she says. But they're great at following orders.

Maybe, it occurs to me, they're even more like lemmings than sheep.

The infamous handrail policy

To illustrate her perspective on all this, Liv tells me about one HSE company policy that sheep and wolves follow differently: the notorious handrail policy. According to this policy – or is it edict? – all employees must hold onto a handrail while walking up or down steps. *No exceptions here.* They must *always* hold onto a handrail. And the policy is enforced not just at offshore facilities, where it makes a lot of sense because of the high winds and general turbulence, but at onshore facilities, too – *and even in administrative company buildings!* Granted, if an employee breaks the handrail policy on land facilities, he's putting himself at risk for slipping and falling. But that's his choice, and his risk. The likelihood of his causing a serious accident is minimal.

But that's not how the sheep see it, maybe because they never even think about it. They'll obey the policy regardless of the situation or the task they're performing precisely because it is policy; they dare not do otherwise. The wolves, though, will often claim to "forget" to hold the rails, especially if focused on completing a task. Or, Liv says, they'll claim to "have a good reason for not wanting to hold the handrails: the germs!" Actually, they're right about that, she concedes. During flu season, the policy can itself be a hazard. Not only does forever holding onto rails increase their chances of getting the flu, but it also necessitates their having to repeatedly sanitize their hands. That's a lot of time wasted right there, and the wolves resent it.

Even if some wolves fabricate the excuse about handrail germs to justify their noncompliant behavior, Liv sees them as mindful even when breaking rules, and she appreciates this sort of active thinking. She also speculates, again in their defense, that the wolves may sometimes forget to hold onto a rail because they're too preoccupied thinking about what's next on their agenda – in other words, they're actively planning ahead. Maybe, she says, they're too focused on figuring out how to make an operation safer, or maybe they're trying to figure out how to complete some critical job before the end of their twelve-hour shift. The latter is important. It's no secret that handing off unfinished tasks to the next crew shift adds an element of risk to already-dangerous operations.

As a compliance officer, Liv is clearly conflicted about having to remind people to hold the rails. The greater problem, she seems to believe, is employees not thinking, and she hates enabling mindless behaviors. Besides, she says, rules like the handrail policy occupy too many intellectual resources that would otherwise be focused on more critical areas. A lot of time, energy, and money are spent training people to follow these rules and reinforcing compliance. If mundane rules like this one *truly* might prevent serious accidents, then they'd be worth it. But otherwise, why not focus on compliance behaviors that prevent riskier, *more* hazardous endeavors?

The STOP game

Despite this internal conflict, Liv accepts that, as HSE manager, she must enforce these rules. And she has a small army of enablers to help her: the employees themselves. Whether it's the handrail policy or another safety rule, her company has implemented a "game" – or so they call it – for monitoring offshore HSE compliance. Called the Safety Training Observation Program (STOP), it was originally created for DuPont. This Orwellian "game" involves employees monitoring and reporting any acts of noncompliance they observe in their co-workers' behavior, regardless of how minor the infraction. The program combines teamwork (an irony there?) with surveillance to control worker behavior.

Here's how it works. If one employee observes another employee breaking a rule, he (or she, but it's typically a he) must follow STOP protocol. First, he's supposed to have an open, honest STOP conversation with the offender. Next, he must complete a STOP card, which documents and spells out the noncompliant behavior, including when and where it occurred offshore.

STOP cards and conversations are meant, of course, to make operations safer. And according to Liv, their quality is far more important than their quantity. Even so, employees are obliged to fill out one card per shift. Again, *no exceptions*. And true to their crafty, rule-breaking nature, the wolves find ways to give the appearance of compliance even while expressing their defiance, at least covertly.

For example, one wolf confided how some of his wolf buddies managed the STOP cards and handrail policy. By intentionally *not* holding the rails, they were breaking an obvious rule, but they also knew that their violation would give their wolf buddies something to write about on their STOP cards, thereby satisfying their daily quota. Through this little game of their own, the wolves were able to check off yet another required task – in this case, a silly one – and then focus their attention on more critical tasks.

Note the teamwork here – though hardly the teamwork that the rule-writers had in mind. These wolves mindfully cooperated with each other in playing this "game." They were aware of what they were doing, and why. Here they were on a platform, faced with plenty of important duties to occupy a twelve-hour work shift. How could they get these tasks completed assertively, wisely, and safely? The wolves had found a way around the onerous STOP cards, and their co-operative strategy worked. Moreover, their sly demeanors and tacit collusion made them look even more conscientious and rule-abiding around the obedient sheep during this façade of a safety procedure.

But the wolves aren't complete scofflaws. In fact, Liv says, they take the STOP card practice very seriously *when they see something really worthy of being reported.* At such times, they genuinely engage in the rules, conversations, and cards. And this extends to their noting serious acts of noncompliance offshore, too. But, like Liv herself, they don't romanticize complying with mundane rules when the potential consequences are small. Unlike the painstaking sheep, the wolves seem to share Liv's sentiment of saving intellectual resources wisely for more hazardous situations.

Short-cuts, near misses, and incidents

Regardless of how mindful their disobedience, Liv is often frustrated that when wolves take short-cuts, they are breaking the rules in the process. She doesn't have a problem with their short-cuts per se, or their crafty ways of thinking. What concerns her is the potential danger for themselves, the lives of others, and the life of the operation itself when they break rules. Even if they manage to complete some task faster, thus saving valuable time, their short-cuts have sometimes compromised the safety of the entire operation.

A couple of years ago, Liv witnessed a wolf start a crane operation without first getting the required approval from management. At the pre-safety meeting that morning, managers had discussed the dangerous nature of all operations, especially since employees were now operating from a critical part of the oil-and-gas well. The managers decided there would be an *absolute minimum* of crane operations that day because of the risks involved. They also decided that before any task could resume, it had to be approved by a platform manager. Yet despite this rule and warning, one wolf who was cleaning and fixing the area started a crane with the intention of resuming operations. Liv explains the crane could have bumped into the reservoir, caused an explosion, and killed everyone involved in the operation, including her and the employees working above. Without a doubt, skipping procedures or overlooking checklists of rule sequences with short-cuts like this could lead to what the industry calls "major accidents," "incidents," or "near misses."

The Norwegian Petroleum Authority defines a "major accident" as "an acute incident, such as a major discharge, emission or a fire or explosion, which immediately or subsequently causes several serious injuries and/or loss of human life, serious harm to the environment and/or loss of substantial material assets"

(Ptil.no). Like the Deepwater Horizon explosion, these accidents involve serious injuries, fatalities, significant property damage and losses, and environmental consequences. According to Statoil, an "incident" is defined as "an event or chain of events that has caused or could have caused injury, illness and/or damage to/loss of property, the environment or a third party" (Statoil.com). Similarly, a "near-miss" is classified as "an event, which under slightly different circumstances, may have resulted in injury … or damage or loss to property, plant, materials, or the environment".

Liv doesn't seem much concerned about near-misses. In fact, she doesn't seem concerned about them at all. Instead, she worries about behaviors and events that can lead to critical incidents and accidents. Overall, her logic is clear: the outcome of not following what she would call "silly rules" is very different from the outcome associated with breaching serious ones. Yet, she would argue, too much time and attention continue to be spent on monitoring compliance with petty policies. To Liv, reminding employees to hold the handrails seems like a waste of "intellectual resources" because the risk associated with going up or down the stairs is minimal compared with the risk associated with more dangerous operations. Liv believes that even more emphasis should be placed on rules that, if broken, could cause serious incidents and accidents.

If a rebellious wolf decided not to hold the handrails, then he might fall and possibly injure himself; but after that, he would probably have learned his lesson, right? He has a brain; he's not stupid. With passion rising in her voice, Liv proclaims, "Our employees shouldn't have to be babied!" And why? Because, she says, they are well trained and competent; everyone has at least one university degree and should be able to judge their own ability to walk safely up or down the stairs, and when they'd best hold those rails for support. If they're carrying a lot of things, then they should consider taking the elevator. But regardless of their options, they should use their common sense and adapt their behavior accordingly. And it's really up to *them* to do this.

As Liv describes incidents and accidents brought about by noncompliance with rules governing dangerous operations, the triviality she associates with the handrail policy becomes even clearer. "If someone cuts their finger," she says, "then they could potentially lose the finger. If someone *lost* a finger, then it is considered to be an accident; but it's not the end of the world. Now if that person did a risky job where they risked the integrity of an *installation*, then managers should focus on *that* and *not* on the lost finger!" With a tiny smile, Liv explains that "where the potential [for harm] is small," managers should realize and understand that "the potential is small. They shouldn't fuss about it! But where the potential for not doing a good job on an installation is larger, managers should focus on what could be critical," because the possibility of having an accident is higher.

"The fact is, people *want* to be safe," Liv argues. Managers want employees to return home with the same number of fingers and the same number of limbs as they came to work with.

All of this being said, Liv says she understands why resources are invested in ensuring compliance with rules, even like the routine handrail policy; after all, minor as it is, it's like a small daily ritual, and it's helped to ingrain more robust HSE practices and to fortify the safety culture throughout Norway. Precisely because using stairs is such a regular activity, it has workers constantly thinking about their safety.

Wolves thrive but sheep suffer

I ask Liv about her own management style. She has a ready, almost parental answer: "I train my employees to think critically – to take responsibility and ownership for their *own* safety, and to use their 'intellectual resources' wisely, rather than wanting to be treated like babies." Liv says she hopes that employees will develop a sense of mindfulness and actively *use* this frame of mind to employ smarter, safer behaviors.

With a smirk, she then roguishly confides, "We talk like we want sheep, but we continue to hire wolves!"

And as it turns out, quite a few wolves occupy management positions. Liv notes that her department, along with the entire Norwegian oil-and-gas industry, happens to be a climate where "wolves thrive and sheep suffer." Liking that phrase, she repeats it for emphasis, then adds, with a grin, "We have *a lot of* wolves here!" Her grin broadens into a wide smile, as though she is admitting a deep secret that is actually no secret at all. Then, preparing me with a loud laugh, she proudly confides, "I'm more of a wolf!"

The irony is that despite her wolf's mindset, she herself must comply with even the most trivial rules, like holding the rails at work, even though she is not on a dangerous platform in the North Sea. In addition, as a compliance officer, she must also enforce and follow-up on compliance with all these practices. She doesn't get to pick and choose.

Stronger together

While Liv identifies with the wolves, she admits that the oil-and-gas industry cannot survive with wolves and their risky behaviors alone. She respects the sheep for their obedience to the rules and the culture of compliance, since they make her life easier and help ensure a safe working environment, but she also respects the wolves for their assertive, goal-oriented mindsets. Liv has faith that the sheep help keep the independent wolves in check, while the wolves help to model mindfulness and critical thinking for their less spunky, and less creative, friends.

She sees her own role not just as an enforcer but also as an explainer. "Rules are *a lot* of words," she says. "No matter how well they are written, communicating them is not always easy." So that's one of her biggest challenges: getting the messages across, intelligibly and persuasively, like a courtroom attorney explaining the relevant rules of law to a jury. And, too, a lot of her world consists of gray areas – areas of compromise, accommodation. As she put it, "Establishing the correct trade-off between operations and safety is *always*, in practice, difficult." That's why the oil-and-gas industry needs *both* sheep and wolves' natural instincts. They keep each other in check through the natural order of the system; the organic mix of dispositions balances control and innovation.

Furthermore, Liv has high respect for Norwegian safety and enforcement regulations. Regardless of whether sheep and wolves are working onshore or offshore, the culture of these standards must be, and will be, robust. So, too, with her follow-up and supervision.

Note

1. Liv is a pseudonym.

Part IV

Fighting for what you believe in

10 Renegade hero for the environment or the King of Bellona?

Just who is Frederic Hauge?

Elizabeth S. Goins, Bodø Graduate School of Business

Frederic Hauge
Photograph by Jarle Vines

"This can't be the place," I think to myself, fishing around in the bottom of my purse for loose cab fare. Instead of the sleek modern office building I imagined befitting an international NGO, the taxi has stopped in front of a charming, white-brick house in Oslo's stylishly youthful Grünerløkka neighborhood. Set off by a lush, green park on the shores of the Akers River, the house is surrounded by sunbathers, picnickers, families, and dogs all enjoying a perfect – and perfectly rare – Oslo summer day. Before paying the driver, I hastily check the address scribbled in my notebook and confirm that, yes, I have in fact arrived at the headquarters of Bellona Foundation, one of the world's premier environmental NGOs.

According to its website, Bellona has "changed both attitudes towards and policies of the environment in Norway and internationally," transitioning from a direct-action protest group to an environmental NGO and think tank. Dubbing itself a "bridge builder between industry and policy makers," Bellona explores the intersections between technology and legislation to fight global warming, its issue of highest priority and "the greatest challenge of our time." In addition to its headquarters in Oslo, Bellona has satellite offices in Brussels, Washington, D.C., St. Petersburg, and Murmansk, has sixty-five employees, and helps scholars in the physical and social sciences to find innovative solutions for Earth's most pressing environmental problems.

Down the gravelly driveway in front of me sits a lush courtyard, enclosed by a lovely wrought-iron gate readily swung aside. Two young men sitting at a picnic table, apparently on a smoke break, look up from their conversation and smile as I walk past, nodding helpfully toward an inviting double front door. I hesitantly press a button there, presumably the doorbell, and a friendly female voice instantly chirps through the intercom.

"Velkommen to Bellona. Hvordan kan jeg hjelpe deg?"

"Hello. I have a noon appointment with Mr. Hauge."

Known for traversing the waters of Norway's fjords in his speedboat-turned-mobile-office, Frederic Hauge (pronounced Ho-gah) has become a strong Norwegian voice in the international fight against climate change. As the co-founder and president of Bellona, he has made progress for the environmental lobby where many others have failed, deftly navigating Norway's political landscape not unlike the Arctic waters he zips through so frequently. Hauge has learned to recognize the competing ideologies of these policy debates, working with oil companies, bureaucrats, and local stakeholders alike to save a warming planet.

"Oh, hei! Yes, of course. Please come in," the voice responds in welcoming English as I hear the door buzz, my cue to open the door and let myself in.

A friendly receptionist, the very picture of organic chic with her flowing braid and stylishly long skirt, stands smiling in the hallway to usher me into the front room of the house. As she directs me to an overstuffed sofa and offers me a freshly brewed latte, I notice paintings, photographs, and ad campaign posters informally mounted on the white walls with no apparent rhyme or reason. The sounds of ringing phones and laughing voices fill the air as employees flow in and out of the lobby, the distinct energy of organized chaos buzzing all around. Sipping my coffee, I attempt to focus on my interview notes one last time.

"Thank you for waiting. I had a very important call from Washington that took longer than I expected," says a booming, friendly voice. Looking up, I see a tall, smiling man, standing in front of me, and realize it's Frederic Hauge. Although I recognized his broad grin and curly mop of hair from his pictures, neither the office's casual exterior nor Hauge himself, in his rumpled jeans and plain white T-shirt, fits one's image of an international organization. As I would soon come to learn, surprises like these are what make Hauge such a fascinating and controversial player in the Arctic oil-and-gas game.

The car of the future

As he leads me down the winding hallways to his rear office, we pause to look at the photo-lined walls, a visual scrapbook of Bellona's twenty-five-year history. These vivid images – of young protesters in bright-orange biohazard suits digging up nuclear waste, or chaining themselves to oil platforms in the middle of oceans despite the dangerous waves surrounding them – are proof that Bellona's environmentalists aren't afraid to stir up trouble in service of their mission.

Hauge, now 48, points to one picture, a younger version of himself dropping an anchor off the side of a speedboat. "I think we made our first action against oil drilling in the Barents Sea in '92," he tells me, eyes twinkling. "We got a huge penalty."

Early battles like this reinforce the origins of the Foundation's name – Bellona, Roman goddess of war and justice – and mission to defend citizens' ecological rights around the world.

"So you were a renegade?" I ask him, laughing at his easy charm.

He smiles nostalgically and nods, "Yes, it was quite fun. The police came on board and arrested us because we were anchoring where Shell wanted to drill. Eight policemen came on board and got really seasick. After half an hour we had to take one of them back to shore."

While unconventional protest tactics like these put Bellona on the map, today the organization gets more attention for its cutting-edge research on the social and scientific implications of climate change and also its influence on global environmental policies. Most media coverage on Hauge focuses on the unique blend of activism he espouses – a willingness to sit down and have a beer with his opponents, but no less willingness to stir up trouble and force action if necessary. *TIME* magazine named Hauge one of 2007's "Heroes of the Environment," and he sits on the board of half a dozen global environmental organizations. Some people question his motives, though, and whether he's making a difference in Norway or just a splash in the papers. He's been accused of manipulating the public sphere, playing both sides of a controversy to keep what some critics have labeled "the Bellona machine" running.

We finally reach the back of the house and Hauge's office, a disheveled but welcoming room full of natural light and friendly clutter. An old television set – complete with rabbit-eared antennae – sits in the corner, while books and reports lie strewn about on every available flat surface, and mismatched wood articles make uneasy peace with traditional office furniture.

"Wait a second," Hauge says as I begin to sit down. Fishing through the papers and empty cigarette packs on his desk, he finally locates what he's searching for: a set of keys. "I have to look and make sure my car is charging," he explains, beckoning me to the window with that mischievous grin.

Outside sits a sleek, ice-blue-and-chrome beauty, something more likely to be parked in Hugh Hefner's garage than an NGO driveway. Squinting through the glass, I see it's a Tesla Roadster! "It's the fastest electric car in the world," Hauge says happily, inviting me to notice the cord connecting it to a wall outlet. "I raced a friend of mine from Pakistan, who drives a Porsche and collects sports cars, that didn't believe me how fast it was. I won that bet."

"Was it expensive?"

"Not for me. They gave it to me for free," he replies, laughing.

Hauge explains that this "car of the future," as he calls it, a vehicle that breaks the mold from its boring, slow, electric counterparts, is symbolic of one of the greater goals of his movement: solving the climate change problem with cutting-edge technologies, not conservation strategies and restrictive regulations. This sexy roadster actually beats its gas-powered competition, going from zero to 60 mph in under four seconds; it merges the realities of a consumer-based society with the lofty goals of environmental sustainability. This is the cornerstone of Hauge's rhetorical agenda. "People don't want to be conserved," he says. "People want *development*."

How does that message, development trumping conservation, translate into the unique brand of environmentalism that Bellona espouses?

From pollution to solution

Although public discourse about expanding petroleum activity into the Barents Sea and Lofoten island region focuses more on environmental sustainability than ever before, Hauge argues, "Bellona has been quite alone for many years in fighting this." With its impressive cadre of brainy experts, Bellona's website says they are searching for "sustainable solutions" to a host of environmental problems like global climate change and post-Cold War nuclear waste in Russia. The foundation sponsors research on everything from biodiversity in drilling waters to algae farms for processing CO_2 emissions, generating reports as fast as they can to back up their arguments with data. Oftentimes, policymakers from around the world actually come to *them* for answers. But this mission strategy wasn't created overnight.

"I started collecting my first signatures against oil drilling back in '79," Hauge begins. "When we started, it was easy. You broke into a factory and you dug up a barrel [of toxic waste]. That was how we created a name. It was on the television news program every week. And if you find mustard gas, you *really* get a lot of attention! But what you *do* with [it]" – Hauge's tone suddenly drops a full register – "is much more complicated."

"So how do you move from direct action to long-term policy influence?"

Hauge allows himself a thoughtful pause. "You use that kind of action when you need to get things up on the agenda and create a kind of momentum. And it takes some years before you manage to create the credibility to have a say.

And when you have that say, *then* you have the basement for the broader public opinion." In other words, real influence comes not only from headline-grabbing protest tactics, but also from building up a reputation over time. Bellona started out in 1986 to raise public awareness about large-scale environmental problems like nuclear waste, but now its focus is "more from pollution to solution." Hauge goes on: "If we don't manage that as an environmental movement, we will end up like the Women's Liberation Movement, where everyone starts to agree, but it's only the most extreme voices that manage to get on the agenda." Instead of being viewed as renegades or environmental extremists, Hauge says, Bellona wants to be a real information source for decision-makers in Norway and abroad.

In order to make comprehensive, credible policy recommendations, Bellona must "pick the right samples to create precedence," he says. That requires collecting and managing huge amounts of data on the economic, social, scientific, and political implications of climate change. This task isn't cheap in terms of money or labor, and Bellona has "put a lot of resources in not only having opinions, but doing the research." According to Hauge, this is one area in which Bellona stands alone in Norway.

"I have spent a lot of time in the U.S.," he says, "and one of the first things I realized when I started working there was that we don't have the think-tank system in Norway. That's awful, because even if the Republicans have their think tanks, and the Democrats have *their* think tanks, they have to work *together* – sit down and think of clever ideas *together*."

This collaborative research network is vital to Bellona's strategy for finding manageable solutions to huge environmental problems, regardless of political ideology or competition. As an example of this network, Hauge cites his work with the Center for American Progress, a liberal think tank in Washington, D.C., chaired by John Podesta, former Chief of Staff for President Clinton.

"John Podesta is a close friend of mine," Hauge says. "We are together in what we call a Global Climate Network .... This is quite high-level, the work that we are doing with these think tanks, when it comes to holistic scenarios on how to combat global warming .... We have been very proactive in creating this kind of clearinghouse" of knowledge to guide international policy. And, in Hauge's opinion, "shared information is a force."

But traditional credibility, packaged in advanced degrees and empirical research, is only part of the equation. While Bellona has worked hard to get the ears of major politicos both in Norway and internationally, now the Foundation focuses on inspiring new approaches to new environmental problems – focusing, he says, "on the issues where we can make a difference, making progress, being able to create momentum, that's needed here." Then adds, matter-of-factly, "We don't need to get the politicians anymore."

The complexity of the issues, too, has evolved since Bellona started out, he says. "First we needed to find the solutions for mustard gas, now for CO_2. That is a different ball game. And no solution is black-and-white. There is always a new environmental challenge within it. So you have to be open. You have to accept that there is not only one answer."

We have no emotions

This openness, a rational and collaborative approach to environmental justice, is what sets Bellona apart from other Norwegian NGOs. "We have no emotions," Hauge insists. "We are not against windmills if there are not too many eagles that will die. Probably they will learn to fly around them. We believe in Darwin. We eat whale meat if there are enough whales to be eaten. We should harvest from what nature gives to us ... within a sustainable limit."

This also means choosing your battles wisely. Rather than blindly following an ideological agenda like many environmental NGOs, Hauge says, Bellona knows when to say when with conservation, limiting the scope of its arguments to manageable levels and constantly challenging its ideas with new information.

"Better to do the job than talk about it," Hauge says.

"What do you mean by that, though?" I ask. "Can you tell me about a time when Bellona took on a challenge and was successful with this approach?"

Hauge pauses, then resumes: "In 2001, there was a very important shift in the discussions" about petroleum activity in Norway, "just before the [national parliamentary] election. Norwegian Hydro [an energy company, later taken over by Statoil, but which then had active operations in the North Sea] had got permission to drill at Røst." Røst, I knew, was a Northern municipality in the Lofoten region, home to the world's largest cod spawning grounds and symbolic of Norway's historic fishing culture. Opening up Lofoten for oil drilling has been a decade-long controversy.

"Before we could appeal to the Ministry of Environment" and demand a formal review of the environmental impacts of new petroleum activity there, Hauge continues, Hydro was ready to start drilling. "And we said, well, this is a lack of democracy and we cannot be arrested" for protesting it. Bellona activists "had just been in the Netherlands and got a new boat, and we sailed directly up and stayed at Røst where the platform was on its way."

After Bellona threw out its anchors, effectively stopping any platform installation, "the Labour Party withdrew the [drilling] permission and said 'we see that this is wrong from a democratic point of view.'" In other words, the government agreed it had been hasty in granting Norsk Hydro their permits without a sufficient public-review process, and that more environmental assessments were needed before any drilling could start.

"That was in September 2001. The Labour Party lost" in the parliamentary elections that year, ceding power to the "Green–Blue" coalition between the Christian Democratic, Liberal, and Conservative parties. But the new coalition, led by prime minister Kjell Magne Bondevik, agreed that Norway needed a "holistic management plan" for the Barents Sea. They started asking, "What is the ship traffic" these petroleum activities bring with them? "What is the global distillation" of organic air and water pollutants occurring from increased traffic? And, perhaps most importantly, "Who are the actors" with the most power over Arctic oil and gas?

"That whole management plan was because Bellona stayed up at Røst, willing to be arrested," Hauge says proudly. But they didn't exactly make friends in the process, he concedes. "Hydro had to turn around their platform, and that cost them 400 million kroners. And the Oil Ministry" – the government agency that serves as a liaison to oil-and-gas companies operating in Norway – "got *furious.*" And according to Hauge, not only had Bellona challenged the government and halted the drilling in Røst, it had changed the way companies like Norsk Hydro would do business in the future. "If you look at the number of people they [the oil industry] have employed since 2001 to do lobby and communication work, it is incredible."

Despite ruffling some major feathers, Bellona's strategy in Røst was also a symbolic victory for Norwegians who questioned the inevitability of Northern petroleum development. Until then, "everyone told us that this was already decided," Hauge recalls. By combining the direct-action protest strategies that made it famous with legal expertise that saved its activists from being arrested, Bellona had "managed to put the issue back on the agenda." Since then, this "ongoing fight" has continued with no clear resolution in sight, but Hauge believes that "if we had not done that work, there would be oil drilling in Lofoten and Vesterålen."

No second dinner

Although stories like Bellona's protests in Røst show that it isn't afraid to stir up trouble and demand action from both the oil industry and the Norwegian government, Hauge is also well known for a more pragmatic approach to environmental activism. He insists that he will sit down with anyone, friend or foe, to hash out innovative solutions for problems like climate change. While its cutting-edge research provides Bellona with a certain level of credibility and authority, Hauge also recognizes the need to forge personal connections with the other stakeholders in these policy-making processes. That means using its international network to influence members of Norwegian Parliament or proving its nautical chops to the fishermen in Lofoten. According to Hauge, many Lofoten residents refuse to deal with the big environmental NGOs, but "when we come up to Lofoten in our boat, they judge us on our seamanship, if the boat is okay, if we are fanatics, if we eat whale meat, and if we can have a beer together."

That's one reason for his mobile speedboat office and why Bellona has been especially successful at grassroots efforts where others have failed. Instead of just swooping in with glitzy marketing campaigns and expensive outreach efforts like Statoil and other petroleum companies, Bellona makes a big effort "to be a part of the daily life, in a way, at Røst, Værøy, Stamsund," Hauge says. Statoil "has the big luxury dinners with a lot of promises," but they "have, in my opinion, misjudged the local attitude completely. It works for a while," until the people realize "there is no second dinner."

Because of the geographic constraints of this region, drilling would be closer to shore than has ever been allowed in Norway. The islands' tourism industry relies on Lofoten's beauty, a symbol of Norway's fjords and mountains. What would oil rigs and tanker ships add to these picturesque views? Lofoten seafood is branded on a history of purity. What could an oil spill do to destroy centuries of fishing tradition?

But five years ago, despite the catastrophic impact that oil drilling might have on their livelihoods, Hauge says the fisherman "had their heads down," feeling "pushed out of the local society" and powerless to effectively voice their stance on the issue. Oil, not fishing, had become the national industry of Norway. Drilling in the North seemed inevitable, and those who opposed it appeared to be fighting the tides of progress. But according to Hauge, it was really only "the leaders of the different political local parties" and "the administration" that wanted drilling in Lofoten. If you sat at a local restaurant and asked around, you would find that "the people don't want it."

Now, with the help of Bellona and other environmental organizations, local residents and fisherman are "allowed to be against" companies drilling oil in their backyards and the government intervening in their daily lives. After working hard to show the locals it means what it says, Bellona has garnered enough support to set up grassroots organizations, led by community members, to continue its mission to keep drilling out of Lofoten. Folkeaksjonen, known as "People's Action Oil-Free Lofoten, Vesterålen, and Senja," is one such "parachute" group that Bellona helped to build from the ground up. Once a small volunteer organization handing out anti-drilling flyers in the local shops to tourists and residents, Folkeaksjonen now has a full-time (paid) leader, sponsors national letter-writing campaigns, and hosts huge weekend protests that draw thousands of supporters from all over Norway.

And when the Fishing Ministry decided to open up a Værøy harbor in 2009, the fishermen mobilized some 70 to 80 boats to block it. This time, Hauge recalls, "it was the fishermen themselves" who organized the protest. "We pulled back." Now Bellona supports the fisherman by providing resources, like expert witnesses to testify on their behalf in legal proceedings and regulatory hearings that these stakeholders could not otherwise afford.

The King of Bellona

Given stories like these, it's easy to see why Hauge has gained international recognition for his pragmatic approach to environmental activism, his willingness to collaborate with industry, and his influence over the Norwegian policymaking system. What remains less clear is why, with such an impressive résumé of accomplishments, Hauge and Bellona are so controversial in Norway.

Despite Bellona's local, regional, national, and international cooperation efforts, Hauge has been accused of opportunistically playing both sides of environmental debates for personal gain. Some argue he's made a business of creating friction between industry, government, and activists rather than facilitating compromises and shared understandings. As a "one-man operation," or "king of the Bellona," as some critics have labeled him, Hauge has kept his organization relevant for almost thirty years in the state oil game. If there were no more issues to fight about, critics argue, Bellona – and Hauge – would lose their power.

One particular sticking point for some opponents is Hauge's signature "development over conservation" rhetoric. For example, other environmentalists have argued the Lofoten island region should be classified as a UNESCO World Heritage Site, effectively restricting any oil-and-gas activity forever. When I ask Hauge about UNESCO, he leans in and slowly whispers, "I … hate … them."

"That strategy is so damaging … people don't want to be conserved. People want *development*," he insists. Rather than basing their strategies on restrictive conservation policies, he says, environmentalists should focus on showing "the alternative industries" to oil and gas, drumming up "investments in seaweed production, or in new technologies for wind or tidal" power as renewable energy sources.

But Hauge's critics offer a different interpretation of his stance on UNESCO. If Lofoten becomes a World Heritage Site, they say, then Bellona is no longer the leader of a national movement. Such tactics have been likened to the anti-whaling campaigns that have become big business for international NGOs like Greenpeace. Despite what those organizations would lead you to believe, Norway actually enforces very tight regulations and quotas on whale hunting; it hasn't been a problem in the country for decades. However, critics argue, misunderstood issues like whaling are great opportunities for environmental organizations to stoke constituent emotions and justify their own existence. As Norway will never likely place an outright ban on whaling – you can even order a whale burger from the food tents at Folkeaksjonen anti-drilling protests – NGOs like Greenpeace can benefit from keeping the issue alive in the public sphere.

Another point of controversy is Bellona's aforementioned stance on promoting alternative energies. Although Hauge asserts that most of the environmental community holds similar priorities, not all organizational agendas for this issue seem aligned. Take carbon capture and storage (CCS) – a technology designed to capture CO_2 emissions from places like fossil-fuel plants and store the emissions underground, deep within geological formations, to prevent atmospheric contamination. Bellona has doubled down on CCS technology as a central component of their organizational strategy to fight climate change. According to their website, the **B**ellona **E**nvironmental CC**S** **T**eam (BEST) partners with European energy companies to produce "Roadmaps for CCS Deployment" – research on developing CCS programs throughout the continent – and lobby the European Union Parliament for legislative funding and support.

While Hauge insists that CCS is a fundamental part of reducing global warming, some green groups scoff at the reliability of its technologies. For example, the leader of Greenpeace Norway has called those who believe in CCS – that is, in its economic potential as an alternative industry for Norway and environmental potential in the global fight against climate change – victims of "false-hope technology." If no clear lines of agreement on CCS can be found in the Norwegian environmental community, it certainly is unclear why government dollars are being taken away from other possible climate-change solution investments, like developing renewable energy, and instead allocated toward CCS-technologies.

Controversies over CCS also point to broader criticisms about Hauge's credibility: Is he really qualified to argue an issue platform based on scientific and technological research? Although Bellona employs experts with advanced degrees in subjects ranging from Russian history to nuclear physics, most of Hauge's own learning hasn't occurred in the classroom. He bristles a little when I hint of this critique, explaining that he quit school at 17 to begin "learning by doing." True, he has "no formal experience," Hauge concedes, but he's well-schooled in "making trouble" and doing "a lot of work."

And to hear Hauge speak, you would never know this is a man without academic training in business, government relations, media strategy, and environmental technology. The international community seems to agree, judging by the contacts in his phone and email address lists – which he showed me, in fact. Regardless of whether or not you agree with his education or methods, it's impossible to deny that Hauge has the ear of some very important people all over the world. However, this connectedness touches on the biggest question posed by critics: Is Bellona in bed with the oil-and-gas industry?

Hauge's been accused of running interference between the state and the oil industry, "selling trust" with Bellona's commissioned research. While he acknowledges that such a relationship exists, he describes it a little differently. Rather than Bellona answering to the oil industry, he insists that *he* is the one asking the questions.

"Yesterday," Hauge exclaims, while excitedly pointing toward his computer, "I fired yesterday 29 questions to Statoil." His voice becomes dramatically hushed as he continues: "And you know, they get scared because they see that we have detailed inside information that never we should have, because we have so many people trusting us."

"What do you mean you have so many people trusting you?" I take the bait and lean closer, ready to receive a top-secret earful.

"We know how to deal with information," Hauge responds enigmatically, giving me a knowing smile.

After a moment, I realize he is implying that Bellona won't sell out its sources. But does it recruit those moles, those sympathizers within Statoil and other industry giants like Shell and Conoco Phillips? No, it's not the other way around, Hauge assures me: "They call us."

Sleeping with the enemy

Overall, does Hauge think these accusations of straddling both sides of the debates detract from Bellona's mission and credibility? Quite the opposite, he says. In fact, Bellona's core strength is its ability to bridge the gap between otherwise disparate stakeholders. To communicate effectively in Lofoten and Vesterålen, "you need to be a fucking seaman," not a conservationist, Hauge argues passionately. From this perspective, Bellona's critics actually help the organization's position with the locals – "the other people [NGOs] become quite extreme, but we are easy to talk with. But we are tough guys; we don't accept [just] anything. And we can take action. They will talk with us because we have an industrial view."

But how can being a tough guy inspire organizational trust from the industry?

According to Hauge, Bellona's relationship with the oil industry has been built on two main factors. First, oil-and-gas companies don't "fuss with science," so it appreciates Bellona's "big reports." In other words, the industry, if not based on research of its own, makes decisions based on established facts, and thereby respects Bellona's data-driven approach to environmentalism. To show me what he means, Hauge pulls a fat report off his bookshelf – a 2005 white paper on CCS, written by Bellona researchers and used by the Norwegian government – and thumbs through it meaningfully as he speaks.

Second, as I have heard over and over from Hauge and Bellona's supporters, he is willing to sit down with industry representatives rather than just mount protests. Although he clearly is willing to stand up to them, Hauge has also sat on committees within some of these companies, working side-by-side with their CEOs to establish environmental best practices. This willingness to collaborate has had a large impact on Bellona's financial viability. The foundation "created a cooperation program with the industry fourteen years ago," and to be accepted, companies must first be a sponsor – that is, make a financial contribution to the NGO – for three years.

"Why the time restriction?"

"Because we don't want the short term," explains Hauge. Rather than viewing this program as a virtual cash machine, however, Hauge describes industry support as a vital part of keeping Bellona's doors open. Compared with "the rest of the Norwegian environmental groups," Bellona has "little governmental funding," Hauge explains, suggesting that his critics' accusations of cozy government relations are unfounded. In fact, Bellona has quite contentious relationships with many Norwegian politicians and ministry officials, a result of giving them what Hauge calls "the fuck-you finger too many times."

However much these political foes may hate Hauge and his organization, though, it doesn't pay to ignore him. Careful not to affiliate with any one political agenda or organization, Bellona falls "very much in between, and we are unpredictable. We can take action, but we can also be the best partner. So people are a little bit afraid of us."

When I ask Hauge about the broader implications of this neutral-but-dangerous strategy, the consequences of playing the middle ground, and whom Bellona is ultimately accountable to, he stops and pauses uncharacteristically. This is the first question to apparently stump him.

"You know, credibility is something you get when you deserve it. But no one really wants to sleep with a prostitute," Hauge replies, that trademark grin slowly spreading across his face after a moment of serious contemplation. We laugh together and I understand his message: all activist organizations need strategic partnerships to survive, but no one wants to be in bed with someone using them for the short term. There have to be relational ties and some mutual degree of loyalty.

On behalf of Norway

Regardless of Hauge's motivations or credibility with critics, his leverage and influence in Norwegian policy-making are hard to deny. Starting with single-issue protests in 1984, Bellona has morphed into an integral cog in the Norwegian policy-making process. Organizations and stakeholders in these environmental debates do not pass go without at least considering Bellona's potential for action, or "stirring up trouble," as Hauge terms it.

For him, Bellona is less about one man or one organization's power than it is about persuading international policy-makers to make sustainable decisions for the future. The "Norwegian government has a big say in the international management of the Arctic. If you look at the Arctic and the challenges we face," he says, you will see "the complexity and the holistic pressure" of regulatory decision-making for these issues. The most important aspect of Bellona's work, he says, is acting "not only on behalf of Norway, but on behalf of the international society." According to Hauge, his organization is filling a massive social need – "the need for independent knowledge" about the environmental consequences of climate change and how to solve them with technological innovation.

As we finish our interview and Hauge walks me back out to the front room, we stop at a wall lined with shelves of Bellona research reports. Pulling two or three from the shelves, he flips through the pages, pointing out facts and images to stress the scope and breadth of information each contains.

"This one," he says in a hushed whisper, clutching the booklet proudly, "is about an issue the government did not have *any* research on, and after our report, they had to produce a white paper in response."

"So that's the heart of your strategy?" I ask. "To be the ones creating these issues to shape how they are discussed, rather than just responding to them?"

He looks up, eyebrows raised, and I worry I've offended him. But then that trademark grin appears and with a wink, he says conspiratorially, "You got it."

11 Easy money

The opportunism of a bootstrapped entrepreneur

Frode Fjelldal-Soelberg, Bodø Graduate School of Business

"We're located on the second floor," he says, "but it's a bit tricky to find the entrance. You'll have to walk through the parking lot in the backyard. The entrance is in the corner on your right as you pass the pub."

Thor,[1] the entrepreneurial founder of NorthWare, a young firm providing ICT services and software consultancy, is on the phone trying to direct me to his office. I manage to find it, but he was right: finding it proved tricky indeed. I've lived in this town for fifteen years and I never knew that this facility was here. It's in an old hotel, and I suspect this part of the building represents unneeded space. In the backyard, plaster has started peeling off the walls, especially close to the ground where rain and snow dissolve it. Yet this is where NorthWare can be found, in the backyard, where you'd expect to find a garage. Hardly ideal for a business consultancy. One would expect a high-end location, shiny cars, dark suits.

There is no such glitter at NorthWare, that's for sure. As I enter the building and climb the narrow staircase, I notice that the wall coloring is a psychedelic pink and creamy white. *Surreal*, I'm thinking. Happily, though, the second floor has gotten itself refurbished and looks considerably better. Thor greets me in the hall and proudly gives me a tour of the premises. The NorthWare office landscape contains seven desks: four grouped in the middle, two by the entrance, and Thor's desk by the windows, slightly elevated above the others. "Not because I like to show that I'm the boss," he explains. "It simply offers a better view of the Arctic scenery outside."

The whole company is fitted into this one rectangular room. Even, off to the right, its conference facilities. Nothing fancy, just a table there that would seat maybe ten people. From the looks of it, it probably also doubles as both a lounge and a lunch room. On the left, standard office hardware (printer, copier, etc.) hides discreetly behind foldable screens. All in all, Thor's venue isn't so bad. I've certainly seen worse, as most new firms are bootstrapped and have to think twice about how to afford even the basics. And what's more, compared with other start-ups, often with just one or two employees, NorthWare is huge. It's got six employees in addition to Thor himself. I fully understand Thor's pride in his start-up achievement. Most new businesses in Norway are one-person operations, and about three-quarters of them go belly up within four years. The survivors typically employ just four people five years after start-up. NorthWare boasts seven, and it's still in its first year. Pretty impressive – and almost no one wears a suit, either.

But observing me gaze curiously around, Thor probably feels that some kind of justification is needed, so he explains himself. "I used to be a car mechanic," he says – all right, that helps explain the backyard location. Quite a career leap, though, from car maintenance to computer software. "But I got sick and tired of it – it bored me and I didn't see any future in it. So I started looking for something new." Pause. Then: "After taking on a position within ICT, I was quickly drawn toward software. During reeducation I realized that I in fact was involved in a criminal activity – you know, piracy. As I figured out how computer systems functioned I became a petty thief. At one point my computer utilized some 12,000 stolen licenses. It didn't fit my moral standards, to say the least. No wonder I got into free software."

Unlike your typical business software, which carries a license fee as well as restricted access to its source code, so-called "free software" is software you may download from the Internet with fully accessible source code, meaning you can modify it freely to suit your particular needs.[2]

It strikes me that Thor probably is a religious man, actually not very common in the secularized culture of Norway. He is discreetly signaling religious belief in his dress, hairstyle, and body language. I can only imagine the moral discomfort Thor must have felt when he realized his crime, leading to this radical shift in thinking.

So how, exactly, did this former car mechanic reinvent himself as a software entrepreneur?

It started with reeducation. Of course, any shift in career requires a major commitment of time and energy, for it sets before you a series of hurdles, one of which involves educational requirements. Because the lack of mobility between careers is a major source of friction in labor markets globally, many countries provide their own ways to ease the problem. Norway, for instance, provides free education for its citizens, thereby eliminating one of the biggest hurdles. In addition, it generously provides a living allowance for those choosing to reeducate, making their career transition even smoother. Thor was eligible for such benefits when he left the garage. So, really, the only barrier Thor had to handle himself was his own motivation to make this bold move. But we've already heard that he was "sick and tired" of car maintenance, and he knew that the government would support him, so his motivation barrier was nil. Later on in the NorthWare story, we'll see that what Thor knows about government will have major implications on the decisions made and the strategies employed by NorthWare.

"You know," Thor goes on, "Norwegians spend way more on software licenses than on developing software. The original idea at NorthWare was to develop software – 'free software.' The whole point is to develop a different ecosystem with a continuous need for further developments and maintenance. NorthWare is going to make money by offering these continuous improvements. And for the moment, NorthWare is without competitors."

What a remarkable demonstration of Marketing Myopia.[3] I hope the no-competition statement is more of a slip of the tongue, and not what he actually believes. Free software and/or open-source software doesn't involve radical innovations; it's rather a unique business idea. This business model depends for its income on profitable add-ons such as customizing, training, and support. It differs from the dominant proprietary model, but the core benefits of the products are equal (word processing, controller functions, etc.). Customers taking the advantage of free software have to purchase training, customization, and modifications, and are therefore usually depending on buying services from software consultants. Customers buying proprietary software pay for the license and subsequent upgrades, but don't necessarily buy services from software consultants. Basically, the software is still performing the same tasks. Thus, from a customer viewpoint these are two ways of satisfying the same need – admittedly with different product structures. I don't think a quick-witted definition of markets and products will make competition disappear. NorthWare is still competing with large global corporations like Microsoft and Apple. That's a tough battle to win.

"Thor, could you please take a look at this?" One of his employees needs his input on some business opportunity or proposition.

"No, that's not interesting to us," Thor says, after hearing him out.

"The money would come in handy, though," the employee says.

"It would," Thor admits, "but it is not consistent with what we are aiming for."

Thor appears to enjoy the luxury of turning down business opportunities that don't fit into his general strategy for NorthWare. This is interesting for two reasons. First, because new ventures commonly depend on short-term adaptation to such opportunities for their very survival, and second, because it's commonly believed that new ventures don't make tactical decisions based on strategic considerations.

This little debate over short-term money continues for another minute or two in the NorthWare office landscape. Might NorthWare have a financial problem? Thor pauses and looks over at me, then says: "I think we should go somewhere else to do the interview. Let's head down to the harbor – I like it at the diner down there."

The harbor is a few blocks away. Once outside, we face a gusty Arctic winter day, with eastern winds sweeping the streets and whipping fine-grained snow in our eyes. I see no car awaiting us in the parking lot.

"I guess we're walking?" I ask, already chilled.

"Yeah, you're right. I like walking when I'm downtown – it's just a short walk anyway."

We walk in silence down to the diner, where we find ourselves a quiet table. Settling in, I'm wondering how best to approach the delicate matter of NorthWare's current health.

"Can you explain to me, as a nonexpert in software, what your business is actually doing – what is your business idea?" I ask him, and to make sure he takes a *grand tour* I add, "The only thing I know about this subject is that it exists."

Thor laughs at my ignorance and launches into a thorough introduction to free software. Then he explains the NorthWare business idea: "There is a lot of free software available on the Internet, but there are still a few missing bits to cover the full range of software that your average company needs. Our business idea is to develop software that covers these gaps, and take care of our customers' needs by using 100 percent free software. We're not quite there yet, I'm afraid."

"Not there yet?" I offer him wriggle room.

"You know, there are two different ways to look at it," he says, then hesitates, like he's making a draft of how he wants to explain it. "You may say that NorthWare is doing great, but at the same time say we're barely coping. It depends on what you focus on."

My worries about how to broach the subject can be put aside, as Thor seemingly needs to talk about it.

"In what respects are you doing great?" I ask, thinking that it's less invasive to be more interested in the successful part of NorthWare.

"As you've seen, we've managed to build a substantial organization. We're able to handle all sorts of customers now. The challenge has been to develop a technologically skilled labor force, and I've personally trained my employees. I'm actually quite happy with that achievement. Additionally, we have formed alliances with other industrial actors. NorthWare is positioned as the main driving force behind free software in our region. In fact, we are the only company that is dedicated to free software and nothing else in Northern Norway." Thor is now talking nonstop. Thank heavens for my digital voice recorder. But if I don't slow him down, I'm going to lose track of where we're going. He modified the no-competition statement, but gave another interesting cue as well.

"You were talking about building an organization?" I'm hoping to force him to rewind a bit.

"Yeah, we're just a small company. But our customers tend to be large. So there is a problem with us being small – you know, these large customers like to deal with equals, and they compare NorthWare with other software consultants. You know, larger and well established ones. If I was the only one employed, customers would definitely doubt NorthWare's ability to deliver. And that I know for a fact; NorthWare has in the past been neglected in competitive bids because the customer didn't trust us. I didn't really have any choice. NorthWare had to grow bigger, in terms of employees, to be able to capture market shares."

Thor had clearly found himself in a catch-22: If your company is too small, it can't enter the really profitable markets, but employing more people creates higher fixed costs, meaning more risk of failure. Prompt success in the marketplace is absolutely critical, then, for sustaining this bolder strategy of organizational development. Choosing to build an organization first and then competing for market share isn't a bad decision, given the market conditions that Thor points to, but it's a high-risk strategy because of the cost structure.

"So, do you think you've got a properly staffed organization now?"

"My first employee was a computer engineer. He started working here the day after sitting the final exam at the University, and has skills that are invaluable to the business. Then I found a fellow that could assist me within management and marketing. This guy was also a university graduate without any impressive CV. These two came to me by way of personal network – recommended by friends. Now there's six people employed here, and the final four were recruited through Employment Services [NAV]: two software specialists, one controller, and a secretary." Thor gives a thorough account of his staff's qualifications, but he seems unwilling to answer yes or no to my question. What strikes me is that there is little-to-no prior experience with free software among the employees. And on top of that, NorthWare personnel are either fresh off the University or previously unemployed. This is what could be labeled "second-tier resources," a predicament common to new ventures. Thor would probably like to have better-skilled staff, but this is what he's got.

"You mentioned earlier that you had to train your staff yourself, didn't you?"

"Yes, I did. I had to teach every one of them about the pros and cons of free software, and how we shall go about doing business at NorthWare. However, my own experience in free software is limited to a couple of years, so I guess there is a lot more that should be done when it comes to training."

Thor relies on his own resources, even though he knows that it will not take him all the way. A characteristic trait of new ventures is limited financial resources. This causes resource leveraging – DIY (Do-It-Yourself) instead of buying services is proverbial.

"But, you know, that is really not the problem," Thor continues. "What is a big problem, however, is that the market isn't ready for our kind of services."

So far, Thor has only mentioned problems that are more or less generic to new ventures. Even successful new ventures must resort to resource leveraging, second-tier resources, and DIY-solutions. What Thor is saying now could mean that NorthWare lacks the kind of success it needs to sustain its bold strategy. This could be what he was talking about when admitting that NorthWare was barely coping.

"What do you mean? Is it a problem with your products or with free software in general?"

"The market isn't ready for free software. Compared to other regions our market hasn't reached the desired level of maturity. We are struggling real hard developing the market, and our numbers are in the red." Thor sighs and looks down at the floor. "You know, reading financial reports is a rather grim experience. Cash flow is bad, too."

I suspect, though, that NorthWare probably faces more than one problem in developing the market. A quick analysis of the market structure will point to at least three major barriers to market entry. First, while free software has been around for some time, customers world-wide have gotten used to computers that employ licensed software from a few major suppliers. Second, customers are familiar with, and have accepted, the business model (licensing) of these same suppliers. This may cause inertia and a general reluctance to adopt alternative software. Third, large corporations also dominate industrial networks, where any hardware is typically infused with their software. Those software products that are successful in the marketplace and that don't come from Apple or Microsoft typically come in two versions and are adaptable to both platforms. So the business concept for successful software businesses doesn't seem to include the concept of free software. The challenges facing NorthWare appear similar to those related to what's called "first-mover advantage" (i.e., the first major occupant of a market segment often enjoys a huge advantage simply by being there first) and substantial financial resources are probably needed to succeed.

"How bad is it? Can you give me the numbers?" I ask, now pressing.

"I'd rather not," he replies. But then admits: "I can put it this way: We haven't paid VAT yet."

I'm stunned. In a way, VAT (value added tax) constitutes a milestone in creating a new venture. Norwegian tax authorities don't find it worthwhile to include a business in the VAT-registry unless there's a minimum revenue. The threshold is currently about NOK 50,000 over twelve months. The median annual net income of Norwegian households is about NOK 400,000, so NOK 50,000 is not a lot of money. In software consultancy you'd expect a new venture to quickly rise above this, since delivering to even a couple of customers would potentially generate a huge cash flow. Bottom line: Things aren't looking good for NorthWare. Still, the company has been in business for only a year, and it's somehow still surviving.

"Is it that bad? How do you cope, Thor?"

"We are focusing on customers with specialized needs, like the public sector who use software that no one else is using. That kind of software need can easily be covered by free software, and at a much lower price. So we've got some cash from a few such customers. But what really keep us afloat are investors, and other sources of funding."

Thor is on a roll, but this needs some elaboration. "Hang on, hang on, hang on," I interrupt. "Investors? What kind of investors do you have and how did you manage to find them?"

"When I was thinking – actually, it was more like daydreaming – about starting this business, I got in touch with Innovation Norway and they sent me off to entrepreneurial training. I attended a program called Europrise, all paid for by Innovation Norway, and two things happened. First, I quit daydreaming and started planning." (As in any other Western country there are special bodies designed to promote and support entrepreneurial efforts. The Norwegian version of it is called Innovation Norway, and entrepreneurs may find support there – both educational and financial.) "Secondly, I learned that the whole business idea must be in tune with Innovation Norway requirements to qualify for support. You know, from the first day of training the instructor made it very clear that Innovation Norway applies a set of rules, and that an application for funding must follow these. Consequently I wrote a business plan, and the instructor helped me get it right. I made a marketing plan, a nice budget, and so on. A while after sending it to Innovation Norway I received a money transfer on my account."

How weird. I had asked about his investors, yet Thor started talking about the supporting system. Entrepreneurs can be working on more than one front simultaneously, sure, but does he really view Innovation Norway as an *investor*? Even so, what he's saying is really telling, as this illuminates how he thinks. Most notably, he apparently views the public new-venture support system as a way to fund NorthWare.

"How do you feel about that?" I ask.

"Great," he says, smiling. "Innovation Norway's contribution is invaluable to us in the current market situation. Writing the business plan and applying for funds was, however, hard work. It's not my cup of tea."

I'm not too surprised by his reply, as a lot of entrepreneurs prefer to work on more tangible aspects of their business than the business plan. "But what about the business plan as such?" I ask. "Is it kept alive through revisions? Does it reflect what the business is doing today?"

"Well, no," Thor admits. "I don't even know where it is. Probably in a drawer somewhere. But, you know, in the beginning it was a really nice document, even though it didn't reflect what I really wanted to achieve with the business. Through the process of training I was advised to adapt to the reigning market conditions, and to create a more standard software consultancy business, and so I did. But as I said: it was more an effort to get funding from Innovation Norway. I actually doubt that I would have taken the trouble if not for the application process. It would be kind of daft not to take the advantage of such easy money, don't you agree?" He is certainly being straightforward. This is plain opportunism. "The business plan has been valuable in a very direct way," Thor continues, "and that is NOK 650,000."

I'm puzzled by Thor's way of thinking. On the one hand, he says he shouldn't have bothered. But on the other hand, writing a business plan has had a valuable and measurable result. However, it doesn't seem like the business plan was important in developing the business. I may be wrong, but I've got a feeling the business plan was actually part of a cunning plan to resolve a critical financial situation. A little earlier, Thor has suggested that investors and other sources of funding were what keep NorthWare in business.

"That's a lot of money, Thor. But what do you mean when you say that was how the business plan was valuable?"

"Oh, yeah, I know it sounds a bit suspect. But what I'm trying to say is that the plan made it easier to attract investors. You know, instead of telling potential investors about it, they could just read the document and make up their mind. I've sold about 20 percent of the shares to investors. Additionally, these investors have contributed with equity. My own investment in NorthWare is about NOK 250,000. Money that I borrowed from a bank. I had to mortgage the house. But the investors are people that I know or are acquainted with."

In other words, NorthWare is financed through bootstrapping. The various sources of equity at NorthWare he's mentioned so far are his own private assets (his house), investors that are part of his personal network, and new-venture support agencies.

"So, the money from Innovation Norway, investors, and your own share is what you are living off at NorthWare?"

"Actually, there is more. You know, all the people I've hired? I couldn't afford to if not for wage subsidy from Unemployment Services [the Norwegian Labour and Welfare Service, or NAV]. We receive subsidies for four of our employees. Unemployment Services is paying half of their salary. The other two are paid very modestly."

Thor certainly knows his way in the new-venture support system. He has exploited the services of both Innovation Norway and NAV, yet he's not successful in the marketplace.

"So that's how you make ends meet. How long do you think you can continue like this, Thor?"

"We can't at all. And the focus on public money and innovation funds has in a way led us astray. Sure, innovation funds can give us time to carve out a market niche, but honestly, the drawback when working with these public sources of funding is that it takes a lot of time and effort, and I'm not the kind of guy who can easily fill in the blanks in lengthy application forms. I've spent hour after hour and usually it comes to naught. Recently I tried to secure funds from North Innovation. Worked day and night for a week only to discover that the deadline was extended and a lot of new applicants had arrived at the scene."

Applying for support is time-consuming, and the thirst for support may move one's focus away from developing the business. This, it seems, is exactly what Thor has experienced. His thorough knowledge of public funds and public institutions supporting new ventures has had a profound effect on the overall strategy of NorthWare. But, as he has realized, it didn't solve the problem. Throughout its first year in business, it appears as if NorthWare has spent far more time looking for public support than it has looking for customers. Viewed from the outside, NorthWare is a relatively large new venture, but its size is financed by funds and investors and unfortunately not substantiated by revenue.

"In a way," he confesses, "we've been out of focus, so we've decided to quit writing applications – you know, it isn't really easy money – and concentrate fully on generating sales and winning competitive bids. Our goal at the moment is to finally break even, and cut loose from new venture support."

Too much of a good thing, he's learned, can hold you back. The opportunistic bootstrapping that Thor utilized to finance NorthWare caused him to focus more on public new-venture support than on gaining a foothold in the marketplace.

Entering the market for software consultancy turned out to be very difficult for several reasons. One problem was that customers prefer to do business with larger companies. The strategy NorthWare employed was to grow its internal ranks (employees) first and then compete for market shares, so the company had to rely on governmental money to fund its growth. But that money came at a stiff price, for, as Thor discovered, it takes a lot of time and effort to secure such funds – time that could have been better spent on other important aspects of building the business. In the case of NorthWare, it took focus away from competing for customers and contracts.

Thor's opportunism involves adapting to a set of rules – what amounts to a fixed formula for creating a new business, namely, the business plan. The new-venture support bodies have simplified the complex process of new-venture creation down to a written document. This is, in part, from a desire to make their own institutional life easier. The problem, though, isn't so much with the simplification as with the implied strategic perspective. The business plan assumes an analytic perspective on strategy – that is, strategic processes based on a rational analysis of the market. Thus, the characteristic entrepreneurial perspective on strategy – strategic thinking that takes advantage of heuristics, intuition, and eventually guessing – is not welcomed by the new-venture support institutions. But entrepreneurs fail or thrive regardless of the mode of their strategic process. It really doesn't seem to matter if the process is analytic or heuristic. What matters is that there is a strategic process.

Furthermore, Thor was blinded by governmental money, and as he put his hand in the cookie jar, customers took their business elsewhere. The business plan he developed for NorthWare was never meant to be implemented. It was a pro forma adaptation done in the process of applying for new-venture support, or "easy money" as Thor described it. But would he, today, still describe it as "easy"?

Notes

1   All names (persons, companies, and cities) are fictitious here.
2   The terms "free software" and "open-source software" are nearly identical, as almost all free software is open-source, and almost all open-source software is free. The philosophical difference between the two movements is, however, appreciated.
3   Translation: A failure to understand the core benefits of products and the profile of customer needs.

12 The whistle-blower

*Joseph McGlynn III, Bodø Graduate School
of Business*

Svartisen Glacier
Photograph by Joseph McGlynn III

"And you knew that they were cooking the books?"

"Yes. At the time, I thought, 'This is strange.' But then it started to bother me, as I realized the company was stealing millions of dollars from their customers."

"What did you do then?"

"I asked my manager, carefully, 'What plans do you have with these millions in the reserve account?' 'None of your business,' he replied."

"It was then that you reported the wrongdoing to the directors of the company?"

"In December, I chose to report the wrongdoing anonymously through a report mailed in an unmarked envelope. Shortly thereafter, the directors of the company began to avoid me. They evaded all interaction with me. Fourteen days later, they summoned me for a meeting with the Board. The agenda for the meeting ... was not revealed." Pausing, the man reaches down with his left hand, grabs a nearby glass, and takes a sip of water.

"Upon entering the building, I was stopped by the division director. He told me I must wait to enter the meeting until he was ready. Minutes later, the two of us in the elevator, I asked him, 'Do you know what this meeting is about?' I felt anxious, and desperately wanted answers to reduce my uncertainty. But he told me nothing."

"At this point, how did you feel?"

"Queasy. I excused myself for a moment, saying I needed a cup of coffee. Really, I needed to work up courage for the meeting. A couple of minutes later, I opened the door to a large room filled with executives from the company. But not a single person was talking. Complete silence. Uncomfortable silence. Unnerving silence .... I was greeted by stares of disdain aimed in my direction. I reluctantly entered the soundless room, awaiting my execution."

"At this point, you knew what the meeting was about?"

His eyes widened as he nodded his head and continued: "I took a seat at the lone empty chair on the far side of the room. Immediately, the CEO threw the anonymous report I had mailed on the table. 'We have a mole in our company!' he screamed, uttering each new word with increased emphasis and volume. He then settled himself, and proceeded to look directly at me. In a narrow-eyed whisper, he declared ominously, 'We will find the man who sent this report. We will expose him. And we will throw him out.'"

"I knew that I was finished. I left the meeting, walked home, and threw up in the toilet."

"How did other people involved in the wrongdoing respond?"

"I received threats on my life. People said they wanted to shoot me. Others threatened to beat me up ... ."

"Because you were a whistle-blower?"

"Because of what I exposed."

The screen emitted a suctioned hiss as Trygve[1] clicked off the television. By now, he was well aware of how things turned out for most whistle-blowers, and, frankly, the stories wearied him. Earlier that day, he had read a newspaper feature on a whistle-blower who, despite uncovering corruption and misbehavior among upper management at his job, suffered a personal financial crisis after a forced resignation, lost contact with most of his friends, and now experiences depression from his sense of isolation and lost professional identity. "It feels like I'm being punished for my honesty," the man said.

Just the week before, he had read a feature on a woman who exposed her boss's embezzlement at a large technology firm. The boss had used company money to pay for private parties and to maintain a lavish personal garden. Despite ample evidence supporting her cause, and admissions from her boss of his unethical behavior, she felt coerced to leave the company, citing a hostile work environment created by what she perceived as distrustful coworkers. "They treated me like a pariah," she said. The woman was still searching for new employment.

And then there had been that television report from the previous month that had featured a man who'd paid a heavy price for exposing corruption in the financial statements of his employer at an oil company. He'd been fired from his job, lost his house, and seen his children suffer negative treatment from certain teachers at their school because of their association with him. Asked if he would blow the whistle again if faced with the same situation, he said, "When I think about what it cost me and my family, both financially and emotionally … it's not something I can recommend for people to do. It's just not worth it."

Trygve was well aware of these and many more reports, detailing the fate of those who exposed organizational wrongdoing. "Why do whistle-blowers suffer?" he wondered. "Why doesn't society *reward* people for exposing lies and corruption? For uncovering unethical behavior?" He didn't know the answers, but he did know the harsh consequences that whistle-blowers often face for exposing wrongdoing in their workplace. The reports were remarkably consistent when discussing the types of retaliation whistle-blowers experience: death threats, physical intimidation, isolation, character defamation, job loss, forced career change, financial difficulties …

Still, when faced with a similar decision about whether to report the unethical behavior of the director at the high school where he'd taught for the previous ten years, Trygve acceded to the demands of his conscience and spoke out. For several years running, the director had created a hostile work environment by playing favorites among the staff, assigning the best sections and benefits to a select inner circle, and by publicly insulting the teachers who chose not to laugh at his obscene jokes, or who whined about his unfair distribution of benefits. An anonymous poll taken by the school's owners found an 80 percent disapproval rate for the director's leadership, and a strong desire from the teachers for a new administration.

The director had received his directorship at the school solely because of his friendship with influential political leaders. He had no formal background as an educator, showed little regard for the aspirations of students, and exhibited even less appreciation for the teachers working diligently on shoestring budgets to promote student learning. There were also whispers of his drinking on the job, and of his "borrowing" tools from the school workshop for home use. "He returns the tools with the same consistency that he treats his employees fairly," Trygve thought.

Of all the director's administrative shortcomings and behavioral offenses, his proclivity to lift tools from the school workshop bothered Trygve the most. Trygve worked there as a shop teacher, and the man's petty thievery had a direct impact on the declining resources available to the students.

But one incident finally proved too much for Trygve. He had received a tip from a security guard that the director had borrowed some missing shop tools for a home project weeks earlier. Frustrated by the lack of tools available to his students, Trygve was determined to get them back.

"Excuse me, Director," Trygve inquired with as much politeness as he could muster, knocking on the man's office door.

"Yes?" the director replied, annoyed by the interruption.

"I am wondering if you know of the whereabouts regarding the shop tools designed to help with leveling furniture. They ... appear to have gone missing."

"Hmm," replied the director impassively. "No idea, sorry."

"But sir ..."

"I said I had no idea! Now if you please, I have important matters that require my attention, and no more of my time can be wasted with your silly quibbling."

"But sir, the students are unable to build a proper foundation for their models without the tools."

"Enough of this nonsense! I suggest you make it work with the tools you do have, and stop wasting my time with your whimpering over lost supplies."

Furious, Trygve stepped back out, slammed the door with every ounce of leverage he could rally, and resolved to prepare a report of the director's unethical behavior.

Once written, the report criticized the school's mismanaged work environment, and the director's apathy toward teachers and students alike. Specifically, it detailed the "lost" tools and noted the unsatisfactory working conditions, the preferential treatment given to the director's favorites, and the hostility felt by teachers not part of the man's inner circle. The report was detailed, but straightforward and concise.

"You must be careful, Trygve," a female friend warned him after reading an advance copy of the report that he had shared with her. "The director has powerful political connections. Don't underestimate the power of his network and the presumed credibility of his status as director."

Sensing his resistance, she then implored him to ignore the wrongdoing. "The costs are high," she said, "and it's not a fair fight. Lawyers and the media will be involved. Trygve, don't *do* this."

"I have to. I *have* to." Declaring that Trygve could be obstinate was like saying that mules had a tendency to be patient rather than stubborn.

"Trygve, please! Consider the consequences. Things do not turn out well for ... for ... for 'whistle-blowers.' They face consequences, Trygve. They receive threats, lose employment, face undue criticism, carry a stigma with them to their next job. Consequences, Trygve!"

"I am not afraid!" Trygve countered. "I am right, and I can prove it."

A week later, he distributed the report to every employee at the school.

Trygve was fired within a year.

Just as his friend had warned him, the response of the school proved less than sympathetic. They sent him a written warning for putting forward "unsubstantiated allegations, disloyalty, and a lack of cooperation." In their view, Trygve was a cause of the untenable work environment, not a victim of it. They demanded his silent compliance.

When he refused, they fired him. Lawyers became involved, and a settlement became a priority for the negotiators. The negative publicity from local media had ensured both parties would emerge the fight as losers.

With the settlement offer nearly in hand, Trygve reminisced about the energy he maintained at the beginning of the battle, nearly two years prior. He had friends then, a support network, but they drifted away over the past 18 months of litigation.

He could hardly blame them, though. They were protecting their jobs. Still, the pain of isolation stung. At the outset, people encouraged him wildly with chants of "We're here for you!" and "The truth will set you free!" He'd been strengthened by their resolve, and felt a responsibility to carry this torch, with visions of placing the union of teachers on his back, and of his heroic return to the school upon completion of the case. He remained motivated by fantasies of potential adulation from peers if he did return, and of the sense of victory he'd feel upon eliminating the director's poison from the school's learning environment. But mostly, Trygve cared about his students, and saw the deleterious effect that poor leadership and administrative greed had had on their fragile minds. With all else stripped away, the students fueled his desire to fight.

But could he return to his position at the school? The answer depended on the terms of the incoming settlement offer.

The morning he was to receive the offer, Trygve breathed deeply and re-knotted his tie. If he weren't so stubborn, he would have changed shirts as well. He understood his clothing wouldn't affect the settlement at this point, but he couldn't sleep anyway.

At 9:00 A.M., in a conference room with his lawyer, Trygve received the school's settlement offer: 500,000 NOK, but with three provisions: (1) he would be barred from returning to his position at the school, (2) he would be barred from applying for alternate positions in the school district, and (3) the director would keep his position at the school.

Being now two years removed from a paycheck, Trygve needed the money desperately. And 500,000 NOK would grant him time to find a new profession without going bankrupt in the process. But the prospect of renouncing his teaching career deflated him like a balloon burst by the sudden pop of a needle. Being a teacher constituted his identity, his sense of self.

Trygve now had to choose between two unappealing options. He could either accept the settlement and begin brainstorming new careers, or he could reject the offer, forsake the money, incur more legal fees, and undergo the duress of a lawsuit, replete with still more of the uncertainty and isolation he had experienced in the previous two years of litigation.

Trygve's lawyer told him he had 48 hours to ponder the offer.

His head cluttered, he needed space to clear his mind. On a whim the following morning, he decided to drive to the Svartisen glacier, a landmark noted for its solitude and peaceful atmosphere, and the second largest in all of Norway. Years ago, a friend had raved about visiting that expansive glacier, and the idea had stuck. A quick search on the map revealed it was only a two-and-a-half-hour drive from Trygve's home in Bodø.

He gathered quickly the items he needed for the trip, packing worn black sunglasses, faded jeans, a loose-fitting navy sweatshirt from college, and a pair of hiking boots. He tossed them into a faded canvas bag that he'd had forever, but like most of his belongings, he'd kept it in good shape throughout the years. Taking a deep breath, he settled in behind the wheel of his eight-year-old Subaru and buckled his seat belt. He smiled as he turned the key.

In the quiet of his car, his thoughts roamed like the curved roads he drove on. "Organizing my thoughts," one of his teachers used to say, though he smirked slightly at the disarray of the "organization." "More like the rush-hour traffic in downtown Oslo," he said to no one. But it felt good to hear a voice, even if it was only his.

Ninety minutes passed, and snow-capped mountains with gusts of fog and clouds dominated his peripheral vision. The heaviness of his thoughts began to lighten as he sorted through the labyrinth of his emotions and focused on the excitement of taking the ferry to the glacier's trail. "This is going to be good," he convinced himself.

As he drove through the final mountain tunnel before arriving at the ferry's point of departure, darkness encapsulated the sedan for nearly 8 kilometers. Despite its inherent uncertainty, the darkness relaxed him in a way, increasing his desire to push forward to the glacier. He certainly could not stop halfway.

Arriving at the Glacier Gift Shop, he parked his car and strolled inside, canvas backpack slung across his right shoulder. He opened the door and stepped into a world of glacier collectibles: picture books, snow globes, even a book offering tips on effective fishing. He nudged through the rectangular display tables and sparse crowd to the service counter, and asked what time the next ferry to the glacier trail departed.

"Hmmm, let me check," replied the middle-aged woman behind the counter.

As he waited, he eyed a rotating postcard display. He spun the display casually, and picked a card at random. Featuring a glorious scene of rolling mountains on top of electric blue water, it read, "Norway: Where Time Stands Still." "A lot like my life the past two years," he thought, placing the card back in the holder.

"Sir?" The clerk had returned to the desk counter.

"Yes."

"You have good timing. The next ferry departs in 12 minutes. It picks up down the trail to the right."

Leaving the shop, he sauntered down a slight hill comprised of more than a few hidden ditches. He stumbled once, but otherwise remained unscathed. He turned his body to the right, and kept close to the side of the road as he approached the dock. Once there, he found a bevy of 8–10 people waiting, all, he imagined, searching for something, be it relaxation, excitement, or clarity. A few minutes passed before they hopped onto a medium-sized passenger boat that rocked lazily with the addition of each new adventurer.

During the 15-minute excursion, Trygve focused his gaze on the boat driver, a bearded man in his mid-40s with a slight build but a full head of hair. He wore charcoal jeans, a blue-striped white knit shirt, and a light red jacket with a grey hood. Trygve appreciated the seeming simplicity of the driver's work, the comforting repetition in bringing adventurers to and from the glacier trail, and the man's carefree attitude. From Trygve's view, the driver had not a single worry at the moment.

Such a possibility warmed Trygve, who was beginning to feel the chill of the wind careering off the sea and into the hair of the passengers, and the thought of working in boat transport brought an agreeable smile to his face. For the life of him, he could not remember how it felt to work without worry, to speak on the phone without hesitation because your words may be collected and used against you, to embrace your daily responsibilities with the fervor of a first-year teacher. He considered the possibilities. Acceptance of the settlement, coupled with a new career as a ferry driver, grew more enticing with the crest of each new wave.

Upon arriving at the glacier trail, Trygve grabbed his bag and began walking. The other adventurers grabbed nearby bicycles to assist their trek, as the sign indicated a three-kilometer path. But he had time and needed to think. The driver yelled out calmly as he drove away, "Last ferry returns at 5!" Trygve looked down at his watch and noted he had six hours to climb.

Even from a distance, the glacier maintained an impressive stature. It featured bold waves of frosted blue water, emerging as though a rush of water cascaded down the mountain as part of an aqueous attack strategy, only to be frozen in place by the single command of a Greek god. As such, it appeared like a moment frozen in time, and reminded Trygve of the postcard he had identified with just minutes before.

The path quivered with gravel divots and uneven rocks. Not enough to make a person lose their footing, but enough to require attention to the paths of your feet. Trygve walked the trail with both anticipation and trepidation. In the past few weeks, he harbored an abundance of pent-up energy bursting for release in anticipation of the settlement offer. Desperate for catharsis, he found the brisk pace a refreshing change from the lethargic tempo of his case against the director. In fact, he almost always yearned to move quickly, preferring swift action to unwarranted hesitation. Still, he made sure to avoid haste through careful deliberation, ensuring a sound foundation for each decision.

As he walked, Trygve pondered the settlement offer but did not feel any resolution. In previous weeks, he had envisioned losing the case, and the crushing blow that would take on his resolve to attack the director's corruption. Of course, he'd also envisioned winning the case, and his glorious return as the man who exposed the director for unethical conduct. But a settlement? He had not considered fully the thought of a settlement, and the unsatisfactory nature of both accepting and rejecting terms of the offer.

"Accepting the settlement would be a victory," he tried to convince himself. "A win. It would be a win. I would get the money. It would be a tacit admission of wrongdoing on their part. I would be exonerated, at least to an extent. It's a no-risk option."

But it was an option that failed to bring the satisfying return of his job. Like many workers, Trygve's employment permeated his identity. Teaching youth about the fundamentals of shop work was his passion, his life's purpose. He emphasized the importance of strong foundations to his students, focusing much of their class projects on the development of sturdy bases. It's what bothered him the most about the underserved placement of the director in his position – unqualified people in leadership positions compromise the capabilities of the entire staff. With the director in charge, the foundation of the school remained inadequate for the promotion of student growth. Accepting the settlement included an acceptance of the director's sustained presence at the school, a thought that screamed injustice.

But when he considered rejection of the settlement, fear shook his bones like an angry landlord asking a tenant for last month's rent. He'd been tortured by this process for nearly two years, and he longed for closure. But renouncing his profession as teacher? "Who am I if I no longer teach? I'll be seen as a whistle-blowing snitch that *used* to teach before he badmouthed his boss and got paid in court to keep quiet. Why did I get myself into this mess in the first place??" When he finished asking the question he realized he was talking aloud, quite demonstrably, and darted his eyes in all directions to see if anyone was listening. As usual, no one was.

Turning his head, he noticed a fork in the trail. To the left required the adventurer to scale a series of jagged rocks set uphill against the mountain. To the right, inclined steps and a semblance of a clear path that promised a smoother trek to the glacier, albeit a mundane smoothness when compared with the compelling uncertainty of a loosely prescribed path on jagged rocks. He feigned consideration of the contrasting options for a brief moment before tightening the laces on his shoes, exhaling deeply, and pulling himself up the first rock on the left.

It was not a decision without consequence. Forty-five minutes into the climb, he began to question his selection. For one thing, the adventurers on the other side looked quite comfortable as they leisurely hopped up each portioned step of the trail. Furthermore, Trygve appeared to be the only person who had chosen the trail to the left. He smiled at the thought of his singularity, but only after allowing himself a hearty sigh and a slight shake of the head. Just as he began to accept his increasing habit for isolation, a small, seemingly nondescript bird with a white body and steel grey wing feathers caught his attention.

The single bird fluttered its wings as it approached, and then perched on, a nearby rock. "How unexpected," Trygve said aloud, savoring the visit. The bird, to its credit, remained perfectly calm despite the strangeness of the situation. Trygve wondered if the bird might listen to his story, something he yearned for desperately. "Why not?" he mused, and so he let it all out: the discrimination faced by teachers at his school, the reckless behavior of the director, his lifelong desire to educate the youth, his obsession with building strong foundations in his shop class, the weight he felt from his responsibility to the other teachers, the forced isolation, the enduring confusion, and his uncertainty following the settlement offer. The full disclosure felt cathartic, and at one point he even forgot he was unloading to a bird. When it appeared that Trygve had vented completely, the bird hopped into the air and resumed its flight to wherever. Trygve grinned as he watched the bird fly off, and considered the folly of his disclosure to a mere bird. But sometimes you just need a friend, no matter how bizarre.

Returning focus to the path, he quickened his pace in anticipation of his goal. At last, the edge of the glacier appeared before him, almost out of nowhere. "Ah! The beauty! The natural beauty!" he exclaimed as he jumped the final hurdles between himself and the massive body of ice. He marveled at the glacier's elegance, and at its persistence in surviving years of brutal conditions, none of which was as detrimental as the previous ten. Signs of wear remained visible, as the melting exterior dripped at an all too steady pace. Trygve's emotions shifted vigorously, from elation at reaching the glacier, to despair upon seeing its shrinking edge, to hope that he could raise awareness of its deterioration, to discouragement upon assessing the likely apathy of others.

"But still," he considered, "the foundation is strong."

Buoyed by the optimism of his thoughts, he marched along the outside of the glacier until he found a crevice, just large enough for him to creep in. Creep in he did, and he immediately found himself in a sort of ice cave, with lucid halls of frozen sky-blue water surrounding him on each side. Underneath his feet, a pattern of rocks gripped his boots, allowing him to mosey between the halls of ice that engulfed him. He ambled forward fifteen steps until he arrived at a patch of ice crystallized to the point of transparency. He paused, tilted his head to the right, and examined the space in detail, whereupon he saw his reflection in the ice. Frightened at first, the moment of startlement turned quickly into a broad smile and a knowing wink of his left eye. Irrational as it sounded, he no longer felt alone.

Strengthened by the resolve of the frozen fortress, Trygve adjusted his knit cap, zipped his jacket to the brim, and began the journey home.

Upon his return, he informed his lawyer he would not accept the settlement offer.

"Trygve, you are against tremendous power. If you allow the case to proceed, there is a chance you receive nothing," his lawyer advised. "There is an imbalance of power here, you've already lost so much, and the settlement offer is generous financially."

"I have the ethical power," Trygve replied. "And my ethics will not fade because of corruption in the system. I am a teacher. And I will not willingly sign that away."

"Okay," said his lawyer. "I admire your courage."

Trygve hung up the phone, and vomited profusely.

Three weeks later, the court restored order into Trygve's world. The judge ruled in Trygve's favor, awarding monetary compensation of 500,000 NOK, and full restoration of his position at the school. In addition, the judge ordered the removal of the director from the school administration, effective immediately.

Trygve nearly fainted, but gathered himself quickly and managed to stand up in a jolt of excitement, forgetting the nausea that dominated his stomach mere minutes before the judge's announcement. Surrounded by friends willing to associate with him for the first time in months, Trygve celebrated the court's ruling with a long series of hugs, handshakes, and eye-to-eye contact. His friends Kirsten and Edvard insisted on scheduling lunch to make up for lost time, and Marta insisted on Trygve's attendance at a victory supper at her house, to be held in his honor. Trygve had ascended from leper to king with a single thump from the judge's gavel.

"Trygve, tell us. How would you describe your emotions when the court ruled in your favor?"

"Of course, I am happy to win the case. Ecstatic. But it wasn't easy. The journey was fraught with difficulty. I lost friends over this. Emotionally, it strained me every day. The costs were many. More than joy, I felt relief."

"What effects has the process had on you?"

"It's made me a stronger person. I am more in-tune with the values I want to stand for, the job I want to do as a teacher. The job I *need* to do."

"Do you have any regrets?"

"Regrets? No. But … if I did it again, I might do things differently."

"What might you do differently?"

"To be honest, I don't know. I'm not sure what I would change. I do know that blowing the whistle is an emotionally harrowing process I would not wish on anyone."

"Knowing what you know now, *would* you blow the whistle again?"

With a private smile, Trygve leaned back in his recliner and clicked off the TV. He already knew how this story ended.

Note

1. Trygve is a pseudonym.

13 Lo–Ve is complicated

Steinar's uneasy co-existence of tourism and petroleum in the Lofoten–Vesterålen archipelago

Ashley Barrett, Bodø Graduate School of Business and Hindertje Hoarau-Heemstra, University of Nordland

Steinar Jøraandstad
Photograph by Kristian Jøraandstad

On a frigid November afternoon in 2010 in the quaint Norwegian town of Kabelvåg, several dozen protestors – mostly locals – filled the ordinarily desolate marketplace, using each other's roars of anti-oil fervor to keep their bodies warm and their attention focused. After a long wait, a rugged man wearing a navy T-shirt emblazoned with the words "Mind-moving Concept" suddenly pushed through the crowd to the speaker's lectern, which he promptly grasped in both hands while sporting a bright toothy smile. The crowd, gathered there that day for a convention supporting an oil-free Lofoten–Vesterålen (Lo–Ve), fell silent.

Although he needed no introduction, the 49-year-old man with an athletic frame and youthful voice announced himself anyway. "Good afternoon, I am Steinar Jøraandstad," he said, grinning broadly. Looking like Indiana Jones sans the rakish fedora, he was tan and fit, no doubt from regular skiing, hiking, and other arduous expeditions on the outer fringes of civilization. His reason for being there? To finally announce his company's stand in the heated oil debate that had consumed Norway's government over the past decade and dominated many a dinner-table conversation as well.

Steinar, co-founder of a popular tourism organization in nearby Svolvær, the capital of the Lofoten archipelago, was somewhat of a local business hero. Admired for his innovative enterprises and his self-proclaimed "crazy guy" attitude, he always seemed to position himself in the front lines of professional success, even if it nudged his personal life to the cooler coals of the back burner. His brainchild, XXLofoten (the name hinting at extra-extra-large tourist experiences), had won several local awards for its customer service and wide-ranging, action-oriented activities, while also gaining momentum and notice in the Norwegian Tourist Board and Trade Council, among other governmental entities. Given the organization's limited number of employees (just six, actually) and growing popularity (or, as Steinar put it, the "dilemma" of being "small, but big locally"), XXLofoten's as yet unstated position on oil drilling in the High North, Norway's most pristine eco-paradise, would undoubtedly influence how other tourism-professionals in Lofoten and Vesterålen viewed their relationship with Nature and its potential contamination through oil drilling and exploration.

The crowd, sensing big news, eagerly awaited his verdict. He began with a long but vibrant portrayal of the vacillating path that he and XXLofoten had each traversed in recent months, and the challenges that had been hurled at them by both the press and public to take a stand on where their values lay. Then he paused, meanwhile slowly shifting his stance and surveying the crowd with the piercing gaze of a raptor. His attentive audience, almost beside itself with anticipation, jointly leaned forward. Seagulls squawked overhead, only adding to the drama.

Finally came his answer: "We have taken a stand. We say no."

Norway can attribute its skyrocketing gross domestic product and its robust economy to its abundant oil-and-gas reserves. In 2010, it ranked as the world's 5th largest oil exporter and 2nd largest gas exporter in Europe, and oil and gas accounted for 46 percent of the nation's total exports (http://www.eia.gov). But, for all that, the country is also environmentally ambitious, as seen in its plan to become the world's first "carbon-neutral" country by 2050. Thus environmental topics are often campaign focuses for candidates, and the dispute over jeopardizing local eco-systems abounding in nutrients, fish, and wildlife with crude-oil exploration and damaging seismic tests has preoccupied Norwegians for decades.

The peak of Norway's oil era actually came and went in the early 2000s, which has left governmental officials and the public with concerns as to where the country will turn when even the newest of extraction technologies cannot revive the exhausted oil fields. For now, however, petroleum feeds the mouths and bank accounts of the better part of the Norwegian population, and many left-wing politicians in the Labour party, with most of Norway's current oil resources nearing depletion, are looking for fresh drilling opportunities, especially in the Norwegian continental shelf. Hence the vulnerability of Lofoten–Vesterålen, a large, beautifully preserved archipelago off the northwest coast of Norway that is both a national treasure and a world fascination.

Because the rich waters surrounding Lo–Ve are home to the world's largest stocks of cod and herring, fishing has been an important part of local traditions for centuries. The characteristic aroma of dried fish can be smelled by anybody travelling along the coasts and into the harbors of each of these small, inviting islands. The unique cold-water habitat encircling the island chain contains one of the world's largest cold-water coral reefs. It's also home to several marine mammal species like the charismatic killer and sperm whales. And above ground it's home to one of the most diverse seabird colonies that ecosystems have to offer. Serving as a playground for Nature enthusiasts, Lo–Ve leaves both its visitors and inhabitants a little different with each passing day. Whether you're just sitting in silence and marveling at the brilliant, incandescent lights shooting from the Midnight Sun and Northern Lights, or scaling a mountain that shoots almost straight up from the very banks of the coast into the bluest of skies, Lo–Ve is "doing something with you," as Steinar puts it. Upon their leaving this paradise, visitors of all ages find their close interaction with Nature leaves them forever changed.

Steinar claims that Lo–Ve's rich national heritage and pulsating fishing and wildlife sanctuaries make it the "world's best classroom" for challenging adventures of both the physical and mental variety. That being almost universally acknowledged, though, does Norway really want to endanger this treasure with the invasive measures of oil exploration, however lucrative?

Anti-oil crusaders see this issue as one that also expands well beyond Norway's borders. Gaute Wahl, founder of "Folkeaksjonen," which he describes as the people's movement for an oil-free Lo–Ve, claimed:

> Seldom has an environmental issue got so much focus. This issue, in itself, is very powerful. It raises some other issues about what is the way forward for this local community, but also Northern Norway, Norway, and perhaps internationally. What is our future? What should every rich country

like Norway do with their resources? And how do we value our renewable resources, which are possible to harvest for hundreds of years?

Also, many protestors speak of marketing Lo–Ve as the area in which the people have finally stood up and said no to oil. They believe that taking such an unbudging stance will bring world-wide publicity to the archipelago's front door and shower it with more tourists than the 300,000 who already visit the area each year.

Unlike the fishing industry, it seems that finding a unified voice proves next to impossible for those who compose the Northern Norway tourism sector. Even an outsider can easily understand the opposing arguments made by the fishing industry. Since the medieval ages, the Lofoten–Vesterålen area has served as a virtual smorgasbord for all manner of fish. Cod, herring, halibut, and pollock are among the forty-plus species of fish that migrate to this area each Spring to feast on the plankton and other nutrients stirred up by the Gulf Stream's collision with local coastal streams. A large slice of Lo–Ve's economy relies on fishing for its livelihood, and drilling for oil in this area would disrupt this major fish-spawning area, if not destroy it with, heaven forbid, an unforeseen spill like the recent one in the Gulf of Mexico. But officials from the Norwegian Oil Industry Association – or, as Steinar likes to call them, "the guys in the pinstriped suits" – argue that drilling for oil will enhance the economy by bringing more jobs and hotel revenue into the area. Yes, they acknowledge, oil carries with it a formidable shadow, but they will protect this sensitive marine environment by operating with stricter environmental requirements and special protection laws.

Yet the tourism industry acts like the quiet kid in the corner who attentively observes the action in the room, but can't find his voice to speak up, and much less, interrupt. Why? Because drilling for oil, like tourism itself, can take several forms, each of which could have a different impact.

For example, if the drilling is subsea, visual pollution is minimized, but you still get urbanization of the nearby coast. "For me, that would be a catastrophe – to have this construction of roads and everything like this in Lofoten," Steinar has said. He also worries about the increased shipping traffic. Then, too, he says, there's the "not-in-my-backyard syndrome." Tourist organizations are often optimistic about the economic benefits of oil until it affects their area and careers personally. "Suddenly I have an oil tanker in my garden," he explains, speaking of his summer house in southeast Norway. "It was just laying there – and this is my place. I have been here for forty-five years fishing and swimming. That's where I grew up." Many don't want this scenario for Lo–Ve.

On the other hand, hospitality (hotel) tourist organizations, as opposed to Nature-based tourism operations, often are pro-oil because they believe it will bring in workers needing a warm bed to sleep in and a place to call home when they aren't slaving away on the rigs. Of course, many compare adopting this outlook with "selling your soul to the devil," as it spells only a short-lived profit; eventually the oil will be drained and the workers will leave. Still, this short-term orientation seems to be a staple in the field. Everyone is living in the here and now, wondering what's next, what's around the corner, but who cares about further down the road?

Steinar's gallant leap off of the fence, where he and XXLofoten had been perched, was unquestionably a momentous occasion at the anti-oil rally in Kabelvåg. And it may well have played a role in the government's later ruling to postpone its decision on the drill-for-oil issue until 2013. (The word "postpone" was, of course, a neat rhetorical ploy, allowing the anti-oil side to read it as a victory, and the pro-oil side to accept it as simply a delay of the inevitable.) In the fall of 2013 a new government was elected, and it too, has postponed drilling. Yet when we talked to Steinar six months later, it was as if the rally was a figment of the oil-protestors' imagination. Steinar had hopped right back up on that fence and taken XXLofoten with him. The organization now had no public stance on the issue. Had he contracted amnesia?

It may have appeared that way to the casual bystander, but the better we came to know Steinar, the more we realized the complexity of his character.

Our second long interview with him commenced on a bench outside of XXLofoten's office in Svolvær. Grabbing a ripe peach out of a basket and tossing it up, Steinar then nonchalantly, and without looking, caught it on its way down and took a large juicy bite. It was a typically Steinaresque piece of showmanship, effortlessly demonstrating the hand–eye coordination of a natural athlete. The beautiful, curving Lofoten landscape lay behind us. We were admiring it when we heard an old man behind us cheerfully mumbling the words and melody to the Elvis song "Are You Lonesome Tonight?" "No, I'm not," Steinar laughingly replied out of the blue. "We'll have to go inside. We're going to attract much more of those."

We continued our interview by asking Steinar about his background and history. He told us that he was born and raised in Oslo. He came from a broken home; his mother was just nineteen at his birth, and it took her only one more year to decide to kick his father to the curb. Because she worked long hours to provide for her family, Steinar was left to raise his younger brother. It was "too much responsibility on my shoulders too early," he admits. "I knew how to make several meals by the time I was six, six and a half."

Though his mother was struggling to put food on the table, Steinar's early education didn't suffer as a result. As a youngster he attended the Rudolf Steiner School, which specialized in something it called "anthroposophic teaching." Steinar made his earliest friends there while learning how to sew and exploring his primal cognitive experiences in an attempt to discover and express his spiritual side. "It's a huge contrast," he acknowledges, from where he wound up years down the road – in the Norwegian Special Forces SEALs, where he was educated in how to "kill in many different ways."

Yet Steinar did not always plan on being a SEAL. His earliest passion was marine biology, and he intended to find a career in it. But one day a friend informed him that it would take eight years to master that field, after which he'd face an ordeal finding a job. Always sensitive to logistics, Steinar dropped the idea and soon redirected his attention to becoming a professional diver like Jacques Cousteau, whose poster decorated his wall about the same time his more "normal" friends had all turned into football fanatics. "OK," he said to himself, "the Navy. That's my new family." Simple as that.

Steinar worked hard, earned his diving-instructor certificate in less than two years, and afterwards dedicated even more blood, sweat, and tears to becoming a member of the legendary Navy SEALs. Thriving in this dangerous environment, he then traveled north to join the Marine Air Commandos. There, he learned how to survive in extreme conditions, developed the mental and physical willpower needed to jump into a hazardous situation where others would instinctively run for their lives, and acquired technical skills in engineering. Welcoming the risks and the idea of living on borrowed time, Steinar shined in, and even flaunted, the eminence that came with the caliber of the men that stood and swam beside him. He bonded with these men and respected them just as he respected himself. "The level of people that I work with today is still high," he assures us, and we get the feeling he wouldn't accept anything less.

After his five years in the Navy expired, Steiner sought to capitalize on his experience as an underwater engineer by working as a North Sea diver. His background afforded him all the credentials he needed for the job, and although the life it promised – spending days and nights in a small pressurized chamber to work in the darkness of the seabed – might strike most people as unthinkable, Steinar saw it as a pioneering position, not to mention a lucrative one. "You made a *lot* of money," he said, "and that was the big goal." He and one of his Navy diving buddies decided to sign on with an oil company, knowing that deep-sea divers are vital for maintaining offshore oil-and-gas platforms, hence are well paid.

But before departing on their life journey, the two men, together with the rest of Steinar's Navy SEAL friends, went to Tromsø to attend a beer-drinking festival put on by the world's northernmost brewery. Steinar merrily admits: "We were invited because we were probably the biggest guests there in recent years. We were drinking way too much. Too many parties." In between those parties, though, Steinar decided to check out a couple of guided tours of the historic city, so he dropped in on a local tourism office. Little did he know that his life was about to take another major turn.

While waiting for a clerk to gather the information he desired, Steinar had plunked himself down in a chair and snatched a magazine from a nearby table, thinking that he might be there a while. The magazine, he recalls, "was called *Campaign*, and I was sitting there just like I do at the dentist, you know? When you are reading something to pass time. And this magazine was about the film industry – the commercial film industry – and advertising marketing. And I looked at it and said, 'This is my new life.' That easy! I was on my way to the North Sea and suddenly, I changed all my plans right there and then ... I figured that if I know how to blow up buildings, and how to parachute with a camera on my helmet to dive, you know ... I had all of these kinds of licenses to do crazy things. Somebody in the civilian world would need me." That and his background in aesthetics from the Rudolph Steiner School gave him the assurance that this time, he had truly found his life's calling. He promptly quit his plans for diving in the North Sea, booked a ticket back to Oslo, and started making phone calls, reinvesting his willpower into pushing his foot in the door of a very exclusive and pragmatic film industry.

It paid off. He soon found a couple of producers who had just come from the U.S. and who, miracle of miracles, were looking for someone with his raw, unique talents. He spent the next couple of years learning the intricacies of the industry from these two tough men, whom he referred to as "sergeants." And before you could say "Lights! Camera! Action!" the three of them had created the biggest commercial film business in Norway. Steinar, a natural in this world, clicked into gear, striking up deals with TV stations and other production companies. When one of these deals fell through, the three owners moved the company to Denmark and sold it there. Steinar was already overflowing with new convictions for the future, and when he returned to his home base, Oslo, he started his own film-business from scratch. Once more, Steinar, a born entrepreneur, had quickly hatched a fresh idea, dedicated his life to it, rearranged his priorities, and settled into a brand new living space – oh, and also had time left over to chug some beer with friends. His new company, REEL Image, soon skyrocketed to success. "And now I'm just trying to tell you how big everything is," he laughed with a wink. And he claims that the next 10 years, spent as managing director, were the best of his life up to this point, as he was always off to shoot on some exotic, challenging location, be it the Sahara or a peak in the Swiss Alps.

Meanwhile, however, Steinar's twelve-year marriage, by which he had had two children, had crumbled under the pressure of his professional success and constant travel. "Being married and working the film industry," he explains, "is like dogs and cats. It's not very easy." It had become apparent that Steinar often found a more immediate, sympathetic "family" in the relationships he carefully constructed in the office.

In fact, after Steinar remarried a few years later, and when his second wife, Benedicte, became pregnant, he left it to his colleagues at REEL to make what many would consider a most private family decision: "I told my board that Benedicte is pregnant at one of our board dinner meetings. And I said, 'I wonder what the name should be?' And this guy said, 'There's only one name. His name is going to be Oscar.' Everyone agreed, 'OK, OK, his name should be Oscar.' So I went to the hospital where Benedicte was lying and I said, 'The name, if it is going to be a boy, is Oscar. Sorry, the decision has been made.'" Luckily, Benedicte agreed with no reservations. Life-long family decisions were being made in the office. One can't help but view this as contradicting his driving desire to create a family atmosphere, but Steinar was simply peeling back another layer of his complexity, and the outsider could soon equate this troubled family situation with Steinar's desire to appease his constant need for exploration. He lived for spontaneity.

With his self-made company now flourishing and his personal life back on track, one might assume that Steinar would start to curtail the frenetic pace of his life. But no. "I cannot work for years with the same thing," he said. "I'm searching for other adventures. So I sold the company, and I felt like now I'm free." Free, it turned out, to start up a new company – an advertising agency in Oslo he named Munter Marketing (English translation: "Happy") in direct response to the impact that the 9/11 attacks had on the advertising industry. "Life isn't that bad," Steinar claimed in his typical buoyant fashion, flashing a smile and shrugging one shoulder toward his ear.

But his involvement with this business was, again, in true Steinar fashion, short-lived. A couple of his Navy buddies, Frank and Geir, then living in northern Norway, were in the midst of creating a tourism organization, using their expertise in climbing, survival, and shooting to give its products a unique twist. Every chance Steinar had, he'd jump on a plane and fly north to help them in marketing and developing their new company. "And every time I put myself back on a plane to Oslo, I felt, 'This is wrong. I belong here,'" referring to the High North.

It all came to a head on Benedicte's birthday that year, when he decided he could no longer ignore that his life was primed for another change. "My focus in Oslo wasn't good enough," he recalled. "My focus was more outdoors – working closely with people, the caring role, you know, instead of running after big clients. I did that for years, and it's nothing to do with values, it's only things." He asked Benedicte, "Shall we move up North?" and Benedicte, seemingly an extraordinarily flexible wife, agreed.

Within a week Steinar had moved, ahead of his family, to Lofoten, although with no warning to his soon-to-be business partners. He simply showed up on their doorstep late one night, set down his two bags, and gave the doorbell a couple of long pokes. Frank groggily opened the door just enough to peer out when Steinar blurted, "Hey, guys, I've just moved up!" Puzzled, Frank, who had yet to even offer Steinar a permanent job, cocked his head and eyebrows simultaneously, and said. "Yea, I think your staying here can be possible."

"I had just arrived in Svolvær and had no place to stay," Steinar explained. "I had nothing in place yet." So his home for the next week would be the cramped basement of Frank's home. And his bed? At least for that night, it was the concrete floor and a down jacket. Later on, he managed to find an apartment, and so began the escapades of his relationship with an innovative tourism industry that would later evolve into XXLofoten.

For the next sixteen years, Steinar merged his military training, love for coaching, and genius for bonding with strangers into his role as a "concept developer" and field operator at XXLofoten, which developed into a close, family-like business. Perhaps because of Steinar's responsibilities during his childhood, he now makes it a point, wherever he works, to take care of the people around him and to create "small groups of families" that he can trust.

This trust is also reflected in the experiences XXLofoten has to offer. The company has received rave reviews for how it manages to engage people into active experiences of Lo–Ve's natural treasures. It has, in fact, reconceptualized tourists from passive knowledge-seekers into interactive doers happy to get their hands dirty while also stimulating their intellects. Steinar designed XXLofoten

to revolve around the "mind-moving concept," which uses emotion, storytelling, physical exertion, and multi-sensory perception to create an experience for
each tourist that will cater to their own specific needs and desires, indefinitely
changing them, even if it is in a way that cannot easily be identified.

Take, for example, the "Seafood Amphitheater," an all-day expedition that
begins at daybreak with a group of tourists packing themselves into an old
wooden boat, much like the ones that fishermen used hundreds of years ago,
and heading out to the deep sea to learn what fishing there is really like.
Why an old wooden boat? May-Britt Paulsen, Sales and Marketing Manager at
XXLofoten, stresses that it's important to create the right historical, cultural,
and natural context for tourists to be fully immersed in the experience; in
fact, aesthetics play just as critical a role as passion and the dissemination of
knowledge. In the midst of the ocean, with no land in sight, the tourists, now
apprentice fishermen, learn how to cast the nets and lines, bait the hooks, and
identify the vast variety of fish swimming beneath them. After each tourist
single-handedly catches the type of fish he or she desires, the old boat heads for
an island where they're greeted with a crackling campfire adorned with a grill
for cooking and an outdoor dining room complete with table and chairs. There
everybody prepares and cooks their procured prey – first using tweezers to pry
the delicate bones from the slimy flesh, then cutting a fillet from its now life-
less body. "When you have blood all the way up your hands," Steinar says, "it
will definitely open up your mind." After choosing the vegetables, spices, and
herbs they want to infuse in their catch of the day, the guests become the chefs
and are instructed in how to cook everything just so. They then share the meal
together as the sun sets over the still waters and reflect on the invigorating day
that they collectively actualized, sharing and echoing each other's acutely acti-
vated senses and stories. This unique XXLofoten service grants the tourists the
opportunity to not only partake in the heritage of the islands, but also to create
a product that is theirs and that could only be achieved by personally interacting with Nature in a way that overcomes the dissociation you experience when
simply buying fish at some supermarket.

Another tourist activity created specifically by Steinar and XXLofoten involves
scaling a mountain with a backpack containing only the bare necessities, and
learning along the way how to survive in the wilderness for a week with only
the primitive tools that Nature provides. When asked about one of his favorite
moments in the field, Steinar reminisced about a time when a CEO of a renowned
oil company in Norway paid for a group of thirty of his employees to participate
in a teamwork navigation expedition created by XXLofoten. One activity that
day involved hiking up a steep mountain, so treacherous in parts it created the
feeling that if you leaned too far backward, you'd pay the ultimate price. With
each movement, bits of rock fell to the earth below, and your mind would start
racing, wondering what would happen if you were to misstep and follow the rocks
over the edge. But Steinar has crafted a method of coaxing tourists into trusting
him by looking them straight in the eyes and saying: "You'll be fine. I'm always
here. I know the way, and I know you can do this."

One of the men on this particular expedition was heavyset and brand new to mountain climbing. He doubted himself from his very first steps, sure that failure was just around the corner. Still, he yearned to succeed, and more than anything else, he didn't want to be seen as the "weak link" in the minds of his boss and coworkers. Steinar, adroit at smelling fear, instantly singled out this fellow and urged him on. "I just kept telling him, 'You can do this,'" Steinar recalled. "'I'm not leaving your side. We will reach the top of this mountain together, and when we do, you'll be a changed man. Don't be embarrassed.'" After some hours had passed, the two men found themselves alone. The rest of the group was now probably miles ahead of them. But Steinar never ceased to encourage the man, whose rosy shirt was now blood red from the sweat that drenched his aching body. Though they took several breaks, Steinar never let the man pause for more than a few minutes, knowing that anything longer could deplete his motivation. Finally, hours later, they reached the top. After a few well-earned minutes of admiring the view, the man turned to Steinar, tears trickling from his eyes, and said, "Every inch of the way I never thought this was possible. I can't believe I'm actually here." Steinar embraced him with a hearty slapping hug, and the man sobbed a few more times before he was able to loosen his grip and detach himself from his guide's shoulders. "Those are the moments I live for," Steinar confessed. "In our age, between 40 and 50, it's not a macho thing anymore. It's really the opposite. It's about giving trust and giving someone the best trip of their life – not because they pay you to do it, but because I choose this kind of work. That's what it's all about. Then you are creating mind-moving moments not only for the guests, but for you as well."

Along with this goal of elevating the contours of the mind through Nature and personal attention, XXLofoten and its employees, Steinar included, are renowned for emphasizing security and safety, creating back-up plans for unanticipated squalls, and even offering their customers a delivery guarantee. If the weather doesn't cooperate, they will relocate the equipment to another location (if possible), transport the clients, and carry out the service with no additional costs. "It's about selling expectations and being honest," May-Britt explains. They have elaborately studied how the land and water interact with the sea in those areas where their activities are offered. If they can circumvent the weather by moving to another location, they gladly will, but if they have so much as a premonition that the ocean isn't safe, they'll forgo the scheduled activity and keep their customers safely ashore.

Given all its emphasis on safety and expectations, though, one has to wonder why XXLofoten won't now take a position in the oil debate. The company pushes its customers to be active, to seek knowledge, to crystalize their values, yet it fails to do any of these things when it comes to forming an opinion on so critical an issue. Granted, doing so could jeopardize the company and its services indefinitely as compared to the brief interruption that a bit of bad weather might bring. Still, why does the careful risk perception and minute planning that the company employs to ensure its customers' safety and success not expand to a larger, more substantial level? Why does the company stand on the sidelines and allow such a monumental decision to be made when their entire organization is based on innovation and taking responsibility?

When asked about the issue months after the inspiring public stance he took at the Kabelvåg rally, Steinar declared, "I'm pretty clear that I'm not 100 percent yes or no .... There are good arguments on both sides." So what happens when the press comes knocking on his door at the XXLofoten headquarters? Steinar said, "In these days, I take the decision of, you know, 'Stand by.' ... If the Norwegian government wanted us to drill, it's going to happen .... For us middle-aged men, it's kind of like 'I don't give a shit.'" By then, he claims, "I'm out of business anyway." Later, he continued, fatalistically, "Fifteen years from now, they will probably take some oil from the ground in Lo–Ve. They will have to do the best of it. But you cannot start crying now and cry for fifteen years. We have to trust in the future, in the way they are going to bring the oil up, and how we are going to secure it." Gazing at the plain back wall of the office, he then suggested, "Maybe with all the things that concern us now, we will somehow make it more safe. All the things we are afraid of now, maybe they are based on what we don't know. At a certain point, you have to trust the next generation, and the equipment they develop. You have to. Otherwise, you start worrying if your life is going to be short."

While it seems Americans often experience spells of bleak skepticism when contemplating their government's next move, Norwegians like Steinar are generally more optimistic and trusting in their government, as can be seen in the aftermath of the terrorist attacks the nation suffered in July 2011. Hysteria did not break out. No war cries of revenge ensued. The nation amazingly trusted its government to take the proper corrective actions and faithfully steer it back onto the path of democracy and peaceful humanity.

At first it's startling to see a hands-on man like Steinar, who values trust and gambles his income on the aesthetics of Nature, figuratively step back from the table and leave to others the hashing out of this critical debate. Yet, his reflexive spontaneity, fascination with what's coming tomorrow, and craving for excitement contribute to his fatalistic, take-it-as-it-comes attitude, and most tourism operators share this quality. Moreover, his diverse background has fashioned him into a man who courts danger and is always on the verge of leaving, looking for his next move in all domains of his life. He is a walking paradox: child coach vs. military man; rugged outdoorsman vs. empathetic motivator; macho man vs. someone who prizes trust and work relationships. It turns out that his company is something of a paradox as well – virtuously high-minded, yes, but also, as Steinar concedes, a "prostitute," for some of XXLofoten's most profitable clients are Statoil and other national oil companies. In a sense, XXLofoten is selling Nature to the very people who are willing to risk putting it in harm's way.

But then again, who doesn't occasionally experience conflicted feelings? Underneath his confident façade, Steinar resembles all of us in that he admires certain qualities that he himself cannot model. On several occasions during our interviews, Steinar reflected on something that happened during a public meeting that, among others, XXLofoten and Statoil were attending. A young man in the public, maybe seventeen, suddenly interrupted the discussion of the men in the pinstriped suits, blurting out, "This matter really doesn't concern any of you anyways. My generation and me will be the ones to decide how Lofoten will be developed. Maybe today I don't have anything. Don't have any money. Don't have a girlfriend. But one day I might be a father, and I don't want my kids going to a school where they look out the window and see oil rigs." The oil execs in the room were speechless. In fact, the room fell so silent, you could hear the people breathing on either side of you, Steinar recalled. "What conviction in that kid! What fearlessness! I really loved that guy," he said. "I wanted to tell him that he could start working at XXLofoten on Monday." Perhaps this is just human nature. We all want what we can't have. The next generation always seems to supply those wants … and then invent fresh ones.

One of Steinar's favorite sayings sheds light on who he is at his core. He regularly mentioned his desire to surround himself with people he could "turn his back against." What he meant, it turned out, was that he wanted people around him who would support him through his rough patches and ensure that his back was never left unprotected. One is reminded of the 1994 film *Forrest Gump* and the enduring bond it portrayed between two men who used each other's backs so they wouldn't have to sleep with their "heads in the mud." When 2013 rolls around, maybe Steinar will have gained enough knowledge and a steward's concern for the future to permanently "turn his back against" the determined youth who personified the anti-oil camp. Is that a contradiction? Only time can tell.

14 The Progress Party in the summer of horror

Matthew B. Morris, Bodø Graduate School of Business

From the July 22nd Terror Attack rose parade
Photograph by Jon Callas

During summer in the High North the sun never sets. It just circles near the horizon, dipping behind the mountains to the west for a few hours every night but keeping the sky constantly bright. This is especially disorienting upon leaving a bar at night, as it makes even the most responsible evening feel like an all-night debauch.

One such evening during the summer of 2011, I sat at a bar in Bodø, a High North city located just above the Arctic Circle. I was there researching the political rhetoric of Norway's Progress Party, a populist party with a uniquely conservative ideology for this Socialist country, and Bodø was my home base. The Progress Party began as an anti-tax movement in 1973 and has since become one of the major parties in Norway. Politics controls the distribution of power and resources in all societies, and the discovery of oil in the North Sea in the late 1960s brought new levels of affluence to Norway. With unprecedented affluence came unprecedented waves of government taxes on private citizens over the next fifty years, and some Norwegians – especially members of the Progress Party – believe the tide has turned too far.

But politics was far from our minds that July night when a few of my American friends and I found ourselves chatting with some Russians over beers. With a lot of jobs in the oil industry here and Bodø's bustling University of Nordland, the High North has attracted people from all over the world, and I found this cosmopolitanism a pleasant surprise. These particular Russians were about our same age; most of them were in Norway studying business and economics. We chatted about fairly innocuous things like the natural beauty of Norway and my surprise at how fast the nearby glacier is melting. Yet I remember thinking how strange it was that as children, we each lived in countries convinced that the other wanted to kill us. Eventually the bar closed and we strolled down to a kebab stand owned by Pakistani immigrants, watching as a young drunk fisherman argued over whether he had already paid for his sandwich.

From my short time living in Bodø, I knew the city's population was changing as more and more people immigrated – mostly from Middle Eastern and African countries – to this cold but wealthy land. These changes were not just isolated to the High North; all over Norway, this historically homogenous culture was becoming more and more diverse. But what I didn't realize on that sunny, late-night walk home was only hours later, the unthinkable would happen.

The summer of horror

On July 22, 2011, Anders Behring Breivik parked a car filled with explosives outside the office of Prime Minister Jens Stoltenberg in downtown Oslo. Eight people died in the subsequent blast and many others were injured. Meanwhile, Breivik, disguised in a police uniform, rode the ferry to the island of Utøya, where the Labor Party was holding its annual youth summer camp. He reportedly told the campers that he was there to brief them on the tragic bombing back in Oslo. Once he had a crowd assembled, he pulled out weapons and began firing. During the chaos that followed, he killed sixty-nine people, mostly adolescents, including many hoping to swim to safety. Many people have called the event "Norway's 9/11."

In a manifesto Breivik reportedly emailed 90 minutes before the Oslo bombing, he called for a new Christian crusade against "cultural Marxists" and Muslims. His targeting of the Labor Party was apparently motivated by his belief that its immigration policies and liberal multiculturalism were deteriorating what he saw as the properly Christian identity of Europe.

It soon came to light that Breivik was a former member of the Progress Party but had left it several years earlier. Party leader Siv Jensen promptly posted this statement on their Website:

> The Progress Party is embarrassed, disgusted and truly sad that the accused terrorist was once a member of the party …. He left the party in 2006, and has probably undergone an extreme radicalization after that time. His actions and beliefs are totally contrary to our policies, beliefs and value-system … .
> We strongly oppose all messages and acts of hatred, violence, bigotry and close-mindedness.

With this message, Jensen attempted to dissociate her party from Breivik and his actions. But she was also reaffirming that despite the Progress Party's sometimes-controversial stance on immigration policy in Norway – some have even called their rhetoric racist – theirs is not a party full of religious extremists.

The party's official website describes the party as "classical liberals" who emphasize the rights of the individual to determine for themselves what to do with these newfound resources. "Centralisation must have its limits," it proclaims. And one of those limits should be on how much the Norwegian government taxes its people and controls public services. In pursuit of "a more free society," the Progress Party embraces policies that promote free market competition, infrastructure investment, and immigration controls.[1]

Leading up to that fateful day in July, I had learned much about how these ideals – their historical basis and changing meaning in a multicultural society – were gaining traction in the High North and beyond in Norway. Municipal elections (similar to congressional races in the United States) were only months away, and the Progress Party was poised to take a majority.

A cold war in the Arctic

Just a month before Breivik's fateful attack, I stood in the old tower of the Norwegian Aviation Museum, gazing out over a peaceful Bodø and thinking about how different life in this Arctic city must have been only decades ago. The Cold War, which Americans like my parents experienced primarily through the media, must have felt far more real so close to the Soviet border. The museum in Bodø no doubt ensures that such memories remain alive. It holds an impressive collection of artifacts from the Cold War era, including a U-2 spy plane similar to one I heard about from Petter Jensen,[2] a Bodø native and Progress Party politician

I interviewed earlier that week. Jensen – currently a Parliament member and second-in-command of the national party – recommended I visit the museum after telling me a fascinating story about an American spy in Norway.

On May 1, 1960, Gary Francis Powers, piloting a U-2 spy plane in the service of the United States Central Intelligence Agency, departed Peshawar, Pakistan, for a military base in Bodø, Norway. His mission? To covertly gather reconnaissance on intercontinental ballistic missile sites in the Soviet Union. Cold War tensions were then high, and the Soviets were leading in both the space and arms races, heightening American paranoia. Norway, as a founding member of the North Atlantic Treaty Organization, staunch ally of the U.S., and arch enemy of neighboring Soviet Russia, had a strong stake in the Cold War, which is why friendly Bodø was Powers' destination on that May Day.

About halfway there, Powers' plane was hit by a surface-to-air missile. Though he managed to safely eject, his plane, loaded with espionage paraphernalia, somehow remained mostly intact after crashing, so the Russians were able both to take him captive and to retrieve ample evidence of his mission. This event only added fresh tension to a previously scheduled summit between U.S. president Dwight Eisenhower and Soviet premier Nikita Khrushchev not long afterward. Eisenhower self-righteously denied that the U.S. was spying on the USSR; Khrushchev called his bluff, and relations between the two nations grew even colder.

Powers' story was heavy on my mind as I scanned the horizon outside of the aviation museum. Looking past the blocks of buildings toward the mountains that line the fjords of Nordland, I imagined the broken line that had connected Bodø and Peshawar, and thought about all those sorties of planes flying out to challenge the Russian MiGs.

Such a view would have been all-to-common for Jensen, a middle-aged man with a thick moustache and distinguished touches of grey on his temples. During our interview, I had asked what it was like as a boy in the Cold War-era High North.

"We were kind of used to airplanes scrambling all through the night just to cut off MiGs or fighters," he recalled with a darkened expression on his face. "They were not fighting, just testing each other's boundaries and stressing each other out. We had as much as 200 sorties – almost one every day – that met Russian fighters in the air. The threat was imminent." The Cold War has been over for about two decades now, but for members of the Progress Party like Jensen, it was formative.

"That's why I'm in the Progress Party," he explained. "When I grew up, the Americans were the good guys and the Russians were the bad guys," he explained. "It was the Cold War. In the northern part of Norway it was *very* cold because of the Soviet border. In the 1970s you were either with the Soviets or you were with the Americans. And I was with the Americans."

Perhaps that's why Jensen spoke proudly of his fondness for the United States, including his taste for American cars, and how the values he identifies with were exemplified by Ronald Reagan's and Margaret Thatcher's defiance of the Soviet threat in the last days of the Cold War. "We won that war. It was not the left that won it. It was *liberals*, liberals in the Norwegian context. It was the right side."

Despite Jensen's adoration of all-things-American, it seemed to me telling of the relationship between Norwegians and their government that I was able to talk to a member of Parliament without too much trouble, whereas in the U.S. you'd almost have to be a celebrity or CEO to meet with a member of Congress.

Waxing nostalgic, he continued, "Freedom was the big thing of the Eighties. When Reagan held his speech in Berlin and told Gorbachev to bring down this Wall, that set the standard for politics." Reagan's influence is one reason Jensen sees a litany of taxation abuses in present-day Norway: "You have tax on sugar. Tax on chocolate. Tax on nearly everything. And taxes are made to control the people." The Progress Party wants to take some of that control away from the government and give it back to Norwegian citizens.

What began humbly as a grassroots anti-tax protest has grown into a powerful voice in government, a situation similar to the Tea (Taxed Enough Already) Party's emergence in U.S. politics. At the time, the Progress Party was the second largest party in Norway's Parliament and was poised to help shape the country's future, especially in the High North.

Socialism isn't all bad, but a Nanny State can kill you

When I walked into the café for our interview, I recognized Jensen from a poster at the Progress Party's Bodø office. The nearly life-sized image depicted him standing with Siv Jensen, illustrating the High North's importance to the national party. Next to the poster and pictures of other candidates hung a rendering of the proposed Bodø *Kulturhus* with a snarky note attached proclaiming, in bright red capitals, "NO!" The *Kulturhus* was a major issue for Bodø's voters in their upcoming election. Progress Party supporters argued the city shouldn't spend money on a concert hall when there were serious infrastructure needs and public services deserving higher priority. When I learned about these debates, I realized even though the party was conservative by Norwegian standards, it still supported a national welfare state.

In a country historically at home with the word "socialist," even members of the Progress Party do not have the same animosity toward government-run services that conservatives express in the U.S. "People don't see freedom as a bad thing," Jensen told me, defending his abhorrence of the "Nanny State." But sometimes, Jensen explained, dealing with the government can interfere with his rights as an individual.

"I can give you a healthcare example," he said, lowering his voice. "My heart, my pulse went really slow. I felt dizzy and fainted, or almost fainted. I went to my doctor and they found some minor problems. And then they told me I could go to the hospital to have [the heart problems] checked out in *nine months*. When you have a heart problem, nine months, that's a long time."

"Oh wow," I replied. "I remember times when I was frustrated at having to wait a month to see a doctor in the United States."

He nodded in agreement and immediately launched into another story about his friend with cancer. "He got diagnosed two years ago and was sent to Tromsø. They operated and it looked very well [at first]. And then they found something bad and he was put on a treatment waiting list. He waited four months and when he went to Tromsø [the cancer] had gone everywhere. There was no way back."

"Those are the problems with government healthcare. If you have a small problem, if you break your hand, it's free and it goes fast. Government healthcare is great." But if you have a bigger problem, like cancer or heart trouble, where "time is of the essence, then government healthcare is a big problem. The government can actually kill you with its Big State socialism."

"Socialism in Norway," Jensen says, "because of the oil money, is a Nanny State, and that is why immigration is an important issue." I must have looked confused, because he leaned forward slightly, eager to clarify. "If you had less government intervention, you could have more immigration. *That's* not a problem. But if you have free immigration in a Nanny State, that's a way to get broke fast."

Immigration, argued Jensen, would not be a problem if the government adopted his party's policy platform. Despite what their opponents have said, the Progress Party is not anti-immigrant, according to Jensen. Instead, the party favors policy reform based on economics: Immigrants should be admitted based strictly upon their useful skills for the workforce, and should not be offered the same social-welfare cushion that tax-burdened Norwegian citizens enjoy (so they are forced to work instead of freeload). According to Jensen and his party, it simply isn't sustainable to keep giving benefits to just anyone who comes to their country.

From Communism to terrorism

The discussion of immigration led us to the topic of terrorism. Jensen emphasized again the Progress Party is not anti-immigrant, reiterating that generous governmental services – for example, education and healthcare – make the country vulnerable to those who would exploit the system.

Another concern is the threat of Islamic terrorism, which the Progress Party took very seriously. According to Jensen, terrorism succeeded Soviet Communism as the great threat of our time, and the problem lies in correctly identifying the enemy. During the Cold War, it was very easy to see the threat of Communism across the border with planes flying overhead almost daily, but today the very mobility that gives peaceful citizens their freedom also allows an enemy to infiltrate from anywhere.

Jensen also worried it was hard for Norwegians to see an ambiguous terrorist threat as real because they had not experienced the same violence as other Westernized countries. "Nothing has happened here, so Norwegians are not afraid of it," he explained. "I think the average Norwegian believes there is absolutely no danger from terrorism, but [we] in the last sixty years, [we] have been one of the most naïve people in the world. We don't believe that anything could happen here."

Just one week later, that ambiguous threat became part of Norwegian reality. Perhaps the biggest surprise? The terrorist was not an immigrant or a Muslim; he was one of their own.

Progress in the streets of Bodø

My last night in Norway was about a week after the Oslo terrorist attack. The city of Bodø announced it would hold a downtown memorial march that evening for the victims. My American colleagues decided to attend, not knowing the path we should take, only to end up in the center of town. As we started out that way from our dormitory, we soon saw masses of people walking toward us. We moved up a few blocks, trying to decide whether we should find a gap in the crowd to join in or just spectate from the curbside. We watched in utter amazement as thousands upon thousands of people streamed toward us, then past us, carrying flowers and torches. Looking back down the street, we saw no end to the procession. Standing there for maybe half an hour, I watched the people passing by – teenagers, small children, women in hijab, senior citizens, soldiers – and the lump in my throat grew as the tears welled up in my eyes.

Turning to my friends, I asked if they saw anyone they knew in the crowd. Just as I said that, Petter came into my view, walking tall alongside some people in military uniform and others in Islamic dress. Eventually we spotted another Norwegian friend, and she invited us to the town center, where everyone had stopped for speeches and songs. Looking around at the thousands of people around me, I saw a city coming together in remembrance and solidarity. The face of Norwegian culture may be changing, but this will always be a country of peace.

Notes

1 From the Progress Party's official website (English version): http://www.frp.no/nor/The-Progress-Party/Principles
2 Jensen's character in this story is a pseudonym and represents the composite reflections, experiences, and opinions of different party members I interviewed for this project.

Part V

The dark side of Norway

15 Norwegian vs. U.S. prisons
A sister's reflections

Brittany Peterson, Bodø Graduate School of Business

Brittany Peterson and her brother Ben
Photograph by Brittany Peterson

I remember looking at families when I was in elementary school, junior high, and high school and thinking how broken so many of them seemed. Family after family haunted by divorce, abuse, death, anger, violence, loss, and rage. How fortunate, I thought, that I had a "normal" family. Sure, my younger brother Ben and I often squabbled, as kids do, but we were the picturesque family of four.

Then things began to change.

Ben entered "the system" more than a decade ago. I was away at college when he started getting into trouble. First, he got caught for underage smoking. Then he got in trouble for swiping a teacher's wallet, which he promptly returned. In the beginning, he'd just spend a few nights in jail. But as his offenses increased in severity, his time behind bars increased exponentially. The petty crimes started to add up, and eventually he found himself sentenced to six years in prison.

As his sister, it was a sentence I symbolically shared with him. My life, too, felt shattered. I remember thinking, *What's going on? How did we get here? And, really, where is here?*

My quest for answers became a good deal more pointed in the spring of 2006, when my personal and professional lives collided. At the time, Ben had been in prison for nearly a year. That spring, as a PhD candidate in Organizational Communication, I was fortunate to attend a week-long qualitative research camp in Port Aransas, Texas. When one of the scholars there presented her fascinating research on victim–offender mediation in Texas prisons, I had an epiphany: I realized I no longer needed, or wanted, to keep my professional and personal lives separate. I wanted to start researching my life and living my research, letting it shape and mature me as both a scholar and a person.

Over the next months and years, then, I began to explore what it was *about prisons* that was interesting from an organizational communication perspective. I came to realize that in all of the extensive archived conversations about prisons among policy makers, protesters, prisoners, scholars, and the media, one thing was regularly overlooked: the importance of communication in the actual experience of incarceration. Moreover, no one had given attention or voice to the very idea of *being involuntary*; that is, having a compulsory membership in an organization against one's will or desire. Accordingly, I began focusing on the communicative experience of involuntary membership in prison. I wanted to explore, at minimum, two penal systems – those of the U.S. and Norway – to better understand the idea of imprisonment, both literal and figurative, in the two nations: the former, reputedly ineffective at best and abhorrent at worst, and the latter, hailed as one of the world's best.

I'll begin by detailing my experiences as a sister of an inmate and then share my thoughts as a scholar of the system.

The broken system

As a sister

In retrospect, I saw that when my brother first became incarcerated, my parents and I became, in a way, incarcerated as well. Though technically "on the outside" and "free," we were no longer able to call him whenever we desired, nor could we visit on a whim, nor could we include him in our family gatherings. In fact, in the years my brother has spent in prison he has missed many of our most joyous life events (graduations, weddings, births) and family tragedies (the deaths of three grandparents).

Our family journey began when Ben was in junior high. After he had repeatedly popped in and out of jail and exhausted the hospitality of several halfway houses, the exasperated Juvenile Court judge finally just threw up his hands and said, "Ben, I don't know what else to do with you." There were only so many programs in our city that helped troubled teens, and my brother had cycled through all of them. Essentially, Ben was sent to prison because the judge ran out of programs for reform. He was sentenced to six years. It devastated our family. I remember the emptiness in our home, the tears staining my mom's cheeks, the sadness in my dad's voice, the bitterness in my brother's heart, and the confusion in my own. And during Ben's time behind bars, I watched and personally encountered some of the frustrating things about the U.S. prison system. Many of them, perhaps even most of them, involve communication issues.

For example, it's really hard to mail items to an inmate. All personal articles like clothing, musical instruments, and electronics must be purchased through a prison catalogue. Books, however, can be sent directly to the prison from a bona fide company like Barnes and Noble. I once tried to send Ben the final volume in the Harry Potter series. I shipped it directly from Barnes and Noble to the prison, being sure to specify the necessity of an itemized receipt. If items did not arrive with the proper receipts, they were returned. For whatever reason the receipt never made it into the package, and *twice* the book was rejected by the prison. Each time some clerk deducted $7 from my brother's account to have it shipped back to the company. No one cared to listen to Ben's questions and concerns. I called the prison but couldn't get anyone to speak to me about the situation. I, too, felt disempowered.

Another communication issue arose shortly after Ben was transferred to a different prison. Unbeknownst to him, some of its Visitors' Room rules were different, too. The new prison had a training kitchen where visitors and inmates could place orders. It being lunchtime, Ben filled out the proper paperwork for himself and my parents and took a visual sweep of the room looking for the posting of any specific instructions about the proper ordering procedures. Neither he nor my parents saw any, so he proceeded to walk up to the correctional officer's desk to present the form. The officer took the form, summarily ripped it up, and coldly told Ben the kitchen wasn't open yet and wouldn't open for ... two more minutes.

Frustrated, Ben went back to my parents' table and filled out a duplicate form. Once the kitchen was officially open, he returned to the desk to present his form only to find a fellow inmate already ahead of him. Unfortunately, Ben was unaware that he wasn't supposed to form a line behind another inmate and was quickly whisked away to a holding room to be questioned about his violation. Ben had actively sought to follow the rules, but they weren't readily accessible, and he suffered the consequences of not having divined them.

Such incidents are hardly unusual. In fact, I heard many similar stories during my research visits to three prisons – Renton, Lawton, and Klayton (pseudonyms) – in the state of Texas. From these interviews, two poignant narratives emerged as characteristic of the communication failures in U.S. prisons.

George's story

When I met George, he had been in incarcerated for more than three years, serving time in Lawton Prison for purchasing goods with counterfeit money. A man with warm but sad eyes, George told me that until he went astray, no one in his family had ever been in trouble with the law. When I asked him how they were handling his incarceration, he volunteered some bitter news: he had actually lost his father a year earlier, almost to the day. His words stole my breath as related details poured out – details of heartache upon heartache. His father, I learned, had been killed by a drunk driver. His sisters called the prison to share the news and were initially met with a surprising accommodation: they were allowed to tell George themselves. Typically, when there's a death in the family, the prison chaplain sits down with an inmate and delivers the news. In this case, the prison actually facilitated direct communication between family members. The correctional officers called George down from his cell and handed him the phone. Such an accommodation is rare, indeed almost unheard of, in U.S. prisons.

Unfortunately, the thoughtfulness stopped there. My heart broke for George as he continued his story:

> So that same day I get told that they come in to say that they're gonna let me go to the funeral. We're gonna make arrangements. At the last minute they told me NO. So after that, I was really kind of mad, you know what I mean? They tell me one thing and then they tell me another … I was preparing that day, 'cause they were giving me phone calls every day and they'd say this is the time you're gonna go and this is the place where they're gonna do it. And I know the place. I could help the guards get there. So they're like, "That fine." And that morning I never got a call, and man, I'm like, I said to the guard, "I suppose to be leaving for my dad's funeral!" and the guard said, "9 o'clock in the morning." I said, "What? I need to talk to the warden." He wasn't here that day. It was the assistant warden, and she's like, oh, we're sorry. We're short on staff. And I'm like, how come they didn't tell me this from the get-go, you know what I mean? I said, "That's fine, that's fine." And then she said, "We can call your family and send a video tape of the funeral." I looked at her and I remember what I told her, the exact words. I said, "Miss, no disrespect to you," I said, "a *videotape*? A person is supposed to sit down here and watch on a video?" I was pretty upset, pretty upset.

The prison had told George he could attend his father's funeral and then had withdrawn the offer without notifying him of the change. What most upset him wasn't that he didn't get to attend the funeral, but that nobody bothered to notify him.

Cullen's story

Unlike George, Cullen's suspicious demeanor set me on edge from the beginning. We chatted at Klayton Prison about his ten years behind bars for possession with intent to deliver amphetamines and manufacturing of a controlled substance. Cullen's conversation with me focused on some of the dire communication situations he has witnessed while incarcerated. Several of them churned my stomach. It started when I asked him what kinds of things happened in a notoriously dangerous prison facility in Texas. Cullen answered emphatically, "What *didn't*? Rapes, killings, stabbings, beatings …" He went on to explain that the correctional officers either couldn't hear inmates' cries for help, or worse, just ignored them:

> And at night they are so short-handed you might have one guard that's in the pickets because you really don't need anybody on the wing, and he's going to be working all four wings. And if they do hear something like that [rape], half of them don't feel like they get paid enough to go down there and do anything about it. Or they might have been paid not to do anything about it. It's wild.

When the inmates' voices were ignored, they had to seek alternate, nonverbal means of communication. Some were unimaginable, like what they felt compelled to do. Here's Cullen conveying the torment of listening to someone getting raped:

> Makes you sick to your stomach. Just feel horrible for whoever it is. I mean, there is absolutely nothing you can do about it. It's just …. And then you hear that when they called "Breakfast," somebody jumped off the third row. And you know why they just jumped off the third row. Somebody just raped him … I guess he was trying to [kill himself], or at least hurt himself bad enough where they would have to take him to the infirmary.

Here, the victim had no way to communicate his terror other than by jumping off the third floor of the cellblock. In theory, there are appropriate ways that inmates can communicate their requests, complaints, and needs. But the system typically moves slowly, if at all, and, my interviewees affirmed, requests often go unanswered.

Ben's experiences, like those of George and Cullen, illustrate that poor communication is among the toughest issues facing both U.S. inmates in prison and their family members. But communication issues seemed rare indeed in Norway's alternative system.

The redemptive system

During the summer of 2009, I travelled to Norway on a fellowship to talk with inmates, correctional officers, prison teachers, and wardens about their experiences in the prison system. I was able to conduct interviews inside one prison, Bollvær Prison in northern Norway, as well as talk with prison teachers who worked for a prison facility in southern Norway, Kongshaugen Prison (pseudonyms).

Kongshaugen Prison looked, and felt, almost surreal. Although the prison had a tall fence with barbed wire that surrounded the building, it did not house any guard towers with guns as was common in the Texas prisons. Moreover, Kongshaugen was located in a residential neighborhood, and it even had a casual, "college dorm room" ambiance in the living quarters. Perhaps most notably, the communicative experience of the incarcerated individuals was markedly different from that of inmates in U.S. prisons. Two specific programs highlight the open flow of communication that occurred in the Norwegian prison.

First, the inmates got to have daily morning meetings with the warden and correctional officers where they could share their concerns, requests, and suggestions. Interestingly, the warden explained to me – and the inmates reaffirmed – that those comments were actively considered. For instance, the warden was attempting to renovate the visitors' area to make it more conducive to family and conjugal visits. At the inmates' request, he also let them prepare meals in a common area near their cells instead of always having to eat in the cafeteria. The inmates voiced appreciation for the warden's respect for their opinions and his efforts to make things as normal as possible under the circumstances.

Second, the prison also facilitated open communication through its rehabilitation and behavior-modification program, most of which centered on inmates' past drug addiction and abuse. Correctional Officer Sandra ran that program. The inmates told me they respected her for her ability to apply the rules uniformly while also giving consideration to any special circumstances at play. Each inmate got assigned a correctional officer mentor. The mentor's role was to talk with them weekly about their addiction and their struggles. This program in particular, and the prison in general, tried to establish constructive, caring relationships between the correctional officers and the inmates. Inmate Erik explained that he viewed the correctional officers' role as being both guards (70 percent) and friends (30 percent). He said that even though it was the correctional officers' job to watch them, they seemed to genuinely care about him and his personal growth.

Inmate Christian concurred. During our conversation, he said that the warden addressed the inmates by name and that the correctional officers took a personal interest in them. Christian struck me as a particularly credible source. He was then 39 years old and had spent most of his life behind bars, thanks to a career in drug trafficking. Being in the international end of that trade, he had managed to experience prison life in Norway, England, Holland, Sweden, Costa Rica, Gambia, and Spain. The Norwegian prisons, he assured me, were more humane and more focused on rehabilitation than their counterparts.

Both the morning meetings and the rehabilitation and behavior-modification program were initiated by Warden Grande. A man who exuded authority while still exhibiting a gentle spirit, Warden Grande talked with me at length about the importance of open communication between all members of his prison. Perhaps most notably, he didn't just talk about it, he practiced it – and got others to as well. Warden Grande took the time to talk with the inmates on a daily basis, listening to their concerns and trying, whenever possible, to resolve them. His aim, he told me, was to do everything in his power to make the experience as comfortable as possible for all parties involved in the incarceration experience, including the inmates' family members. He really wanted to improve, and ultimately transform, the lives of everyone coming through his doors. His model of open communication was distinctly different from the typical practices of U.S. prison organizations.

Let me now identify a core tension found in U.S. and Norwegian prisons and explain how its handling contributes to the very different communicative practices one finds in the two nations.

The inevitable tension

In my several years of researching prisons, I have witnessed one core tension manifest itself in prison organizations: I'll call it *participative decision-making (PDM) vs. authoritative control*. This tension, also found throughout society at large, is particularly problematic in prisons, where the goal is to confine law-breakers in order to protect society while still hoping to rehabilitate them enough to minimize recidivism, a task that involves according them as much respect and dignity as possible. But given some inmates' self-destructive pathology, prison administrators face a high challenge with respect to treating them "normally" and facilitating open communication. In general, the Norwegian prison I visited tended to allow far more PDM, perhaps because of its largely nonviolent, amenable clientele, whereas U.S. prison organizations typically leaned decisively toward authoritarian control. In my experience, two Norwegian prisons did a more effective job of managing this tension. But this no doubt partly reflects the kind of prisoners it incarcerates (largely nonviolent) and the relatively small size of its prison population, not to mention certain financial and cultural differences there.

In the Norwegian prison, both the staff and the inmates praised the warden's efforts to facilitate open discussion and encourage participation across all members of the prison. As explained earlier, Warden Grande not only listened to inmates' and correctional officers' qualms but also attempted to involve them in fixing the problems. He solicited suggestions from *all* individuals either in or immediately affected by the prison (e.g., suggestions about conjugal visits and the Visitors Room), and he worked tirelessly to see their ideas implemented. Moreover, incarcerated individuals and correctional officers alike discussed how they felt their voices were both noted and acted upon.

U.S. prisons, meanwhile, far from striving for PDM, prefer a military-type hierarchical command structure, with the wardens and assistant wardens almost exclusively making unilateral decisions. Staff input, I found, is minimal; inmate input is even less. In the cases of Ben, George, and Cullen, the three found themselves with virtually no communicative recourse to their respective situations. Their mouths were figuratively sealed. They could give no feedback on posting rules in visiting rooms, handling funeral transport, or dealing with prison rape. The "non-rank" prison staff also seemed to simply toe the company line as opposed to having a voice in the daily life of the prison. The wardens at the U.S. prisons expressed varying degrees of authority and control – everything from overtly stating "I'm a mayor of a small town" to discussing their rules for allowing or restricting the inmate's "freedoms" or "privileges" such as watching TV, getting out into the exercise yard, and purchasing items from the prison commissary.

All other things being equal, it seems clear that PDM is the optimal choice for effective prison management. Its practice seemed to elicit far more positive feedback from interviewees than the alternative. But of course all other things typically aren't equal. Managing this tension is more complicated than it might first appear. Consider just the logistics: the more prisoners, the more time is needed to hear them out. U.S. prisons are typically huge facilities. The ones I visited in Texas housed 1,800, 1,000, and 500 inmates respectively, while the Norwegian prison I visited held just 54. Given these numbers, it's easy to see where a Norwegian warden's best intentions have the best hope for success.

Money also plays a big role. In the U.S., Warden Tex explained that one of the only reasons that they embrace change and engage in levels of PDM is linked to monetary concerns. For example, several years back the state legislature passed a law allowing inmates to make phone calls to family members. (Previously, they had been able to communicate solely through the U.S. Mail.) Why that new freedom? The explanation would delight any cynic: the state could earn a lot of money by charging the inmates for each call.

Another variable that affects this tension is cultural. The social distance between officers and inmates in the Norwegian prison was extremely low. The two groups often shared meals at the same table. They'd joke and laugh together. They obviously felt a sense of community. And as inmate Erik explained, friendships often developed between them. In U.S. prisons, meanwhile, the distance – emotional and physical – between "offenders" and correctional officers is designed to be as distant as possible. The wardens often told me stories about correctional officers gone "rogue." And why rogue? According to the wardens, those officers were always the ones that got too close to the inmates and blurred the boundaries between their professional and personal lives.

In sum, while the PDM strategy is more widely accepted and praised in Norwegian prisons, applying it to maxed-out U.S. prisons would inevitably prove far more complicated. But should complication necessitate surrender? I think not. In fact, as evidenced by the stories I've told here, there is still much to be learned from the communication methods enacted in Norwegian prisons.

The hope

Scholars, practitioners, and politicians often agree that a total overhaul of U.S. prison policy is needed. Prisons are being maxed out and the costs of incarceration keep rising. In fact, the U.S. spends more on prisons than it does on education. Clearly, something is broken in this system. And although adopting PDM will not alleviate all of these concerns, it certainly has the ability to improve the situation.

There are two small steps that U.S. prisons can take to move them toward Norway's successful PDM model. First, U.S. prisons can start involving inmates in the conversation. Although daily morning meetings are impractical in a facility of 1,500, a semi-annual survey or series of focus groups in already established classes (e.g., General Educational Development classes) could serve to open the lines of communication between the inmates and the prison administration. Anecdotally, the inmates in Norway were more amendable to the warden's decisions because of the mutual respect established through PDM. Norway also boasts one of the lowest recidivism rates in the world, perhaps in part due to its humane approach to incarceration. Its prisons are not as isolated from society; so Norwegian inmates likely face more manageable reintegration challenges than their U.S. counterparts.

Second, the U.S. can better equip incarcerated individuals for successful reintegration. In the Norwegian prison I visited, inmates are mentored on a one-on-one basis in the rehabilitation and behavior-modification program. This mentoring is consistent with PDM as it opens the lines of communication and equips inmates for successful transition. The U.S. correctional system can also benefit from similar mentoring partnerships; however, from a financial perspective, these may be unrealizable behind bars. Because of the impracticality of reaching inmates while incarcerated (e.g., issues of access, cost, time, etc.), programs are popping up in communities across the U.S. to address this mentorship need post-release.

One such organization, FOCUS reentry of Boulder, Colorado, pairs community citizens with inmates just prior to release to help with the reintegration process. These mentors provide informational, instrumental, and emotional support to their mentees by connecting them to social-service organizations, helping them fill out paperwork, transporting them to jobs, and listening to some of the challenges during the transitional time. Mentoring partnerships like those in Norway's behavior-modification program and FOCUS's reentry program help prepare incarcerated individuals for their post-release life and increase the probability of successful reintegration.

In the short run these changes would cost money. Yet, the possibility of reduced recidivism, which could mean decreased costs over time, makes this a model worth fighting for. Perhaps more importantly, implementation of these changes could humanize the incarceration experience and equip individuals like my brother to make it on the outside.

16 The Norwegian workplace hustle
A crisis of shifting national identity

*Ashley Barrett, Bodø Graduate School of Business and
Dawna Ballard, The University of Texas at Austin*

Her bustling workplace is a virtual sea of gray cubicles stretching as far as the eye can see, and it's as loud as it is soulless, the room's concrete walls and steel rafters magnifying all the normal office sounds. But Eldrid[1] is oblivious. Seemingly immune to the ringing phones, busy foot traffic, and clicking computer keyboards, she keeps glancing at the to-do list propped up just to the right of her computer. Eldrid is the consummate multi-tasker; nothing holds her attention for very long, but of course it can't, for there's so much, really much too much, needing doing. Peering over her thick, black-framed reading glasses, she restlessly scrolls through her latest emails. Does she have time to squeeze in a few more phone calls? She slides her chair around to double-check the deadline dates she has scribbled on the white board behind her, and then – as if by habit – steals a glance up at the big clock over the elevators on the north entrance wall. It's always struck her as a cruel juxtaposition – a dictatorial device positioned directly over the elevators, with their promise of liberation. Seeing the clock's big sweep hand ticking away the seconds, she sighs, putting her hands over her eyes and frowning in frustration and despair. There's no way she'll have enough time to meet that last deadline, is there?

Co-workers walk by and occasionally attempt to trade greetings, but Eldrid appears deaf. It's as if they're talking to a robot; as one task is completed, another gets entered into the big database marked "pending." There's hardly a trace of a unique individual left in her mechanistic movements; even her eyes appear glazed. This is her first real job since graduating from college, and "job" describes it all too well. The corporate world has swallowed her whole.

Everything in that world – deadline to deadline to deadline – has an order, but it still feels like chaos. There are never enough minutes in the day, she feels, and every minute carries a sense of high urgency. It's enough to drive a conscientious person crazy.

At one point her boss knocks peremptorily on the sliding door to her cubicle, only to burst in before she can answer. He is a man of considerable intellectual stature, but he's always made her uneasy with his counterfeit smile and demanding nature. Eldrid looks up, then reflexively shrinks back in her chair, instantly on the defensive. She speaks first.

"I'm almost done with the layout of that brochure," she assures him, thinking to anticipate his latest demand. "I just need another hour or so."

"Oh, that? You were supposed to be done with that this morning, weren't you? That's not what I'm here for. I need you to get me a better picture of the fjords in Romsdal and Sogn to go in the pamphlets for the Western Norway Fjord tour. Also, get me the details on the Haugesund International Jazz festival coming up this August. Oh, and before you leave, decide on a pitch for the Innovative Norway campaign – one that will really grab people's attention. Remember to record your hours on each project. You'll need to stay late again."

As he speaks, Eldrid nervously taps on her desk with one hand and covers her mouth with the other, then searches frantically for her pen. She finally finds it, buried under a stack of loose papers, and adds these new tasks to her to-do list. She feels a little better whenever she can relieve an exhausted memory with pen and paper.

But before she can even think to ask him a question of clarification, her boss scurries out and away like the White Rabbit in *Alice's Adventures in Wonderland*.

She sighs, but then realizes there's no time for sighing, so it's back to work. This time, reaching too quickly for her mouse to get restarted on her chores, she manages to bump her forearm hard on the sharp edge of the desk and reflexively emits a muffled scream. *That darn arm again.* Over the past few months, she has not been able to fend off a nagging pain there. After consulting some medical info sites on the Internet (for who has time to make a doctor's appointment anymore?), she's learned that the pain is likely tendonitis resulting from overuse of her computer mouse. She had meant to buy a wrist pad to help minimize the problem, but she'd forgotten to. She had also meant to buy an anti-inflammatory med, but she hadn't gotten around to it, either. Somehow, neither had made it onto her list.

Eldrid's hectic work environment is still something of an anomaly in Norway, a country renowned for its flexible and "feminine" workplace culture. Yet there are recent signs of a drifting away from that traditional culture. Frenzied workers and a cult of time efficiency are becoming increasingly commonplace in organizations across the country, the result, mostly, of the major urbanization that has accompanied the radical economic changes spurred by the oil strikes in Norway's continental shelf. While money can solve many problems, experience teaches that it often manages to create newer, more complicated ones, too. Consider Norwegians "experienced."

Oil and gas have brought unprecedented wealth to the country, and, along with it, a crisis of national identity. For well over half a century the storybook original "Norwegian Dream" was a simple one, and typically agrarian, too: a hard-working person laboring with his hands in the earth, aspiring only to secure the basic necessities – a sound roof overhead, nutritious food on the table, a cow or two out in the pasture, maybe a few chickens, and a close-knit, healthy family. So exemplary of Norwegian culture was this ideal that it was even showcased in 1988 in the "Norway Pavilion" at the Epcot Theme Park's World Showcase (aka Walt Disney World). This was the image of Norwegian life that had been sold to people all over the world. Even though Norway's economic growth in the twentieth century had largely come from industries such as textile mills funded by banks in the late nineteeth century, its agricultural sector had always been a staple, with farming, timber, and fishing persisting as the backbone of Norway's economy.

But a lucrative transformation awaited the country. In May 1963, Norway claimed sovereign rights over its sector of the oil-rich North Sea. By the 1980s, Norway was experiencing skyrocketing profits from its engineering and construction investments in the oil-and-gas sector, pushing the country's collective identity away from past accomplishments and toward new ones fuelled by its black gold. Norway has now revamped its once commodity-based economy to one reaping the benefits of windfall cash. Not only has the old "Norwegian Dream" of a modestly comfortable livelihood been fulfilled many times over, it has been overshot as displays of materialism have begun to creep into the country in the form of pricey pads and weekend cabins. The per capita income for the country now stands at $86,440 US, which is the third highest in the world, surpassed only by that of Monaco and Lichtenstein. This, incidentally, is almost double the per capita income of the US, which, at $47,240, is the seventeenth-highest in the world (http://data.worldbank.org/indicator/NY.GDP.PCAP.CD).

Yet, as history shows, more money can spawn fresh problems, and as Norway has been transformed in the last four decades by its black gold and urban expansion, this focus on money and material success has begun to leak into other domains, none more so than the urban Norwegian organization. Some call it the "resource curse." You also hear scholars invoking the catchy phrase "petroleum perpetuates patriarchy" to help explain the shift in socio-cultural dynamics that's increasingly seen in Norwegian workplaces. The oil discoveries greatly augmented net family income, but, equally significant, they also greatly increased the father's salary – and with it, his authority. The labor jobs tied to offshore drilling are often male-dominated, as are many oil occupations for the highly educated such as engineering, trading, legal services, and architecture.

Stories like Eldrid's, now proliferating, suggest that adaptation to the patriarchal oil industry in Norway is at least indirectly responsible for "masculinizing" the Norwegian organization in the form of stricter hierarchies, more labor-intensive demands, and lots more deadlines and overtime. While this shift toward a highly competitive, masculine workplace is not yet the norm in Norway, it's gaining momentum and can be observed most commonly in organizations affiliated with petroleum production, including governmental ones and, in Eldrid's case, tourism operations. Evidence of unprecedented modern workplace stressors tiptoeing into the organization can further be found in the recent increase in Norwegians working hours well beyond the traditional work window of Monday through Friday, 6:00 A.M. to 6:00 P.M. A 2010 poll indicated that one out of three Norwegians logs time on the weekend, maybe even burning the midnight oil on weeknights as well (Statistics Norway, Labor Force Survey, 2010). Since 37 percent of those working outside normal business hours are women, Eldrid appears hardly alone in the pressures she faces in this brave new world.

Reflecting on her job as a project manager for a tourism center near the Norwegian–Swedish border, Eldrid recalls the acute pressure she faced daily: "I had to write down every hour that I was using. The problem was that I was using too much [time] because I was new. My boss had an impossible time schedule for me. I ended up working a lot of spare ... all of my free time, and because I was single at the time, I could of course do it. So I got this inflammation in one arm." But would that slow her down? Not a chance. She adds, stoically, "It was not a problem because I could switch the mouse on the computer to the other arm and just learn that." It appears that Eldrid's professional zeal and her need to keep her job by staying "productive" sometimes overshadowed her physical health. Eldrid casually mentioned in our interview that her boss's knowing she was unmarried may have been at least "indirectly" related to the added pressures she encountered there. "I think this happens quite often," she says, referring to the presumption that single employees have more free time out of the office, "but it is not out in the open." Thus, even her social needs were frequently subjugated to the demands of her occupation.

After working all of her available overtime and beyond, the result of an ever-growing to-do list dictated by her boss and reinforced by her confessedly "very ambitious" nature, Eldrid claims she "almost hit a wall. I was millimeters away from crashing because you get so tired because you never have time off. I sort of, like, worked myself into a corner .... You have these periods of really high stress, and then you sort of collapse. You can't function."

Nor was she alone in the acute discomfort she felt in the grinder of the workplace. Heidi, (pseudonym) a coworker, actually had what Eldrid called a true burnout: "She was on a sick leave for many months, and continued to work half-time for months after in order to recover." Eldrid then reflected on the sustainability of asking employees to give 100 percent day in and day out: "You can have a work environment giving you 95 percent during the day for 8 hours. [But] that's the best you can get. I mean, that's really an effective day. If you push people too much, they could max out and give you 60 percent, and they have to work for more and more hours to get it in. With more pressure, the percent effectiveness will go down gradually, so what's the point?" Hearing from lived experience is often more persuasive than reading theoretical accounts about it in a book, but in this case the two merge as Eldrid's description exemplifies the price of workplace burnout that scholars have been warning managers and employees about for decades. ("Burnout," interestingly, was coined in 1974.) Chronically pushing workers too hard can eventually take a debilitating toll on them, causing emotional exhaustion, the depersonalized treatment of one's peers, and a lost sense of personal accomplishment – all of which increase worker apathy while simultaneously decreasing their output.

Norwegian legislators have recently taken up this issue, reflecting a crisis of national identity as concerns with workplace norms grow. Last amended in December 2012, the Working Environment Act is an effort to more tightly regulate the quality of working life in Norway. Addressing critical workplace issues such as workplace flexibility, working hours/overtime, autonomy, and protection from discrimination, this legislation has served as a cautionary lighthouse to the escalating anxiety and burdens felt by employees in certain Norwegian organizations; it validated their distress calls, much as a lighthouse warns of nearby hazards. But this legislation was more than just a warning. It instructed Norwegians how to avoid the trenches of an impending disaster.[2]

Even with the noblest of intentions, though, legislation can be effective only if enforced, and the workplace standards spelled out in this Act are both complex and nearly impossible to enforce, as Eldrid's experiences illustrate. Specifically, the Working Environment Act attempts to police five areas:

(1) *Work content.* It must be varied and give control to workers. (Did Eldrid's to-do list give her some sense of control? Was it varied?)
(2) *Social relationships.* Employers must permit employee contact with other persons. (How does one define "contact"? Does working the same long hours together qualify?)
(3) *Compensation.* Pay systems must not lead to the risk of mental or physical damage. (Did Eldrid's boss take advantage of her by implementing a pay system that demanded she work more hours than the company could actually fund?)
(4) *Work planning.* Employers must ensure personal and professional development for their employees. (Did all of the experience Eldrid gained in such a high-velocity work environment offer professional development?)
(5) *Conditions under which the work is done.* Employers must standardize working hours so that those hours don't cause mental or physical damage. (Given that Eldrid had to work well beyond her overtime allotment, often into the late-night hours, this is one metric that she might have had difficulty bringing a suit over – though, on paper, it would look to be the easiest standard to measure.)

The issue of working hours is also impacted by the larger workplace norms and culture. Take, for example, Eldrid's boss, Bjørn, (pseudonym) who was intentionally underbidding Ministry of Agriculture jobs in order to knock out the competition. To "win" this battle, he had to accept a sometimes significant reduction in the amount of revenue his company would receive for a given project. Less revenue, of course, meant fewer paid working hours to complete the job. Yet because any such project is contractually required to be finished, Bjørn's underbidding resulted in stealing money from the pockets of his employees and also strapping them with lots of uncompensated overtime.

The result was Eldrid's typical experience on the job. She recalls the time demands and her indispensable, unforgiving, imperious to-do list: "Often I would start the day thinking about and planning how much I would manage to get done during the day, but realizing at the end of the day that my plan had been too ambitious but at the same time thinking that it wouldn't have been possible for me to work any faster or feel more concentrated. That is a frustrating feeling, again inducing stress. Because I had to clock my hours, it also becomes very visible that you are using more hours than is expected of you, more hours than you have in the budget. The result is that you end up pulling overtime hours that you don't report but that continue to wear you down."

At this point, it seemed as if our interview was almost cathartic for Eldrid. She continued: "Sometimes you just have to admit that you can't do it all. It's not a good feeling and you get really stressed when you see that you have to deliver this by Friday, and you just can't do it." Eldrid found that this sensation of failure bleeds into other aspects of life and creates a residual negative feeling that is hard to shake even when home with family and friends. She recalls walking home at the end of the day "feeling inadequate, being so tired that even shopping for groceries feels like a drag." While this admission would likely alarm the average person, it's particularly telling in Norway, as Norwegians traditionally are big celebrators of food and the shopping for food. Food brings people together, creates and strengthens friendships, and breaks patterns of reticence. Food is often associated here with entertaining guests and enjoying several rounds of cheerful toasts and bouts of roaring laughter. Yet Eldrid's experience clearly undermined this prominent cultural value.

While her workplace frustration has all the ingredients of an engrossing story, what's even more interesting is her diagnosis of the underlying source of that frustration. One would think she would blame her martinet of a boss, yet Eldrid chooses to see most of her stress coming from a piece of paper. Make that a list.

While it's still common for many Norwegians to cock their head in confusion when asked about their use of to-do lists, Eldrid's case illustrates at least one example of an increased orientation toward, and outward insistence on, a particular type of success. This orientation engenders an increased need to *remember* what those criteria for "success" are. Thus, to-do lists appear a sign of the changing times. Aptly so, because – symbolically – with the list comes the good and the evil. As an example, while Eldrid said that the efficiency of a list allowed her to get a "good night's sleep," she also admitted, "In stressed periods, I may have to make notes of all of the things coming to mind after going to bed." So, at such times, she is regularly getting in bed, thinking of something important, getting up, writing it down, feeling relieved, getting back in bed, and repeating this terribly redundant, restless process throughout the night. The list is her salvation, but also her curse. It resolves her worries, but is itself the chief producer of them as it grows and grows, becoming monstrous in both size and effect, consuming all her spare time and distancing her from friends and a social life.

In the same way that Norwegians' "resource curse" is associated with a crisis of national identity, reflecting their ambivalence about their very prosperity, Eldrid shares a similar ambivalence about the to-do list. The list is what guides her, yet it's also the monster that has her by the throat and seems to dominate her every thought. The list is there after the boss has left, and the list keeps the score of her daily achievement, which inevitably is always less than complete. The list sets the standards regarding both reward and reprimand. It determines both how her time will be spent and how far she is from ever feeling "done." When a day is particularly hectic, she says, "then I am more true to my 'to-do' lists because then I really need to be efficient. And it is more important to structure. And then you have these horrible periods of really high stress. And then you sort of, like, collapse from the stress. You know, you just can't function that much. You just need a moment to exhale, and suddenly an hour has gone by and you were just checking the news on the Web, you know, and you shouldn't be doing that because that was not on my to-do list."

Yet we all know the importance of scheduling time in our day to relax and do something we enjoy. Eleanor Roosevelt, America's former First Lady, once observed: "Sometimes it is extremely good for you to forget that there is anything in the world which needs to be done, and to do some particular thing that you want to do. Every human being needs a certain amount of time in which he can be peaceful." One cannot help but wonder if the urbanization of Norway that accompanied oil production and economic growth has introduced a dangerous new tempo into the country, stealing the rural, seasonal pace that used to stabilize and temper the typical Norwegian organization. Can we assume that with more *kroner* and more workers come more competition, more responsibilities, more fear of failure ... and thus more self-protective, increasingly neurotic list-making?

Eldrid now concedes that "living by the list" is not the best way to carry out the responsibilities of one's job. "I think it is really valuable not to be *too* busy if you have to be innovative like I do in my work," she says, "because it is development work, and you need to have time to talk to people and to be inspired. To-do lists are not very inspiring. They are sort of like action things ... I can't have an exciting phone call with somebody I don't know yet. You can't put that on your to-do list, but you have to prioritize it when it happens because that's where the goals are. I think a lot of things happen when you are busy making other plans. I think it's more about being present in the moment. Instead of a to-do list, it is sort of like working half in the future. You cross out things that you have done in the past, but [you] also need to be able to see things when they come." After a few moments' reflection, she continued: "If you say, 'That's very valuable but I have to do this,' then you miss out. So I think that sometimes it is really positive when you have to put chores over to the next week because maybe something else more important happened. That's why I was really unhappy with this job. It really wasn't development work. It was just *getting the job done*. I hated that."

The thought of routine work makes Eldrid bridle. She despises mindless patterns. So it's no surprise that she works in tourism, an industry accustomed to unpredictable weather, new anthropological and geographical discoveries, and endless streams of adventurous folk from all over the world, no two alike. In her opinion, lists become a form of abuse, a weapon in the toolbox of the manager, since most items on the list carry deadlines, and implicit standards set by others, and also carry a heavy price if they aren't met properly. Lists become, finally, balls and chains that weigh employees down, leaving them stressed and stripped of that sense of well-being and self-esteem that come with self-achievement and others' appreciation.

Accordingly, Eldrid believes that lists should be modified, diversified. Besides tasks, they should also record exploratory directions, newly discovered interests, ideas for motivation, and activities for inspiration. And the template of the list should be individualized, reflecting how each employee *specifically chooses* to organize his or her time. This would undoubtedly help honor the regulations spelled out in the Working Environment Act, specifically the one that restrains employers from assigning work content that is monotonous and steals control from the workers themselves. Like the "control of work content" issue addressed in the Act, many of the laws put into effect by this piece of important legislation were grossly violated by Eldrid's boss, and she is sure he was pretty typical. Because he assigned her an endless stream of tasks, each with a strict timeline, he also left no room for ensuring her personal and professional development at work. Because he unethically assigned her more hours than the firm had money to finance, he employed a rigged compensation system that impaired the mental and physical health of his subordinates. And because he exploited Eldrid's unmarried status and eagerness to please by drowning her in overtime hours, he poked and prodded her to the edge – but expected her not to jump.

Did she?

Eventually, yes she did. Her job had been conditional anyway. When hired for it, she had been informed that she'd be replacing a woman on maternity leave and therefore the position would be guaranteed for only twelve months, after which it would be "up for discussion." Disgusted with her treatment in the weeks leading up to that twelfth-month decision point, Eldrid decided to finally take her life back into her own hands and revoke her allegiance to her now vilified boss.

"I knew I had the job for twelve months until she returned," Eldrid recalls. "When the end date was approaching, my boss was still not talking to me about how they liked my work and if they wanted to keep me. I found this irritating and not respectful. At the same time, I had a friend advocating jobs in Bodø and asking me to return to my home county in order to spend time with her, living in the same city. I decided to start applying for other jobs. I got an interview with the Nordland Country Administration and told my boss, and *then* he reacted. He told me that they wanted me to stay and that he expected me to continue. I responded that if this was true, I think he should have talked to me about it .... I interpreted his silence about the time after the contract would expire as a signal that they didn't want me to stay. He offered me a pay raise, but at this time I had an option. The combination of constant stress in my current job, the promise of a new job, and moving back to Bodø to be with family and friends all affected my decision to leave. I felt *good* when I made my decision to leave."

While lack of appreciative feedback, not stress, turned out to be the deciding factor leading Eldrid to finally pack her bags, she confessed that she had been too young to thoroughly understand just how poor her work situation really was: "I think when you are young – this was my first real job – you don't have the experience or anything to compare it to, and you are less conscious of the fact that this job is not a good one." Yet her final decision to leave, and the culmination of events that led to it, turned out to be for the best. Once she finally took back the reins to her life and found her own direction, she would not be so foolish as to easily hand them over again.

It's now four years down the road, and Eldrid's work life as well as her personal life have dramatically changed. She's now married. And when arriving at her workplace these days, she's now invariably highly spirited and vivacious. She and her lively coworkers at the Nordland Tourist Board spend the first half hour of each morning engaged in personal and collective brainstorming exercises. They'll drink spiced green tea together, scan the newspaper for interesting events, and chat about their weekend and any upcoming work activities and opportunities that spike their enthusiasm. It's all part of what she calls simply "emptying your brain" and getting it ready to think and work creatively. Her new boss, Erik, is super conscious about not letting his workers slip into the bottomless pit of burnout. For example, he refuses to let them punch the clock any time other than Monday through Friday, 8:00 A.M. to 3:30 P.M. "He is really clear on that," Eldrid says. "He often says, 'I think it is important that you go home and relax because I need you here tomorrow and you need to be alert and ready to work.' So that is the work ethic of this company. You work like hell when you are here, and then you go home and have a life outside of work."

The daily to-do lists that used to rule Eldrid's life and pin her to a piece of paper have now been replaced by weekly to-do lists, which, she says, are "more flexible." "If I don't get everything that I want to get accomplished in one day," she says happily, "I just let it roll over to the next, and I don't let it haunt me. After all, I have all week to get it done."

In Eldrid's present organization, no employees can be found on company grounds between Christmas Eve and New Year's Day. Easter brings an equally ghostly vacant office. Eldrid points out that most of her co-workers have been with the company for ten or more years. It appears a warm and welcoming place, just like one would expect a Norwegian workplace to be. "If you are in it for the long run, you need to have strict rules and you need to help employees manage stress and the amount of stress that lingers in the office," Eldrid insists, with a wisdom born of experience. "I think people need a life. Working life is important, but it's not *everything*."

Eldrid was lucky to escape from the previous toxic working situation when she did, and she knows it. Speaking of her former boss, she wonders now if his start in the professional domain was actually not so different from her own. Did he also burst out of the gates fueled by a driving desire to prove himself and his credentials and capability? Did stress become second-nature to him? Did that same stress blind him to the stress he was causing in others? "It's easy to get used to the stress," she warns me, and for a split second, I could again see her fresh eyes go hazy in remembrance. "You get so used to it that you can't stress down. Really, you can't."

While riches have revamped the Norwegian economy and the business of oil and gas has perhaps upped the testosterone climate of the Norwegian work culture, Norwegians still have it pretty good in terms of their working environment. If some overbearing boss bites you too hard, you can nearly always opt out; Eldrid's story is certainly a testament to this. But her experience also illustrates how the Norwegian work environment is changing, and some would argue this change is a ruthless one.

With the last of the oil money being drilled out of the Barents Sea coming not far ahead, Norway has recently focused hard on reexamining its national reputation, or "*omdømme*," and the global stance it wants to establish in the post-oil era. It is prepared to launch a new identity. In fact, the government has recently toyed with updating its "Norway Pavilion" exhibit at Disney World in Orlando, Florida. That exhibit currently offers rides and entertainment that paint Norway as a land of great environmental beauty where polar bears lurk in the streets, Vikings sail its icy coastal waters, and trickster trolls are hiding in the snow-capped mountains. Over ten million visitors flock to this child-friendly spectacle each year. The cash required to renovate the exhibit is next to nothing for the Norwegian government's coffers, so money isn't at issue here. What's stalling the update is indecision about what Norwegian identity to project.

No matter how its people choose to re-define their prospective "Norwegian Dream," new socio-cultural dynamics will surface, and with every paradigm shift comes the fog that hovers over change. Until Norway discovers what exactly this identity will be, or should be, its national work environment will continue to evolve and be reconstructed, perhaps even get pushed back toward the "femininity" which long made it so congenial. It is impossible to see the end result while in the middle of such a sea change. Some questions now lingering over Norway are these: How do we want to define "hard work"? And how does a country known for its workplace flexibility go about demanding "hard work" without being excessively demanding, thereby undercutting its very goal?

"I think there are stressful times in all jobs," Eldrid admits. "I just don't want to walk home every day after work crying."

We think that's a fair request.

Notes

1 Eldrid is a pseudonym.
2 To view the most updated Working Environment Act, visit: http://www.arbeidstil-synet.no/binfil/download2.php?tid=92156

17 It is hard to be suave when you fish for cod

Belonging, identity, and future in Norway

Nicholas A. Merola, Bodø Graduate School of Business

Guttorm Sivertsen (to the left) and his girlfriend
Photograph by Guttorm Sivertsen

On a summer evening, I walk through the deserted downtown of Bodø, in Northern Norway. A light breeze creeps down every street and alley, turning the air chilly, though the midnight sun lights the world brightly. Much of the rest of the town is at a bonfire, celebrating the Summer Solstice, the longest day of the year. I got tired of watching families grill hot dogs around portable grills, so I'm off to figure out where the rest of the twenty-somethings are tonight.

I walk to *Dama Di*, a hip bar with a sign that roughly translates to "Girlfriend." A sign outside announces that *Dama Di* is the place for "Art and Chaos," and just inside, a long bar shoots down the length of the space. I've been here before, and have come back because I know I can get Salmiakki, vodka flavored by the salty black licorice beloved by Scandinavians. On weekends, there's jazz and a packed dance floor, but tonight the patrons and bartenders are free to queue up whatever music they wish. Johnny Cash plays often, on request.

It's dim inside, the few bulbs lighting mainly the bar and walls of posters and paintings for sale. Tonight, there are around twenty or thirty people filling out the sofas, stools, and high chairs throughout the bar. The young crowd chatters in small groups, each discussion animated more by the bond between the participants than the substance of the conversation. Bodø's nightlife scene seems to be dominated by techno, hiphop, and laser shows, and this place is an oasis in that sonic jungle.

The bar is manned by three cute blonde bartenders, who serve drinks with admirable dispatch. I step up and order my shot, and a beer. A rowdy group of three guys next to me seems unable to decide between having a wrestling match and ordering drinks. I think they may have the wrong bar. I sip my beer while one of the guys eventually rattles off an order of Norwegian beers, like Mack and Ringnes. The bartender nods and snaps away sharply to begin filling glasses. Beers in Norway are a bit larger than those served in the United States, and sometimes drunk with a glass of traditional aquavit, a schnapps tasting mildly of aniseed and bitter herbs. Tonight, though, the accompaniment of choice for these guys seems to be Jack Daniel's whiskey.

"Hey, are you American?" The leader approaches me, colleagues in tow. I tell him that I am, and that I'm studying Norway and oil. We begin a half-shouted discussion. His name Guttorm, which means, he adds without prompting, "serpent boy" and is from the old times. I look it up later and find that it's an old Norse name that he shares with several long-deceased Norwegian kings.

Guttorm's a fisherman, a fact I could not have divined from his outward presentation. His smooth skin belies the years he has spent fishing on the Norwegian Sea with his brother – six, since he's twenty-four now. He could pass for younger, in appearance and demeanor. Dressed in jeans and a black T-shirt, with gelled, spiked hair the same dark brown color of his heavy eyebrows, it would be hard to differentiate him from the "mainlanders" on a night out without talking to him about his life. One might never guess that he had stepped off of his boat, the *Eros*, earlier today.

Looking at him, one also wouldn't guess that Guttorm is a (fisher)man with a problem. Guttorm's problem starts with the fact that he works on a boat roughly 300 days a year. This leaves him just 65 days on land. After deducting time for family obligations and catching up on mundane stuff like paying his bills and running miscellaneous errands, he doesn't have a lot of time for himself. Certainly, not enough time for the things that mean most to a young fisherman long away from port: girls, friends, and drinking. Guttorm has tonight and tomorrow off, but this hardly solves his problems. It's only a respite, and it's unclear whether it will satisfy like a cool drink on a warm day or just tantalize, like an alcoholic's first sip. Regardless, it's all he is getting and that, in itself, is a problem. He's got one shot at making the most of what he's got. How can he make the most of tonight?

In many ways, Guttorm's problem resembles a problem Norway is facing: how best to handle a limited resource. In Norway's case, it's the country's oil-and-gas reserves. However, these resources, though still huge, are non-sustainable and, thanks to heavy production, steadily declining. So basically the country gets one shot with the money they generate, and that's it.

Many credit the oil fields with Norway's metamorphosis from one of the poorer countries in Europe at the start of the twentieth century to one of the richest by the end. Currently, oil accounts for some 30 percent of its GDP. The boost from oil, combined with a low population, gives Norway a remarkable and enviable per capita GDP of ~ $52,000, the fourth highest in the world. And unlike other countries that have discovered great oil resources, Norway has not allowed a few oligarchs to profiteer, or otherwise mismanaged its national treasure. Instead, it has put the bulk of that treasure in an ethically guided investment fund that excludes companies that contribute to human rights abuses.

There is much debate within Norway regarding how to continue to manage the money they've made from oil. The sovereign wealth fund formed from this capital is the largest such fund in the world, at more than $700 billion. Parties within the government want to reserve this money, and any to come, for future citizens. This means leaving the bulk of it largely alone and continuing to invest it with care. Others want to pour it into the economy by reducing taxes and increasing spending on infrastructure. They argue that spending it now will pay dividends later, stimulating economic growth in other areas. Both views should be lauded for their future-oriented perspective, though they do differ sharply in how they propose to achieve their goals.

Guttorm's shots appear on the bar, only to vanish promptly with a loud "Skål!" I join him and his cohorts, Morten and Kim Andreas, on a sofa near the entrance. Morten works on a fishing boat, too, but not the *Eros*. He is blond, a couple inches taller than Guttorm's 5'-10", with a square jaw. His height advantage would make him the natural leader, but Guttorm is clearly running the show tonight.

Kim Andreas has a nice watch on, which flashes as he punctuates his speech with gestures. His oval face and broad jaw look typically Scandinavian. He says his father buys fish from Guttorm and Morten's fathers, both of whom are fishermen. Kim Andreas spends a lot more time on land than Guttorm does, learning his father's trade. He lacks the zeal and fails to match the frenetic pace set by Guttorm, perhaps because Kim Andreas gets more time for bars and girls.

Guttorm and Norway thus share the problem of managing a scarce resource, although in Guttorm's mind there is no debate on what to do with his own commodity, which is time. He's going to splurge it on drinking, hanging out with friends, and chasing girls.

If only Norway's problem were as simple as this.

I've been in Norway for months, trying to understand the complex perspectives that every citizen seems to have on this issue. After how to spend (or conserve) the money, the second great debate within Norway revolves around what action should be taken regarding Norway's remaining oil fields. Should they be developed? Or should laws be passed blocking further testing and exploration? There are a number of nuanced economic, environmental, and cultural arguments both for and against these perspectives. Environmentalists note the myriad hazards of drilling and oil production, thinking of the all too recent BP oil spill in the Gulf of Mexico and other such catastrophes worldwide. Others fear for the fishing and marine life populations. Still others worry about protecting the unspoiled landscape of the North. "Pristine" is a word that is used often, and a pristine wilderness is dear to the Norwegian heart.

Proponents of development, meanwhile, note the economic benefits that the oil industry has already brought to Norway. Discovery of new large fields could mean further growth. More development, particularly in northern Norway, would mean fresh, well-paying jobs and upgraded infrastructure, both badly needed. Norway has done well with its current funds, but could do a lot more with the discovery of another large field. This is a debate that everyone can provide an opinion on. It's talked about so much that it's impossible not to.

I ask Guttorm what he thinks about oil and the future. After thinking for a moment, he tells me, "Seismic location of oil scares away the fish for a year. If there are no fish for the year, I don't make any money. I don't give a damn about oil, but fuck seismic tests." Guttorm's brisk assessment is refreshing to me. His buddies nod their assent. His opinion is either widely shared, or they're of the opinion that it's good to have an opinion.

Guttorm's answer to the debate leads to a toast. Glasses are raised, and Morten and Kim Andreas join in, yelling "Fuck seismic tests! Fuck oil!"

A bout of shoving and general roughhousing breaks out between Guttorm and Morten. The two of them seem in a constant contest, testing their strength. Guttorm evidently has something to prove. He grew up in a tiny community on a small island, Landegode. Kim Andreas and Morten, meanwhile, are from Helligvær, a chain of islands. Their island is more densely populated and considered less rural, perhaps less backward, than Guttorm's.

Landegode is north and just six miles west of Bodø. It is a rugged, mountainous island, less than 12 square miles in size, roughly half the size of Manhattan, covered in the black rock and forests common to the coast. Sailors used to find shelter there from storms, which is likely how the island got its name, the "Good Land." These days, its population totals just forty-two people. They share the island with herds of sheep and a family of walruses.

Along with seven or so other local kids, Guttorm attended primary school on Landegode, taught by a teacher and her aide. While an American parent might envy this level of individual attention in grade school, island life lacks appeal to many young people, who feel cut off and lonely. For a time, Guttorm had his older brother for company, but that lad soon followed in their father and grandfather's footsteps as a fisherman. Nowadays, their father, after fishing for twenty-five years, is too beat up to go on the boats himself, so he acts as a middle man between the fishermen and fish buyers.

Guttorm says fishing is a tough job. He himself started out right after high school, and has been toiling on the boat from dawn to dusk since then. Even schooled by generations of experience, fishing proves a perilous life. *Deadliest Catch*, a Discovery Channel show on Alaskan fishermen, documents the risk and adventure of the fishing lifestyle. Guttorm has seen the show, and points out proudly that the boat run by Norwegian descendants is routinely the most productive.

The *Eros*, a jaunty red fishing boat, is the boat Guttorm calls home. Out in the vast water, it looks tiny, though it's longer than a school bus. Much of the space on deck is taken up by the massive bridge, and the rest filled with the accoutrements of commercial fishing: nets and ropes, winches, and fish processing stations. Guttorm tells me that he suits up every morning in thick neon raingear, gloves, and a hat, and works up on deck all day clearing fish from lengths of netting.

Guttorm fishes for Atlantic cod, distinguishable from other species of cod by their matched anal and dorsal fins and dangling chin whisker. The cod the *Eros* pulls up are usually 7 to 10 kilos (15 to 20 pounds), and a meter or more (4 to 5 feet) in length. When Guttorm comes upon a fish trapped in the net, he carefully removes it. Then, he inserts the tip of a long, thin blade into the fish's anus and slices upwards. This splits the belly of the fish end to end. After ripping out its guts, he tosses what remains of the fish into the hold for storage. This continues all day. Once, a whale shark got caught in the nets, and the crew spent hours freeing it. Though it broke up the routine, Guttorm found this vexing. You don't get paid to clear whale sharks from the net.

From six years of working on the boat, Guttorm is stronger than he looks and likes to prove it, as when, alpha-like, he impulsively grabs the back of Morten's neck, attempting to shove him down, and crows, "I get all the women, isn't that right, you son of a bitch?" Morten breaks free, laughing, and throws a punch into Guttorm's chest. Kim Andreas rolls his eyes and gets up to collect the next round.

In the meantime, Guttorm and Morten get to enjoy the sight of several youthful women strolling happily into the bar. The majority are garbed in light sweaters or trendy jean jackets. Blonde hair is a recurring theme, though it's not clear whether nature or nurture is responsible. The women array themselves on a nearby couch. They are noticed.

The guys move over to join the new arrivals, sitting down next to two women, both of whom turn out to be aspiring nurses. One is a pretty blonde, the other a redhead, which is not as uncommon in Scandinavia as elsewhere. Tonight, the ladies are celebrating completion of a grueling final nursing exam. Kim Andreas soon joins them, bringing fresh drinks.

Guttorm leans in toward the blonde, speaking rapid Norwegian. One can imagine the conversation progressing in a typical manner: "Who are you, what do you do, where are you from?" I'm content to observe and interpret body language. The signs aren't good. At some point, Guttorm laughs too loudly and goes to buy another round.

We all toast. And toast some more.

Schmoozing with the nurses doesn't progress as the guys would hope. Perhaps they have drunk too much by this time, or maybe the women are just more interested in celebrating their collective scholastic achievement. It may also be true that they aren't keen on getting chummy with some island fishermen who are growing increasingly rowdy on their only night off from work.

Returning to the sofa they'd abandoned, Guttorm and Morten are momentarily dejected, but soon forget their woes.

"Fishing pays well," Guttorm tells me. "Not everyone can do it." And, he might have added, not everyone can throw money around like he can. For me as an American graduate student, buying what translates to a $12 beer for myself, much less covering beers for everyone else, is a struggle, so I imagine cod fishing must pay well indeed. That, or when you live on a boat, there isn't much to spend your money on. By any measure, though, Guttorm is a generous guy.

Fishing is a source of pride for Guttorm. It's his family's trade, and has been for generations. He is proud because it is manly, demanding work, work that not everyone can do. It is important work, too, as the industry makes up a significant portion of Norway's exports. Norway supplies countries throughout Europe and Africa with dried fish. Its stockfish – mostly unsalted, air-dried cod – is considered a delicacy in Italy and eaten with great relish there. It's also a special treat in Croatia. And, of course, other Scandinavians savor Norwegian cod, too.

Fishing has been a source of distinction for Norway, long before its oil fields were discovered. In fact, stockfish has been a chief export of Norway since the twelth century, and some historians date it as a source of trade as far as back to the ninth century, or even earlier. Then, as now, the large amount of cod relying on the waters around Norway as a spawning ground, particularly the Lofoten Islands north of Bodø, ensures a bountiful supply of fish – well, for now, at least. The Norwegian climate is also ideal for drying fish outdoors. Consistent cool, dry temperatures and sunlight mean the best conditions for stockfish production in the world. If, at least to some, oil represents Norway's future, fishing represents its past, a centuries-old way of life.

Now, though, Norway is at a crossroads. Since 2000, fishing fleets have declined by 50 percent as the traditional fishing industry contracts in favor of farmed fish and other work (www.ssb.no). Though Norway is internationally known for its fish exports, they actually account for only 1 percent of its GDP. But while the rich oil fields discovered in the late 1960s are slowing their production, many Norwegians continue to dream of a future fired by oil.

Researchers have written extensively about the positive ripple effects of oil development in the High North. Permanent infrastructure will be installed, jobs created, and depopulation checked. In the eyes of young people, this industrial development will in turn bring a perception of urbanity to rival the cities in southern Norway, where many youths might otherwise relocate. In 2010, less than a quarter of municipalities in the north of Norway showed population growth. The declining population is a problem for those who want to develop the north for tourism and industry.

The interest of oil companies has turned to an area outside of the beautiful Lofoten islands as the next likely strike zone – the Nordland VII and Troms-II blocks of the continental shelf. But this area is home to spawning Atlantic cod, and some fear that oil-related activity will scare the fish, interrupt the spawning, and possibly even lead to the loss of the cod-fishing economy entirely. This, of course, would be catastrophic for the fishermen who rely on cod for their livelihood. The choice, as some put it, is: fishing or oil.

To some Norwegians, fishing represents more than a career; it represents Norway's traditional trade and history. Last winter, a bonfire lighting was organized by groups opposed to oil and development of the North. Bonfires were lit all across the mountains, and blazed in the dark hills all day. In times of war and danger bonfires were lit to tell the people to come together, to rally – the symbolism here is that it's time to defend the North again.

Earlier that week, I'd taken a ferry trip from Bodø up to the Lofoten islands to meet the leader of People's Action for Oil-Free Lofoten, Vesterålen and Senja and an organizer of the bonfire rallies, Gaute Wahl. Gaute said that his organization is there to protect tradition, to protect the islands. He looks like what Hollywood imagines environmental activists to look: light stubble and a fleece and denim wardrobe. In a soft-spoken manner at odds with his leadership position, he told me, "Our life is nature. Everything we need, we have …. We must live centrally, renewably, not exploit resources." He's concerned because oil raises challenges to this life, and so he wonders "what is the way forward, for the local community, and nationally?" Moving oil development into the area around Lofoten is a disruption – to fishing, to tradition, and to the lifestyle of High North locals. Families have lived for generations in the towns that dot Lofoten, and see oil development putting their lifestyle at risk.

For his part, Guttorm says he couldn't wait to get off his island when he was younger. He is aware of the international role of Norway in fish production, and the traditional ways it symbolizes. He grew up in it. But fishing for him was not a choice. As a young man, Guttorm had few options other than to follow his family onto a fishing boat. Now, with some age and experience, his options and priorities have changed. Rather than simply getting off the island, he wants to get off the boat and onto the mainland.

As often as fishing makes Guttorm proud, it also makes him unhappy. The fisherman's lifestyle has become a yoke. Lately, mainlanders no longer respect his kind. Women, especially, aren't impressed that he is a fisherman. And, of course, he can't live the life he wants to live. Cooped up in his boat, he has no shot at the modern lifestyle he desires. Fishermen, while important, are viewed in the cities perhaps the way some residents of Manhattan might view a farmer from upstate New York who shows up in boots and overalls for a night out in the Meatpacking District. A bit rustic, pleasant, and thoroughly out of place. Of course, a Manhattanite on a farm might stick out a bit, too.

A bout of arm wrestling breaks out at our table in the bar. I grip up with Guttorm. His forearm is strong, and he offers a light challenge. I press his arm down, but he cocks his wrist at the last moment, refusing to give in. "When you throw fish all day, every day, you build the endurance. I can outlast any man," he boasts. Slowly, surely, I roll his knuckles to the table. No matter. Guttorm insists that after fifteen more contests, he'll be the one winning. Kim Andreas is elected the next challenger. He crushes me, soundly. I think to myself that my arm was probably tired.

I tell Guttorm I'm hungry, and ask what we should eat. Dried cod, perhaps? He laughs and says we should go to the kebab stand down the street. We all get up, leaving the passel of empty glasses and bottles strewn about our table as testament to a night of accomplishment and distinction.

The bar is closing anyway. Though it's now 3 A.M., daylight shines bright as the *Dama Di* and neighboring bars disgorge their squinting patrons. G, the club just down the street, leaks a steady line of hungry people toward the food stands. Kim Andreas has had enough and takes a cab home. Meanwhile, Guttorm and Morten chat up another blonde as I join that flow of night owls, making sure we have a place in line and salivating at the inviting photos of kebabs and burgers just ahead.

Guttorm and Morten join me shortly. They didn't get any traction with the latest girl, either. Another night, maybe. Guttorm demonstrates more of his largesse, offering to pay for my kebab. I decline, but he insists, saying, "I have 200,000 NOK in the bank right now." We eat, and then part ways with promises to keep in touch.

I trudge back to my apartment, reflecting. What have I learned about this Norwegian fisherman? He shows great pride in the demands of his work, and in the fact that not many can do what he does. It pays well, he says. It is important work, according to Gauthe Wahl, and many others. It's Norway's heritage. But, for other mainlanders, the young ones that Guttorm wants to impress, fishing isn't so big a deal. They only know a Norway flush with oil money and international interest. There also are universities and businesses and culture to be concerned with. The Internet has shrunk everything – no matter how far above the Arctic Circle you live, pop culture and modern entertainment media reach there. Nowadays, young people dream beyond simply getting off an island. They want the rest of Europe and the rest of the world.

These are the things Guttorm wants. He misses girls and free time and parties, the things that the media and Internet have shown him. Things that you cannot get living on a boat.

A month passes, and I return to Austin, Texas. I have little substantive contact with Guttorm, Morten, or Kim Andreas, though we keep in touch through Facebook. But one night Guttorm messages me, urging me to come to Trondheim. He has just returned from a party. I ask what he is doing in Trondheim, and when he will return to the boat. I don't ask why he's been partying until 7 A.M. Norwegian time. That doesn't need an explanation.

"I stopped working on the boat," he replies. "Too much work, and too little money."

"So what are you doing for a living?" I ask him.

He says that he's going to find work on dry land so he can get some privacy – and "maybe a girlfriend."

"Well, girls are pretty important," I concede.

"No," he proclaims, "they are the meaning of life!" He wants me to know that he is enjoying himself, and living off of savings. I don't ask what his family thinks of this. Really, I am glad that he was able to get to the mainland while still a young man. In thirty years, I can't imagine Guttorm looking back and wishing he had stayed on the boat. I tell him I'm glad he's having a good time.

But I can't help asking him what he'll do when the money runs out.

"I don't know, but it won't be fishing," he says.

18 Norway under attack

Melissa Murphy and Maegan Stephens, Bodø Graduate School of Business

Jørgen Bikset
Photograph by Thor Wiggo Skille

5 July 2011 @ 08:00

Buzz ... buzz ... buzz ...

Jørgen reached over for his phone, which rested conveniently between his pillow and the edge of the bed. With eyes still closed, he switched off the alarm but kept the phone in his hand. Almost without thinking he wiped the sleep from his eyes and quickly worked his fingertips across the touch screen. It was still early, so few of his friends had updated yet, but this was his morning ritual. Scrolling with his thumb, he scanned the news feed of his Facebook page and then noticed the red flag in the upper-left corner of his screen. Other Young Labour Party members, knowing it was useless to try and contact him late at night, often left him Facebook messages that he would find upon waking. Being the party's County Secretary of Nordland, which was a full-time position, entailed a lot of work, but Jørgen wouldn't have it any other way.

He got out of bed while never putting the phone down. Making his way to the bathroom, he grabbed his glasses off the nightstand and began confirming his morning meetings, liking a few friends' Facebook statuses from the night before, and checking the Young Labour Party's group page, AUF, short for Arbeidernes Ungdomsfylking. Jørgen managed to look like the stereotypical Norwegian politician – glasses, side-parted thick brown hair, a full face. But he also still looked like a kid, too, with kind, big brown eyes. His mature demeanor and articulateness belied his twenty years. One of the most professionally dressed among his peers, he tucked in his oxford button-down and slipped into his shoes.

After he was finished getting ready for the day he headed downstairs for a breakfast of bread and strawberry jam, plus of course a very strong Norwegian coffee blend lightened with milk. Sure, he needed to check his email, but that was better done at the office. For now, it was time to close Facebook and get an overview of the day's news stories. Instead of pulling up a news website or turning on the television, he opened his Twitter feed. Facebook and Twitter – those were websites he was always connected to. He read the headlines from various news sources and Tweets from the numerous journalists he was following. Since he lived in Bodø, he felt very connected to the political issues in his immediate surroundings. He used Facebook and Twitter as a way to stay in touch with Labour Party supporters and opposition members in other parts of Norway, especially Oslo. His online relationship with journalists and politicians all over Norway provided a chance for them to see what was going on in the High North, too. It wasn't a completely reciprocal relationship since Oslo was the epicenter of political activity and the High North seemed less crucial to those in the capital, but at least it was a start. His generation was sure to change this imbalance; the youngest members of the AUF believed that social media could do anything and *everything*.

5 July 2011 @ 12:30

Even as the barista set a steaming ceramic red mug on the granite bar top in front of him, Jørgen was already reaching for his HTC Incredible S cellphone in the back pocket of his jeans to update his status. It had been a long morning of meetings, taking care of the economy of the Young Labour Party, contacting potential members, organizing seminars, and planning others, so he was grateful for the chance to get some work done in the comfort of a familiar, relaxed setting. He wanted to brag to his online social network about the decadence he would soon enjoy. While the foam on the mocha cappuccino was thicker than normal – his usual barista was away on holiday – Jørgen was still relieved to be taking a break from work. The planning and preparation from the previous weeks had left him tired but restless. By this time in the afternoon, he needed a pick-me-up, and this was the best place in town to get it. He carefully carried the mug down the winding staircase lined with books and trinkets and over to his favorite spot – an old lime-green upholstered couch in the back corner. This spot also had a great little foot table where the lighting was just right, and he liked to put his feet up for a break. It was adjacent to the pool table where a few of the locals would shoot corner pockets and Aquavit in the evenings. He found this corner to be a great place to relax and recharge. He had written several speeches in this corner and met many travelers enjoying their expensive hamburgers and crispy french fries with mayonnaise at the nearby tables.

No sooner had he sat down when his HTC Incredible S began vibrating in his back pocket. It seems his friend Aslak had "liked" his status on Facebook. Jørgen smiled. Weeks earlier, Aslak and Jørgen had enjoyed orange ice teas with cherry flavoring (and Cafe Kafka's signature splash of Sprite) while talking about this year's upcoming AUF summer camp. Aslak had been down from Longyearbyen, an island close to the North Pole, visiting his grandparents when he met up with Jørgen downtown near the shopping center. Aslak had just finished telling Jørgen about the latest polar bear sighting in downtown Longyearbyen, where they were released from school early to ride their skateboards to catch a glimpse of the mama and her cub – from a far distance, of course. Aslak was fair-skinned, tall, and lanky, weighing barely 115 pounds. Jørgen was grateful to have Aslak's fearless, outgoing energy in the Young Labour Party to help push the party's views.

Buzz … Buzz. Jørgen was caught mid-daydream as his phone went off again.

It was his boss messaging about setting up a meeting to strategize ways to get the word out about the upcoming school debates and mock elections. Jørgen, his coworkers, and other members of the organization had spent months pushing their social-media campaign, trying to recruit more members for the AUF's cause. The group had been gradually gaining membership via their Facebook page with about ten people joining a week. Slowly but surely the number of supporters was rising from just a few hundred to into the thousands, and, finally, just a few weeks ago, reaching the 2,000 mark. Jørgen, logged in at all times to the world's biggest social networking site, tried not to check the membership too frequently, but he loved watching the number climb.

As he jotted down the newly scheduled meeting, he noticed that the paper he was writing on was his check-list for camp. Young Labour Party members including Jørgen were preparing for their annual trip in July to Utøya Island, some 100 kilometers northwest of Oslo, where they would spend five days in tents and cabins discussing politics. AUF was the biggest political youth organization in Norway, "*fighting for a fairer world.*" Close to 1,000 AUF members would attend what some called the best summer camp in Norway, and what Aslak and the tabloids called the best place to meet someone, or "hook up." Jørgen loved the island of Utøya; he found it magical and fairytale-like. Some of his best memories were staying in the cabins by the water and telling stories by the campfire. After returning from the camp every year, campers' Facebook in-boxes were flooded with friend requests. Not only was there a chance to talk about important democracy and leadership issues, but it was a place where a thousand young Norwegians, ages 13–30, could make new friends in a social setting. Perhaps more exciting, depending on your taste, was the visit by the Prime Minister and leader of the Labour Party. Jens Stoltenberg always attended a portion of the camp and chatted informally with the Young Labour Party members. The trip was getting so close, *so close*. As Jørgen packed up his work he smiled at the thought of Aslak. Soon Jørgen would get to spend some quality time with his friend, but for now he had to work. Only two weeks away.

19 July 2011 @ 6:00

In the weeks leading up to camp, Jørgen and the other county secretaries were at one of their four annual conferences. When the computer pinged, Jørgen was just stowing his favorite gray sweatshirt into his duffle bag. And then another one: *Ping!* It was early Tuesday, 19 July, and he would be making his way to Oslo on the 08:30 flight. The sun was out and shinning, as it never goes to bed this time of year. And last night, neither did Jørgen. He was hurrying to finish breakfast and packing while waiting for his ride to the airport. He stuffed another few pairs of socks into the side compartment, just in case. While he was wrestling with his giant pack, his mobile device began to buzz, and the computer continued to talk at him.

Buzz … Ping! … Buzz … Ping! Jørgen glanced at the screen, and saw several blue chat windows flashing back at him.

He hammered a few sentences into his keyboard and started closing applications on his bright green laptop as he was already running late. Once the computer had shut down, he slid his HTC Incredible S into his back pocket and snapped on his watch, a graduation gift from his grandmother. Then he grabbed his glasses case, threw the black laptop bag strap over his shoulder, and grabbed his bread with his free hand. As he was balancing his breakfast he grabbed his pack and began dragging it down the two flights of stairs. *Thump … thump … thump.*

Sporting his new Asics tennis shoes, he hopped into the car, where he got a whiff of his friend's "new car smell" air freshener. Ebulliently taking a swing at it dangling from the rear-view mirror, he shouted, "Let's go!" He had waited an entire year for this week and had barely slept the night before. He turned up the radio as his friend sped off to the airport with the air freshener swinging in the wind.

19 July 2011 @ 08:00

At the airport terminal, he reviewed some of the pictures from last year's camp on his friend's Facebook "mobile uploads" album. His entire career was working for the AUF. Even his free time was spent volunteering with affiliated organizations and the Norwegian Red Cross Search and Rescue Group, so this camp was one place where he could see all the hard work pay off. He was going to be able to see his friends from all over the country and return to the magical Utøya. The weather forecast looked promising, so maybe they'd escape rain. Camping in the rain made for wet socks and cold feet, and he hated that. It was also a recipe for unhappy campers, especially the little ones. But in Norway they say there is no such thing as bad weather, only poor clothing. He was glad he had packed that extra pair of socks.

When he landed in Oslo after listening to a political podcast and enjoying a complimentary tomato juice and peanuts, he met a couple of the other AUF county secretaries from Troms and Finnmark standing outside Baggage Claim. Almost immediately the crew climbed into the bus, but not before his colleagues smoked a couple of cigarettes. He disliked being on his mobile phone in front of them, specifically Facebook, as he thought it was impolite, especially since he saw them so infrequently. But while his friends took a few last drags, he had a chance to update his status:

> On the bus to Utøya! Wooopwooop!
> July 19th at 10:56 via Facebook mobile
> 8 people like this.

As soon as he put his phone away, his friend turned to Jørgen, cleared his throat a bit impatiently, and asked, "You ready?"

"Just waiting on you guys!" Jørgen replied.

"Let's do this!" the boy said, gesturing at the bus.

The loud bus ride from Oslo was just over 100 kilometers, and the ferry ride was less than 5 minutes. The bus was full of old friends and new faces. Some sang Norwegian songs, others were glued to their mobile phones, and still others just chatted away. During the time that the bus wound through the countryside, two girls seated behind Jørgen chatted incessantly about an ex-boyfriend and a rude text message. As he tried to block them out, he hoped that the drama would be kept to a minimum this year, but every year some couple would break up, or someone would start a rumor that caused a fuss, mostly among the young teen set. While Jørgen reached in his backpack under the seat in front of him to grab a stick of gum, he overheard one of the youngest campers with red hair and freckles, who looked no older than eleven, scream, "Look! There it is!!" Jørgen turned his head toward the window and, sure enough, there it was: *Utøya*! Shades of green and blue with the sunlight dancing on the waves – paradise on earth. Returning members looked forward to camp from the minute they left the previous year. First-timers had heard years of stories and couldn't contain themselves. Everyone howled with excitement.

Jørgen's seat-mate leaned to him and asked, "What campsite are you at?"

"Oh, I have a bad back so I'll be in one of the dorms in the lower levels of the old barn."

"Cool, yeah … I'll be in the bright green tent. We normally pitch up near the grills. Hey, maybe I will see you around?"

"Absolutely! It was good to meet you, Ole," Jørgen said, reaching out his right hand to shake the boy's hand, but instead they bumped fists. *Ole Ole Ole*. Jørgen silently repeated the new acquaintance's name and made a mental connection to an Ole he knew back in Bodø so he could remember it. It was a trick one of his mentors taught him when he started his job. It served very useful at networking events, and it was key for working in politics.

The island was in the distance as the bus pulled up to the dock. The historical ferry owned and operated by AUF, called MS *Thorbjørn*, carried fifty campers at a time over to the island. Veteran campers were accustomed to standing at the dock, waiting for its arrival – there was no telling when it would come. The anticipation was all part of the fun. As everyone single-filed off the bus and waited in line for registration, the shoreside crew worked feverishly, checking luggage and providing color-coded armbands for the campers. Before Jørgen jumped into help, he pulled out his phone to take a photo to share with his friends and family back home.

22 July 2011 @ 17:26

It had been a busy day at camp, just like the previous three days. Jørgen had been working shoreside in the pouring rain making room for the visit from Gro Harlem Brundtland, Norway's first female prime minister, by moving cars out of the deep, wet mud. He was finally able to slip away for a nap in his cabin after eating a quick dinner. His back had been bothering him, and he was looking forward to lying down and catching up on some reading. He had been asleep for almost two hours when his phone rang. Still exhausted from the day's events, and knowing that there was a lot of work still ahead of him, he sent the call to voicemail with the hope of getting just a bit more sleep. Within minutes the phone transitioned between text message, voicemail, and incoming call alerts. *Buzz … Ring … Buzz … Ring … Buzz*. In that instant, the camp had changed forever.

22 July 2011 @ 17:50

I need to know what is going on, Jørgen thought. The string of text messages and voicemails from friends and family that he initially ignored were about a bombing in Oslo. On any other day a bombing in his country would have been enough to shock him – *Norway is a safe place.* At this very moment, however, the situation at camp had him paralyzed. Text messages about a gunman ... shooting ... campers died ... in the cafeteria... – *This doesn't make sense.*

As he hid in his cabin he realized that any noise, even a hushed whisper, could be a deadly mistake. He needed to keep his friends safe and call the police. Initially, helping others was the *only* thing he was focused on. His phone had already started going off as the attack began and he just kept silencing calls in an attempt to stay quiet. Although text messaging was an option, that could tie up the lines for people who needed help, more help than he needed at the moment. Plus, how would he be able to reach all his family and friends? The only connection to the rest of Norway was the Internet, but that was failing him too. Connections had been slow at camp since he arrived and they only continued to be. Avoiding the windows and walking quietly, he was crawling around his cabin, searching for a usable signal.

The corner by the bed was a good hiding spot, but the signal was intermittent – he hadn't been able to access a stable Internet connection from there for the previous three days. Without thinking, he grabbed one of the beds and lodged it up against the door. The center of the room had worked before as a spot for Internet connection but that seemed like unprotected territory now. He peered out the window but could see no one. Finally, he inched his way to the hinged side of the doorframe. He refreshed the Web browser on his phone, hoping for a strong enough signal from his new hiding place.

Five minutes passed. His brow and palms were sweating profusely and his heart pounded. He stared hard at the two-inch screen while shaking the device impatiently, mouthing the words *c'mon, c'mon* ... He could hear gunshots in the distance – *crack, crack, pop* – and people running around yelling to go into hiding. He tried to remain as still as possible, trying not to think about what was happening just meters away. He did not want to make any false moves. Ten minutes passed ... He tried to remain calm to catch the precious signal. *C'mon, c'mon, work!* After he'd been crouched for fifteen minutes, the progress bar fully loaded. *Finally!* The connection got stronger and stronger as that familiar blue-and-white screen appeared. He quickly scanned his Facebook news feed, looking for updates on the situation. Several messages were desperate calls for help, giving details of their location and the horror they were witnessing. Most were attempting to contact authorities: "OMG *there is a shooting at Utøya,*" "I see *people swimming,*" "I see *people dead,*" "I am hiding, *please send help. Please send help!*" "*Please call the police,*" "I am in the school cabin,*" "I am hiding in the toilet, with *others, please send help!!!*"

It appeared that the news media had not been covering the story yet. Surely they would, once more information was made available, but fearful of causing more panic he chose not to post anything about his seemingly safe hiding place just yet. Campers across the island had updated Facebook saying that the shooter was dressed as a police officer. *Good to know.*

22 July 2011 @ 18:10

Several minutes had passed before the news media finally picked up the story, but it had felt like an eternity. The room was getting stuffy and the gunshots were more frequent. At that point, Jørgen had made a conscious decision to let his friends and family know he was okay, at least for now. The decision of updating via Facebook over Twitter was an easy one. While his Facebook page was full of friends and his large family, his Twitter connections were mostly journalists, who were incessantly trying to contact him while he was hiding. By this time they, too, had heard about all the shooting at Utøya. He didn't want to deal with their questions or risk having their alerts make too much noise. He began to type, sharing his status with his Facebook friends:

> I am ok and safe. Will keep FB updated
> July 22 at 18:43 via facebook mobile
> 120 likes like this.
> 44 comments.

After posting, he decided to send a separate text message to his mom. Almost instantly, friends in Bodø began liking and commenting on his status, including Joakim Sennesvik, Veronica Christiansen, and Stian Hiis Bergh, members of the young Conservative Party and his opposing candidates for the county election that was only weeks away. Within moments forty-four people had commented, asking if others were okay, and sending prayers and love his way. It appeared Norwegians everywhere were glued to their Facebook newsfeeds. Hoping to get some more information about the situation, Jørgen continued to try and access news websites. Although he was able to keep the connection to Facebook from his spot next to the doorframe, the standard news websites were giving him trouble. Facebook required only a fraction of the bandwidth that the other websites took in order to load. His go-to news site, vg.no, was just not going to work this time. *This is getting me exactly nowhere*, he thought. Across the island a few campers were continuing to update from the forest and from other cabins, others from the beach. He read that some of his friends there were still safe. *Thank God.* He read that several people were swimming to get away in the freezing water, and there were messages that instructed people to get into *any* boat that was off the coast. Text messages were flying back and forth between his friends and the campers hiding for their lives. Inside the main cafeteria building, six campers were hiding in each of the bathroom stalls, with at least one device connected to Facebook. Quickly doing the math in his head, it seemed that about 150 people at the camp were connected to Facebook at this very moment. Brothers and sisters, boyfriends and girlfriends of campers, all were starting to post updates too. News was spreading on Facebook about who was safe. *But what about those who weren't?*

24 July 2011 @ 08:00

Buzz … buzz … buzz.

Jørgen reached over to his phone at the edge of the bed, only on this morning he was awake even before the alarm went off. *I am so lucky to be alive*, he thought. As he had done hundreds of Monday mornings before, he opened his Facebook. He noticed the new group immediately, as many of those in his social network had joined. Someone had started a group suggesting a march in Oslo for the victims of the attacks. Jørgen clicked the icon to join the group. He scrolled through the rest of his news-feed, and then checked the AUF group page. He could hardly believe his eyes: 36,369. *Is that right?* Although still in a bit of shock he realized why the number was so high. Many people were astonished, angry, and crestfallen at the attacks and wanted to support each other somehow. Joining the AUF Facebook page was one way for them to do so. Realizing he hadn't noticed the number of people who had agreed to join the march in Oslo, he returned to that group page: *60,000?!*

While staring at the screen in amazement, he noticed the red flag in the corner of his Facebook, signaling that he had messages waiting. This would be the case for weeks to come; his camp friends leaned heavily upon one another trying to process the attack. While the country, his co-workers, family, and friends provided huge support, it was only his friends at Utøya that truly understood what he had been through – *what they all had been through*. The attack had happened so fast, the evacuation so swift, that the only way to get in touch with his camp friends, from all over the country, was through Facebook. His friends would spend hours chatting through private messages about their mixed emotions: anger, sadness, gratitude, and fear. The strongest connections he made, and the strongest support he received, was through the very medium that quite possibly saved hundreds of children's lives. It was clear, the technology continued to impact lives in the aftermath.

His inbox was also flooded with event invitations for memorial walks in over thirty municipalities in Norway, as well as friend requests from campers all over the island, some of whom he had met and some he hadn't. Additionally, a private Facebook page had been created for the survivors of the attack on Utøya. It was only here that the campers could talk each other through the tragedy and coordinate future meet-ups, including the return to Utøya in August. Jørgen was looking forward to taking back the island. Citizens from all over Norway were coming together in Facebook groups to show their solidarity, and his hometown of Bodø was no different. In a few days, he would march for the country of Norway and his friends who were no longer with him.

27 July 2011 @ 19:00

It was a clear night and the march began promptly at 19:00. Jørgen walked to the starting location with his arm around his mom. The procession began near the middle school and would finish near the town hall in the center of his hometown. He saw everyone – his old teachers, his neighbors, his coworkers, his barber, his barista, his postman, his friends. The march continued for three kilometers, mostly in silence. He would forever remember the shuffling of the thousands of feet that night, approximately 15,000 mourners, in a town of 50,000 people. He stood tall and carried a bright, burning torch while his mother held three beautiful, long-stemmed red roses close to her chest. She had tears welling in her eyes, but was staying strong. He was proud of her. As the duo walked closer than ever, thousands of people – babies, mommies, families, tourists, and dogs, in rows of a dozen or more – continued to join and fill the entire width of the street carrying candles, Norwegian flags, and flowers of all kinds. Jørgen smiled and nodded his head solemnly when he spotted a group of visiting researchers from the University of Texas, whom he had been interviewed by only weeks earlier about the upcoming county elections. They, too, had come out to show their support.

Marchers gathered for a beautiful concert where a few of his friends performed while the Norwegian flag flew at half-mast in the chilly wind. The crowd was still and somber, raising thousands of red, yellow, and white roses high in the air. Heartfelt speeches were made and salutes were strong, especially for two of Bodø's very own losses. Smartphones captured the scene, and images were shared from Norwegian Facebook and Twitter pages with people all over the world who were watching the event. *Who would have thought that one guy could have organized such an outpouring of support with a Facebook group?*

As the midnight sun began its temporary descent behind the mountains in the High North, the weather turned cooler and the leaves began to blow. As he zipped up his navy blue Helly Hansen fleece and as the last prayer was made, he said to himself, *We will be stronger than ever. We will show that hatred is not a force we want. AUF is a big family, and we'll forever be each other's brothers and sisters. We will use that to build the society we want. There is some legacy to those we have lost, and we shall fight for the society they believed in.*

19 Doubly disadvantaged

Ethnic and gender bias in Norway's engineering sector

Matthew S. McGlone, Bodø Graduate School of Business

Nasrin's[1] résumé boasts a bachelor's degree in physics (with distinction), master's degrees in both industrial engineering and robotics, and management experience at a prominent Norwegian construction firm in Oslo.

But when she tried to raise money for a nanotech start-up she co-founded in 2007, she recalled one venture capitalist frankly telling her it didn't matter that she hadn't yet made up business cards, because any serious investor in Norway would see her Pakistani name and politely pass.

Another financier invited this tall, attractive, second-generation Pakistani–Norwegian woman, then in her early 30s, to discuss the matter over lunch at the Royal Norwegian Yacht Club in Oslo. Flattered, she agreed, but changed her mind a few minutes later after he flashed her a picture of himself standing at the helm of his own yacht, nude and aroused. When a third potential backer learned she's a biking enthusiast, he seemed less curious about her business plan than about how Pakistanis prevent their *kameez* – traditional long tunics that Nasrin herself rarely wears – from getting caught in the spokes.

Not one of more than twenty firms she pitched was inclined to finance her company. Disappointed but not defeated, she asked Vytek, her Polish-born co-founder, to try his luck. Though an introverted electrical engineer with only passing proficiency in Norwegian and a flimsy grasp of finance, he managed to secure the necessary capital that his natively fluent, former executive of a partner could not. Vytek thought that sexism had hindered her fundraising efforts, but Nasrin thinks her ethnicity was the bigger obstacle.

"In truth, both might have worked against me," she concedes, then quips, "Brenton Wood would say that I am a two-time loser." I miss the allusion, but let it pass, content to simply enjoy Nasrin's fluent English, which she delivers with an exotic blend of Subcontinental and Nordic accents.

Nasrin and I are chatting about her work experiences over coffee at an out-door café in Tromsø. It's a cloudy, cool day in early August. She moved here six months ago after her nanotech start-up in Oslo went bust, a victim of "industrial espionage," she says, declining to elaborate. Nasrin was drawn here in part by an attractive offer from a subsea engineering firm to conduct research on "well integrity" – that is, maintenance and safety in underwater oil-drilling operations. The other draw was her older sister Rezeya, an IT specialist at a local hospital.

Although they are native Norwegians, Nasrin and Rezeya are among only a few hundred people of Pakistani descent in this High North municipality of 70,000. Throughout the country, however, Pakistanis constitute the third largest minority group, surpassed only by ethnic Poles and Swedes.

Rezeya has accompanied Nasrin to our coffee date because she said it would be "scandalous" if anyone in their small ethnic local community were to see the single Nasrin alone with me. The two women pair up well; in fact, they could pass for fraternal twins, physically and behaviorally. Neither sister is an observant Muslim, although both occasionally attend functions at the Islamic Centre of Northern Norway downtown. They also proudly trumpet Tromsø's possession of *Alnor Senter*, the northernmost mosque in the world. Rezeya's Caucasian husband, a onetime Lutheran missionary who lost his faith and learned carpentry, recently did some grout and tile repair in the mosque. But neither Rezeya nor Nasrin has ever been inside, despite being encouraged to visit by its moderate imam.

Both sisters are smoking while we sip our coffee in the café courtyard, and nervously look down and hide their cigarettes under the table when people pass by. "We don't want to be recognized," Rezeya says, "because what we are doing is, well, prohibited."

"That's too strong," Nasrin corrects. "It's considered *improper*. But many Pakistani girls do it. And drink alcohol too. Of course *that* is truly prohibited by the older generation. They see it as unforgivable." She later admits to "accidentally" sipping a beer at university, but claims to have never developed a taste for it.

I find their jumpiness about being recognized and preoccupation with proper behavior as perplexing as it is endearing. These are not "traditional" Pakistani women by any means. Neither attends mosque. Both work outside the home in stereotypically male professions (engineering, IT) that demand frequent social contact with men not of their kin. The older sister is married to a man who is neither Pakistani nor even a Muslim, but instead a Nordic non-believer. She is in her mid-30s and has no children. Nasrin, although of marriageable age, is single and has no plans to marry. And they both agreed to meet with a perfect stranger – an American and a male stranger at that – at an outdoor café in the middle of town to discuss their work experiences, over coffee and cigarettes. Given their iconoclastic choices past and present, why would they be so worried about public perceptions and propriety?

When I put this question to them, they laugh nervously and then are silent for several seconds. Nasrin chimes in first. "It's not the perception that bothers me," she says. "It's the gossip."

Rezeya agrees. "That's quite right. Forget what you've heard about Pakistan's passion for cricket. Gossip is the true national sport, and our parents' generation brought it with them to this country."

"Our mother is definitely proud of what my sister and I do and how we live, and our father is tolerant of it," Nasrin adds. "What they cannot abide is knowing that people are whispering about us behind their backs, asking 'Why does Rezeya not have children?' or 'Will no man ask Nasrin for her hand?' Or they over-hear some old crone chattering about us smoking in a café whilst talking to an American man. This gossip gives them great pain, and it pains me to know that."

I'm still puzzled. "Your parents live in Oslo, over a thousand kilometers away. How often do whispers about you up here make it down to your parents?"

"Does your mother not have a phone, sir?" Nasrin prods. "My mother carries hers around in her *hijab*" – the traditional head scarf – "like every other mother in Little Karachi [the predominantly Pakistani enclave of the multicultural Grønland neighborhood where the sisters grew up]. And every day these women are on the phone with their children, chattering about this neighbor's pregnant daughter or that one's ungrateful son. And just about every Pakistani we know in Tromsø has family ties in Grønland."

"Yes!" Rezeya agrees. "Several of the doctors at my hospital grew up down the street from me. My dentist is a dear childhood friend. Half the cabbies in town are our cousins! All of them talk to their mothers every day, and the mothers talk to one another, and then my mother hears a rumor about us doing something prohibited."

"Improper," Nasrin again corrects.

The cabbie cousins have followed in the footsteps of their fathers, who immigrated to Norway in the early 1970s. At the time, Norway itself was following the lead of other European countries by importing cheap, unskilled laborers for its most menial tasks. The sisters' father and his four brothers were among several planeloads brought over from Lahore to work sanitation details. After injuring his back, however, their father turned to taxi driving, and eventually all of his brothers joined him in a trade that may have been less strenuous but required longer shifts.

The sisters recall listening to their father and uncles bitterly complain about the monotony of days spent shuttling between Fornebu (the principal international airport in Oslo for many years, replaced by Gardermoen in 1998) and downtown Oslo, and about their shabby treatment by travelers. "Tourists come to Norway expecting to see blond, blue-eyed Vikings, and were dismayed that their driver was a brown man with a thick foreign accent," Nasrin recalls. "Many of the natives were dismayed as well, at least in the 1980s."

As I later learned in my research following the interview, a ban on labor migration to the country was imposed in 1975. Until it was lifted in the late 1980s, it temporarily brought the growth of the Pakistani community to a halt. Since then, the growth has been driven chiefly by in-country births and family reunifications, the rules for which remained relatively lax even during the ban.

The Pakistani community in Norway is in a special position not only because it is the largest non-white immigrant community, but also because it was the first. Since the ban was lifted, the migration flow has consisted mainly of refugees from war-torn or politically authoritarian societies such as Somalia, Vietnam, Iran, and Sri Lanka. These communities are still quite insular. In contrast, thousands of ethnic Pakistani children have grown up in Norway, speak the language without an accent, and consider themselves Norwegians.

These circumstances pose some new challenges, though, for the construction of Norwegian nationalism, not to mention the integration of immigrants into Norwegian society.

Until the 1990s, the country had been geographically and economically marginal and relatively isolated. Apart from the indigenous Sami in the High North, the population was considered – and considered itself – homogeneous. In fact, the entire trajectory of Norway's national development, as it evolved from the late nineteenth century until its independence from Sweden in 1905, emphasized the indivisible nature of the country's populace.

Norwegian nationalism also continues to be oriented toward a pastoral mythology. The indigenous traditional peasant is portrayed as the archetypal Norwegian, and although four-fifths of the population now lives in urbanized areas, Norwegians still portray themselves as an essentially rural population of peasants and fishermen. This kind of national identity, which stresses continuity with the past and the rural way of life, is not obviously compatible with an urban minority of Urdu-speaking Muslims.

Nonetheless, the Norwegian government has pursued a straightforward policy of assimilation vis-à-vis the Pakistanis and other immigrant groups. Their integration into the labor market has been taken for granted; they did come here to work, after all. Their children attend ordinary Norwegian public schools, although some concessions have been made over the years by granting them a few classes in Urdu. In general, a successful Pakistani, according to the values of the majority, is a "Norwegianized" Pakistani.

Nasrin and Rezeya surely surpass this criterion for success. They are secular Muslims, they speak Norwegian fluently ("better than Urdu," claims Rezeya), they are highly skilled workers in the country's rapidly expanding technical professions, and they express great loyalty for their country as well as contentment with the High North municipality they call home. However, they also regret the bias against them that they perceive in the job market, although the unflappable Nasrin philosophically characterizes it as a "disadvantage" of her ethnicity rather than "discrimination."

"Norwegians prefer to hire people who look like them, like anywhere else in the world," she explains calmly. "In Pakistan, employers prefer people who look like them, too. But the employers who fail to see beyond my appearance are not those I want to work for anyway. The ones who make a genuine effort to appraise my skills and assess my personality tend to like me, and those are the employers I seek."

Both sisters credit their choice of technical professions as "shielding" them somewhat from the prejudice experienced by many ethnic Pakistanis in the Norwegian workforce. "My degrees, skill sets, and experience are what get me interviews," Nasrin says, "because there are not that many with the combination I have. If I am invited to interview and it is conducted professionally, then I have a good chance [of being hired]."

I remind Nasrin of the rather unprofessional interactions with financiers she had told me about earlier. "Ah, well, the wealthy are a different matter altogether," she says. "The people I encounter every day – engineers, chemists, construction managers, office workers, neighbors, diners in this café – I don't think so many of them are racists. Working and living with us shows them that we are not so different. But the wealthy rarely mingle with the minorities, especially the Muslims. So they still don't think of us as genuine Norwegians."

Nasrin's generalizations are based on personal experience, but there is research that partially corroborates her claims. In 2008, sociologist Anders Vassenden at the University of Bergen published an interesting study on how contact with minority ethnic groups influences Norwegians' attitudes toward them. Among the working class, Vassenden observed the typical pattern of contact-based attitude change – that is, working-class Norwegians expressed more positive attitudes toward minorities after having them as neighbors. Thus "working and living with" ethnic minorities appears to generally soften working-class sentiments toward these groups, as Nasrin suggested. Curiously, however, Vassenden found just the opposite trend among highly educated, wealthier Norwegians: they tend to express more negative attitudes toward minorities after having them as neighbors.

Vassenden attributes these contradictory trends to the nuancing of simple group-oriented attitudes that contact may bring about, a phenomenon he calls "double discrediting." Less educated working-class Norwegians start out with little knowledge about minorities and a reflexive prejudice against them as "others," meaning "different." But living close to minorities teaches them that these groups value family and hard work just as they do, resulting in a softening of their prejudice. In contrast, more educated Norwegians, taught an "enlightened" cultural relativism in school, initially view minorities as culturally different but nonetheless equal. After actual contact, though, they tend to focus on the *differences* between a minority's culture and their own – language, religion, rituals, social structures such as caste systems, and the like – which in turn qualify the multicultural pieties they had been taught. Thus contact with Pakistanis and other ethnic minorities serves to promote greater cultural tolerance among some Norwegian classes but undercut it among others.

Given that I had asked Nasrin and her sister to discuss their work experiences, I fully expected the topic of employer bias to come up, but expected to hear more about gender than ethnic discrimination. That expectation reflects my experience in the United States, where Asian ethnic groups (Chinese and Indians as well as Pakistanis) are overrepresented in technical professions and women are grossly underrepresented, relative to Caucasian males. In Norway, women are underrepresented in technical professions as well, but the government identified this disparity as a problem over a decade ago, and has since taken significant steps toward fixing it.

"Oil helps, but women are the key to Norway's prosperity," asserted Mie Opjordsmoen, President of the Norwegian Confederation of Trade and mother of two, in a 2011 press statement. "Norwegian women work, pay taxes, and have babies. That's our secret." This union leader's confidence reflects a government policy of *state feminism*, in which gender equality in the technical professions is seen as a national competitive advantage. By law, 40 percent of Norwegian boardroom seats are filled by women. Two male cabinet members at the time, Knut Storberget, the justice minister, and Audun Lysbakken, the minister of equality (a position with no counterpart in the U.S. or most of Europe), recently took several months off to look after newborn children. When they went back to work, they could take advantage of state-subsidized child care with a price cap of 60 Norwegian Kroner (~$10) per day.

Oil helps make these subsidies possible, as union leader Opjordsmoen concedes. But the Scandinavian success story can't be pegged simply to lucrative natural resources. After all, Sweden, Finland, and Denmark have no significant fossil-fuel reserves to exploit, but still have thriving economies. Scandinavia's human resources are the key: the region combines the world's highest female employment rates with some of the most impressive fertility rates among developed countries. Economists credit this combination to the region's ability to weather the global economic crisis with solid public finances and respectable growth, Iceland being the notable exception.

"One Norwegian lesson," claims Jens Stoltenberg, the country's Prime Minister, "is that if you can raise female participation, it helps the economy, birth rates, and the budget." Many Norwegian women work part-time and for the public sector. Approximately 75 percent of Norwegian women work outside the home, compared with 68 percent in the U.S. and 65 percent in the European Union.

Women's impressive workforce participation in the country stems in part from a public policy directed at men. Norway was the first country to invent a "fathers' quota" that since 1993 has reserved a growing part of the yearlong paid parental leave for fathers. In 2011, the quota rose from 10 to 12 weeks. Nine in ten fathers now share parental leave with their spouses, up from just 2 percent only twenty years ago, enabling mothers who have recently given birth to return to work sooner.

Another benefit of the program derives from the peace of mind it provides to young women as they prepare to enter the workforce. Labor analysts speculate that single young women are now more apt to consider careers requiring longer hours and greater responsibilities by virtue of knowing that when they do decide to have children, the government will support the extended work leaves they need to build and maintain their families.

Neither Nasrin nor Rezeya intends to have children and so won't directly benefit from Norway's generous parental-leave program. But Nasrin believes she has reaped indirect benefits from it.

"The women I work with all have demanding careers," she says. "Most of them are also mothers, or soon plan to be. I seriously doubt many of them would be working in my firm if they couldn't get time off for having children. Infant leave is the main reason I have any female peers at all."

Nasrin also credits the program with softening sexist attitudes among her male colleagues. "When fathers take parental leave, it changes them," she says with a grin. "One of my project managers just returned from a 3-month leave to care for his first child, a son. Before he left he was talking about all the things he planned to do while tending to the baby – catch up on his reading, resume his exercise routine, remodel his kitchen, and the like. He achieved none of these things, of course. Caring for the child took up all his time and energy. When he came back to work, he went on and on about how hard it was and how he couldn't fathom how his mother was able to raise five children with so little assistance from his father, an airline pilot who was away all the time. I think that this experience has genuinely changed the way he looks at women."

"Well, maybe women who have babies, dear sister," Rezeya teases. "Not a spinster like you!"

"Yes, you're probably right. He also doesn't care for Pakistanis, I think. So I'm still a two-time loser," Nasrin replies, more amused than bitter, "or so Brenton Wood would say."

Nasrin's self-deprecating humor is charming, but it saddens me nonetheless. The woman I've spent the last two hours chatting with is hardly a "loser." What she has managed to achieve academically and professionally is humbling, especially for someone still in her early 30s. What's more, she achieved these things despite the social stigma attached to her ethnicity and gender, which she minimizes as a mere "disadvantage" that she doesn't bemoan but instead seems rather bemused by. Very curious. I wonder if her levity about the matter stems from the wisdom of Brenton Wood, an unfamiliar name she has now mentioned twice in our conversation. I let it pass the first time, but now inquire: "This Wood fellow, is he a writer?"

Nasrin smiles warmly, embarrassed for me. "No, Brenton Wood is a singer. An American singer, in the '60s. Of the Motown school, I believe. My girlfriends and I sing his songs all the time. 'Two-Time Loser' is my favorite, but he recorded many others too. You know 'Oogum Boogum,' perhaps?"

She pronounces the title slowly, elongating the initial syllables (*oooo-gum boooo-gum*); she's probably just trying to pronounce it precisely, but I still feel implicitly insulted. Yes, I do know this song, and feel stupid for not initially recognizing a singer from my own soil. Attempting to reclaim some dignity, I try to put her on the spot: "Oh, sure! I know 'Oogum Boogum.' But I don't recall that first song you mentioned. Can you sing it for me?"

Nasrin briefly glares at me, then looks nervously from side to side, then stubs out her cigarette. She closes her eyes, opens her mouth, and starts to sing softly. Rezeya joins in on the second verse. They sing beautifully together.

Note

1 Nasrin is a pseudonym.

References

Bennhold, K. (2011, June 28). Working women are the key to Norway's prosperity. *The New York Times*, p. A8.

Vassenden, A. (2008). *Flerkulturelle forståelsesformer: En studie av majoritetsnordmenn i multietniske boligområder*. Universitetet i Oslo, Oslo.

Part VI

Mayors by surprise

20 The Indian bride who became deputy-mayor of Røst

Preeti Mudliar, Bodø Graduate School of Business

Harjeet Kaur Jassal
Photograph by Harjeet Kaur Jassal

As an undergraduate student in India, Harjeet found herself so fascinated with political science that she elected it as her major. Some of her course work, naturally enough, involved closely studying her country's constitution and political structure. But as interesting as those topics were to her, they had to remain a purely academic interest, for like most other young women her age growing up in a small town in India, she was essentially in a marital holding pattern, awaiting the inevitable match that her parents would arrange for her when it was time for marriage. Her studies were simply a way to add to her attractiveness as an accomplished young girl of marriageable age. Harjeet's practice of politics was thus limited to the times when her fountain pen would furiously scratch across the ruled sheets of foolscap paper during her three-hour-long final exams.

Yet, life has the strangest ways of making us marvel, in retrospect, at the clear tunnel it has provided for the journey from our past to our present. In Harjeet's case, the tunnel that led her from those classes in college to the Harjeet of today ends on the island of Røst, the southernmost point of the Lofoten archipelago in the High North region of Norway. While she bustles in the kitchen of *Fiskarheimen Havly* ("Fisherman's Lodge"), where she's the manager, Harjeet often thinks back to her native India and how the textbook politics that had remained shut within her were gently coaxed open on a remote island just 5 km^2 in area.

Here, in 2003, Harjeet, despite never once campaigning, managed to win the maximum number of individual votes for election to her town council. More wondrous still, she was then asked to serve as deputy-mayor of the Røst *kommune* (local municipality). This event, along with her Indian passport, propelled her straight into the national limelight in Norway. It is not every day that a woman from the land stereotypically known for its elephants, snake charmers, royal maharajas, and grinding poverty can enter a municipal election in a foreign country and win by acclamation. "I was suddenly dealing with television crews and giving sound bites, and it was all very bewildering for me," she recalls.

To understand her bewilderment, let us rewind a bit. Going back to the start slides us back on the timeline, changes our geography, and introduces us to a new protagonist. This is because, unbeknown to her, Harjeet's ascension to the post of deputy mayor had been set in motion by events that occurred many years earlier.

These events begin in the fertile alluvial plains of northwestern India, in the state of Punjab. There, in the small city of Ahmedgarh, a father angrily tore up the admission letter that his 18-year-old son, Kulwant, had secured to an art school. The year was 1971, and like most Indian fathers, this father nursed white-collar dreams for his son. He himself was a tailor, but for his son he wanted better, in fact nothing less than an MBBS degree. That would turn his son into a medical doctor professionally and into a revered god-like figure socially. But the son, dreamy yet strong-willed, was more inclined toward the arts. He liked using his hands, but they were not meant for the discipline of precise incisions inside operating rooms. Instead, he wanted to draw and sketch. He wanted to bend strips of cane and weave beautiful baskets out of them. He wanted to press leaves of the peepal tree between pages and use their fragile translucence many months later to spray paint designs on sheets of paper.

And so it happened that when Kulwant picked up the pen to write, he did a better job with his application to art school than with the pre-med exams that his father made him take. It is not hard to guess what happened next. The postman delivered two sets of envelopes to their home one day. One set carried the news of his failing the pre-medical entrance; the other delivered the validation of his artistic potential. Enraged, Kulwant's father tore up both envelopes and went back to joining the strips of cloth under the sewing machine that kept their home fires burning.

For days Kulwant wandered around town dejected and nursing feelings of guilt. Though pained with having let down his father, he still wanted to believe in his natural abilities and follow his dreams. The close-knit ties that characterize Indian families also keep the gossip grapevine perpetually warm. And soon, a relative working in the Indian embassy in Tehran, Iran, heard of the "black sheep" that was not toeing papa's line. "Send him to me for a few days. The change will do him good," said the relative to the father. The father looked at Kulwant and packed him off to Tehran hoping that foreign shores would lead to better prospects for his son.

That was the first time Kulwant left India. The journey that took him to Tehran would eventually end in Norway on the island of Røst where he now lives. In 1994, giving in to his family's constant nagging, Kulwant decided to get married. His parents chose Harjeet. She was 18 years his junior, but in the tradition of Indian marriages she obediently followed the path her parents picked for her, unwavering in the belief that they knew best.

This story is as much Kulwant's as it is Harjeet's. If Harjeet's journey to Norway was emblematic of the traditional Indian woman dutifully following her husband's lead wherever, then Kulwant's journey to Norway is emblematic of a young man's rebelling against an imperious father and boldly charting his own destiny in the outside world. In Kulwant's case, this adventurism proved quite literal. So in the telling of Harjeet's story, we find embedded many stories: of a young man's rebellion, of sailing far across unknown seas, of an Indian marriage, of a young woman who left behind her comfortable homeland in order to build a new home in a new land, and, most importantly, of an island in the High North of Norway – a country halfway across the world where the couple continues to live with their three children. How did this happen?

Let's go back to Tehran. Here, Kulwant found employment as a dye fitter in a car-manufacturing plant. He wasn't unhappy. He was working with his hands, so he enjoyed the hands-on aspect of his trade. Moreover, he was acquiring a particular skill through the training that his job provided. And his relative, with whom he was staying, was proving pleasant company. Tehran, too, in the 1970s was a merry place to be. Kulwant, with little to complain about, felt content. He would write regularly to his father and would receive his letters through the official attaché of the Indian embassy. There was a set pattern to their communication. His father would generally enclose letters to Kulwant and his cousin in a single envelope and the two would respond in kind, enclosing both their replies in a return envelope. But one day Kulwant's sharp eye noticed that for the first time his father had used separate envelopes for the letters. Kulwant knew his father well. Despite all their conflicts over a son's suitable career path, Kulwant speaks with gleeful delight about the friendship he shared with his father. "My mother would often scold him," he recalls. "He would forever be asking me about girlfriends and my relationships, and my mother thought that these conversations were wholly inappropriate for a father to have with his son."

The two envelopes alerted Kulwant to the fact that his father was again plotting a plan that might be less than palatable. Self-preservation dictated that he sneak a peek at the letter addressed to his cousin. Aha, he was right! His father wanted him back to help with their tailoring business. Kulwant cunningly decided to pretend compliance. In a scene that was played out many years later as a father–daughter conversation in the cult Hindi film *Dilwale Dulhania Le Jayenge* ("The Braveheart Will Take the Bride") – one of the biggest hits of Hindi cinema ever – Kulwant made an emotional appeal to his father. "Let me please go see the world once," he pleaded. "I am young and there is no better time for me to visit Europe. I have saved enough money and I can fund my trip there. I will return once I have had some fun." The time he spent in Tehran had given Kulwant a taste of life abroad. He was in no mood to return to provincial Ahmedgarh. Assisting his father in the business would mean cutting and sewing pieces of cloth. It seemed a dreary way to spend the rest of his life.

And so, upon getting his father's blessing, Kulwant set forth to Europe. He spent four months hopping from place to place only to arrive nearly penniless in Switzerland. Wiring home for fresh funds was not an option. It would mean giving up his location, and Kulwant was not prepared to reveal his whereabouts. Fortunately, his social gregariousness came to his rescue. He met a prosperous Swiss family of four who were road-tripping across Europe, and they were needing a person to drive their caravan. Would Kulwant like the job? Yes, he would. For Kulwant, the deal was heaven-sent. He was offered lodging, boarding, and a small amount of money, so he could continue traveling without having to worry about where his next meal would come from or where he would sleep.

Country-hopping through Europe, Kulwant at last reached Athens. Here, he had to bid the family goodbye. By now, it was 1975 – four years since he had left India. What next?

Well, one good thing about being an Indian is that you can find a compatriot in any corner of the world. Greece was no exception. After all, if there could be an Indian on a 5 km^2 island above the Arctic Circle, Greece was bound to have an Indian presence too. Kulwant soon made friends with a group of young men from the motherland. They, too, had left home for various reasons and were now trying to figure out a good way to subsist. Through contacts, they learned that an agent could fetch them jobs on a ship for a sum of $200 US per head. Done! So Kulwant joined them and clambered aboard the ship. The job also gave him the confidence to write to his family. Sailing the world's oceans, he was now sure of having escaped any overbearing expectations his father may have had of him. Kulwant was truly his own man now.

Kulwant takes great delight in telling his story. He enjoys the life he has led and prides himself on having survived solely on his wits. His eyes twinkle and he laughs as he throws his head back while recounting his many adventures. His travel also serves as a commentary on the times of yore. He asks rhetorically, "Do you think you would be able to hoodwink your parents the way I did in *this* day and age?" For Kulwant, technology is the enemy of many younger Kulwant-wannabes across the globe. Shaking his head, he answers his own question: "One swipe of a credit card and you will be tracked down." With one finger on his chin he adds, "Can you shake off your social network on Facebook? Can you stop using your cellphone? Even if you want to do without modern communication technology, can you? The world today is not built to function without these tools. You have to use [the technology], and the moment you do, you give up yourself." With a wicked glint in his eye, he challenges me: "Try it." And winks.

While sailing on that ship, Kulwant recalls visiting almost every port in the world. And then he arrived at the U.S. "You cannot reach America and not pay your homage," he says, laughing. So Kulwant decided to be dramatic and contribute to becoming part of the Great American Dream. While sailing the Great Lakes he jumped ship in Wisconsin by simply not returning to it on its departure day.

Fascinated with the adventurous life he was unfolding for me, I pressed him for details. How on earth did you accomplish this? Working on the ship surely meant surrendering your passport to the captain, right? Whenever anybody jumped ship, the captain would merely hand over the passport to the local police so that the errant sailor could be caught and extradited, right?

That's correct, Kulwant says. "You [also] need the passport if you have to leave the country," Kulwant reminded me. "And how long can someone survive without money?"

But not to worry. This was Kulwant. And this was America. The land of gold-paved streets. The land of opportunities. The land of freedom and liberty. He might just have found the port of his calling. Yet, wasn't being an illegal alien pushing the boundaries of adventure? Not really. Kulwant explains the convenient way that American immigration laws were structured back in the 1980s: "Your immigration status and your tax histories were not linked. I did not need a passport to get a job. I got a job legally and paid my taxes just like everybody else. With time, people would get naturalized."

In Wisconsin, Kulwant chose a wholly new business venue to try his hand in: a beer factory. He has fond memories of both it and Wisconsin. "I found people from all over the world there," he recalls. "It was very diverse. It was all beautiful. The women especially." He sighs. Kulwant does not share too many details, though. "Suffice to say that I led the sailor's life. I lived the saying of 'a wife at every port.' I lived it up."

Until, that is, one day when he realized he was humming Hindi film songs a little too frequently. "I said to hell with this job, I want to go home!" he exclaims, and roars with laughter when recalling the expression of the police officer when he walked up to him and demanded his passport back. "The police officer said, 'You are probably the first one I have encountered who, having successfully jumped ship, is wanting to leave the United States of America.' I paid the $20 fine that he demanded and left the U.S."

And returned home.

It had been nearly six years. Father and son had another conversation. Falling into the old pattern, the father asked the son to stay. The son of course refused. "By now it was too late for me to be redeemed," Kulwant remembers. "I told him that if you had to tie me down you should have done that earlier. It is too late for it now." The year was 1982, and Kulwant was now 29 years old. This time around when Kulwant left home, he found company in his younger brother who, fascinated by the elder brother's adventure, wanted to try some of it himself. Kulwant was anxious to shake off his brother as soon as he could. The two of them flew out of India and landed in Bangkok, a relatively cheap city where Kulwant would have time to plot his way forward. He decided to stay there for a couple of weeks to fix his brother up with a job on a ship.

Meanwhile, Kulwant had made up his mind about wanting to put down roots somewhere – somewhere really special. He had two destinations in mind. One was Costa Rica. The other was Anchorage. He says, "By now I had had my fun. I wanted to be someplace peaceful and beautiful. I love nature, and in my travels both Costa Rica and Anchorage had made a deep impression on me."

"Why not India?" I ask.

"You have to go with life's flow. This wasn't so much about the country as it was about familiarity. It's difficult to break the cycle of family and social status no matter where in the world you come from. I love my family and my relatives, but from a distance. If I had stayed in India, I would have been bound by social rules. This is true for any country. If you want to break free of the social rules by which you have grown up, you have to leave."

Since Kulwant had decided to make either Anchorage or Costa Rica his home, he was determined to enter the United States legally this time around. He was also determined not to board a ship again, for he was tired of that life. No, he would fly to some other country and apply for a visa from there. In those days, Aeroflot was the cheapest airline, and it had fares that he could afford that would take him to a place where he knew fellow Indians willing to briefly host him. This place was Norway.

And that is how Kulwant Jassal, now all of 29 years, landed in Oslo. He recalls, "A girl from Ahmedgarh was staying in Drammen with her husband. I got in touch with them and told them that I needed a place to stay until my visa for Anchorage came through." The United States, however, rejected his initial application and advised him to reapply in three months. That meant trouble, for with Norway's high cost of living, Kulwant couldn't afford to be without an income for three months. His friends in Drammen had a suggestion: Why not enroll in a school that would enable him to learn both a trade and the Norwegian language? The very next day Kulwant started making calls to different schools in

Norway. As it happened, the semester was already underway and he feared not getting a seat, but the principal of a vocational school in Rowland, in southern Norway, invited him to join immediately, so Kulwant set off to stay in a dorm, learn shipbuilding, and also learn a new language in a new country.

Not surprisingly, he enjoyed his time in the school – so much so, in fact, that he now considered making Norway his home. But Rowland in the south is still far from the Lofoten islands. How did he get to little Røst?

Kulwant answers: "In Rowland, I realized that I got along fabulously well with people who were from the northern parts of Norway. I found them very open, warm, and friendly. There was a lack of guile in them. Their trust in people was touching. The southerners were a little more strait-laced and closed. I fell in love with northerners and their qualities and decided to give up the thought of going to Anchorage or Costa Rica. It was as if I had found what I was looking for here. From Rowland, I wanted to move up north, so I applied to some more schools so that I could learn the language properly. I got offers from schools in Oslo, Tromsø, and Bodø. However, I was determined to move far away from all Indians. I knew I would never be able to learn Norwegian if there were Indians and Pakistanis around me. We are a very close-knit community here and I would always stay in my comfort zone if I were around them. I wanted to integrate in Norwegian society and settle here, so even though the school in Bodø put me on the waiting list, I still came down here to convince the principal to accept me. Luckily, he did. I continued to learn shipbuilding and the language. I never wanted to go back. I wanted to be in a place that would accept me, and I found that here. It was quiet, peaceful, and the people were wonderful. [Eventually] there was an opening for a job at a shipyard in Røst, and that is how I came to this island. And here I am still, many years later."

The acceptance that Kulwant speaks of from people in the High North is demonstrated in various ways. For instance, one of the jobs that he held was that of the altar server in the church at Røst. He says, "Growing up in India, with so many different religions around you, teaches you secularism. As Indians, we imbibe this from birth. When I came to Røst, I saw the same secularism around me. I have never been questioned about my religion. I happily served as the priest's assistant for a while." Even the current position that Kulwant and Harjeet hold is for a Christian mission. Fiskarheimen Havly was begun by the church to provide refuge to fishermen during the harsh winter season. They still line up during the fishing season in winter, but the lodge remains open year-round for tourists and other visitors.

Both Kulwant and Harjeet stress how their religion was never an issue for any of the Norwegians, either in Røst or elsewhere. Their own religion is Sikhism. Traditionally, Sikhs never cut their hair, it being a symbol of their devotion to God. So the men, for instance, never shave their beards, and they maintain their long hair on top by knotting it in a turban. Many Sikhs today, though, choose not to carry these visible markers of their faith. For Kulwant, maintaining his hair became a dreary chore when he was a vagabond in Europe, and he decided to cut it off in Bulgaria. Harjeet, too, opted for a change. Once in Norway, she found that she wanted to style her hair in a more fashionable way. Her decision upset Kulwant, if only for aesthetic reasons. "It used to be so long and beautiful," he sighs. Both, however, remain proud Sikhs. Traditionally a martial race, the Sikhs are valorized for their bravery, and the community forms an important component of the Indian Armed Forces.

Among the other things that Kulwant is proud of is the social trust that Røst immediately reposed in him even though he was both a foreigner and a bachelor to boot. He recalls that when he took over as manager of Fiskarheimen Havly, young girls of the island would visit him for a chat and their parents would never be worried. "I have been a babysitter and a friend to so many girls on the island. They all knew they could trust me. This is an island with only 600 inhabitants. Everyone knows each other very well."

But that same social trust that was given to Kulwant in Røst turned into a bit of a joke for him during his visits home. With him now pushing 40, Kulwant's friends in India would rib him, saying that as a bachelor he was not fit to be socializing with their wives and young daughters. Kulwant, who had successfully resisted marriage for so long, now began to soften toward the idea of his father scouting for a bride for him. Kulwant's cousin had recently gotten married to a girl from the state of West Bengal, which is as far to the east in India as Punjab is to the west. The family that his cousin had married into, now satisfied with his prospects and lineage, and having themselves a comely daughter with excellent credentials, then offered a marriage proposal to Kulwant's father through him. That girl was Harjeet.

And so they met, and their courtship began. Kulwant tried his honest best to prepare Harjeet for Røst. He told her about the island, about its 600 residents, about how bad the weather could get, about the six months of continuous daylight followed by six months of dark. When he got back to Røst after a shortened wooing, he supplemented his word pictures with picture postcards from the island. In the days before the Internet, those words and those pictures became the slivers that would help her put together her own expectations of the country.

November is hardly the best time to introduce a girl from the tropical climate of India to Norway, but that was when Harjeet arrived in the country as a newlywed nervously fingering the bright red bangles that Punjabi brides traditionally wear. Their first stop was Drammen, where Harjeet wondered why Kulwant was loading up on the rice, spices, and other pulses that are an integral part of Indian cooking. She was soon to discover. It was dark and cold there, and as they set out for Bodø, the weather got progressively worse. In the end, Harjeet and Kulwant found themselves stranded in Bodø for four days, with all transportation and communication to Røst breaking down.

Of her early days, Harjeet recalls that the weather was the toughest to get used to – that, and the food. Accustomed to the spice-laden, aromatic flavors of Indian cuisine, she found the salt-and-peppered, steamed Norwegian fare notably bland and unsatisfying. And feeling periodically marooned on a small island only made everything worse. But, she says, "The situation has improved tremendously. Not only are spices now available, but there is a greater variety in the kind of produce that is there in the markets. Sometimes, Røst gets completely cut off from the mainland. In those days, we would not get any stock of food. It used to be quite difficult."

I ask Harjeet if she remembers the first meal she cooked in Norway.

She smiles. "It was *masoor dal*, rice, and some vegetables. Along with spicy fried green chilies. There was also another Indian who was visiting us from another island. He hadn't been home in 11 years, and he cried when I served him food."

For a while, life continued to remain tough for Harjeet in Røst. It only eased when she returned to Røst from her first trip back home to India. "Things immediately got better," she recalls. "My homesickness was more bearable after that."

I ask her how she socialized herself into Norwegian society.

She says it was thanks to the questions that came her way. Kulwant, with his gregariousness, already had a very strong social circle in place, so "everyone was curious about me. They all knew that Kulwant would be returning with a bride and they all wanted to know me. I was very busy the first few days in Røst paying social visits and receiving neighbors and guests at home." Everything about her was a cause for curiosity. Indian women, especially as newlyweds, are a sight to behold, and there was a lot about Harjeet's appearance that made her neighbors curious. As a Punjabi bride, she was expected to follow tradition and wear her red bangles for forty days. That became a talking point for the island, with everyone agog at the glitter and shine around her wrists. The henna designs on her hands and feet were another talking point, as were her earrings and the big red dot adorning her forehead. One neighbor, puzzled by that dot, actually asked her if she had been shot through the head! Yes, Harjeet indeed was a curiosity.

"Did the Norwegians on the island know about India?" I ask.

"It was mostly about the poverty. That was all they had heard about," she says. "One of the children actually asked me if the water in our taps came from India and if it was safe to drink." Children were Harjeet's first friends. They would often stop by Fiskarheimen Havly to holler hellos to her. She was that adult who would giddily slide down the snow with them on black polythene bags and aim snowballs with devastating precision at their fleeing backs. Today those children have babies of their own and they often drop by for a cup of afternoon tea in the Fiskarheimen Havly kitchen, a sight I witnessed myself during my own visit to Røst.

Not many people on Røst spoke English when Harjeet first arrived. This proved a blessing in the long run, she says. "There were only two people who knew English here. One was the lady in the post office and another was a man who used to work in the lodge. I grew very close to both of them. They are still my best friends to this day. With the rest, I was forced to speak in Norwegian. I did my utmost to learn the language. The children would be my natural allies in this. I would practice what I learned from watching the TV with them. I also enrolled in Norwegian classes for three months in the school here. I was soon speaking fluently. I deputed my two closest friends to constantly correct my grammar. They were a big help to me in picking up the language so quickly."

For Harjeet, the people on the island soon became family almost by default. "It is not as if I had parents here or my siblings with whom I could talk my heart out," she says. "The people on the island became my stand-ins. They assumed the different roles of mother, father, brother, and sisters. In fact, I think that my relationship with them is more genuine because these are not blood bonds. I met these people as a 23-year-old, and we have all grown together through the years." Like Kulwant, Harjeet herself was outgoing. She made it a point to participate in all activities on the island, most of which were voluntary. She says, "The kind of activities here would mostly involve children. Either the church or the local school would organize them and they would always need volunteers to help out. I would attend all of them. I felt that it was a good way to meet people and learn something new."

With every outing, Harjeet was also deepening her roots on the island. She soon became a popular person among the locals. In fact, according to Harjeet, being elected as the island's deputy-mayor is meaningful to her because it formally validated her popularity. She says, "I suspected that people liked me because not only would they come to my help, but would also call me when they needed help. I was running a lodge with three small children. Kulwant also fell very ill at one point and was in the hospital. So, my friend from the post office moved into our house for a month to help me out. Similarly, I was also called on to help folks many times. This symbiosis was very important. It meant that I was accepted as someone who could be counted on. So I knew that I was liked. The day the votes were counted, it was like a formal seal of approval from the island."

Kulwant has never given up his Indian passport, and neither has Harjeet. Their three children, though born and raised in Norway, also hold Indian passports, and the family visits India often. It was during one such all-family vacation there that Kulwant took a long-distance call for Harjeet from Røst. It was a neighbor calling to ask Harjeet's permission to nominate her as a candidate on the voting list for the island's council elections. Harjeet was out making social visits that day, so Kulwant answered on her behalf. "Of course, you can nominate her. She won't mind," he assured the caller. When Harjeet returned, Kulwant mentioned the call, but then they both promptly forgot about it in the holiday spirit of their vacation.

They returned to Røst in late August, and the elections rolled around in October. I ask Harjeet if she campaigned. "No, nobody really campaigns here," she says. "The island is so small and the population is so scarce. We all know everybody. There was no formal campaigning of any kind by any candidate."

The morning of the elections, Harjeet went to the polling booth. She cast a vote, but not for herself. She laughs: "I was very sure nobody would vote for me. So I didn't vote for myself because that would have been the single vote against my name and the whole island would have thought that I voted for myself."

Her vote now cast, Harjeet went home. The elections were hardly on her mind because she figured nothing would come of it. Later, when the phone rang and the caller congratulated her, Harjeet's first thought was, *Did I forget my birthday or wedding anniversary today?*

"Congratulations for what?" she asked.

"Haven't you been listening to the radio?" the caller demanded.

"What happened?" Harjeet still couldn't divine what was going on.

"You have received the highest number of votes on the island!" the caller exclaimed.

Harjeet's confusion turned to incredulousness. Convinced that she was being prank-called, she humored her friend and quickly hung up. But before she had a chance to switch on the radio, the phone rang again. This time it was a journalist. Harjeet was now convinced that something was up, and soon the phone calls turned into a steady stream. The phone rarely stayed on the hook after that.

When the elected members met the next day, the coalition wanted Harjeet to accept the post of deputy-mayor. Røst was receiving a lot of attention in the national press and they wanted to further showcase Harjeet. She herself, though, had doubts. She felt overwhelmed. Moreover, Kulwant was in the hospital with cardiac issues and she didn't know if she could juggle the responsibility of home, hearth, and running the lodge without him. But then Kulwant called from the hospital, encouraging her to accept the post. "He told me to try it for two years and then reconsider it after that," she says. Thus emboldened, Harjeet accepted the position. And that is how the island of Røst was put on the national map for electing an Indian woman as its deputy-mayor.

What happens once the journalists fade away from your doorstep? What happens when the phone stops ringing and the cameras train their flashes on someone else? What do the nitty-gritties of everyday political work look like in Norway?

Harjeet says that the publicity continued unabated in some form or the other for the first two years of her tenure. Not only was she being interviewed, but she suddenly experienced a sudden increase in travel. By this time, the mayor who was elected along with her had been diagnosed with cancer. Harjeet had to stand in for him a lot and the workload was far more than she had anticipated, especially with the travel. She was often away on business to Oslo and other municipalities around Norway.

Two incidents vividly stand out in her mind. Once, at a convocation of women leaders in Italy, she was asked to give a speech on her experience as a woman politician in Norway. For Harjeet the speech was one of the biggest accomplishments of her life. "I am not a big-city girl," she says. "I am from a very small town in India. To stand up in public and speak was a very big deal for me." An even more significant speech was to follow in 2004, in Bodø. There, Harjeet was asked to represent the average North Norwegian. This time, she titled her speech with an intriguing question: "Who Is a North Norwegian?" It was a momentous occasion. Here was a woman who had come from India in 1994, yet just ten years later, she was speaking on behalf of her island and attempting to describe the people who had so warmly welcomed her and made her one of their own.

So who *are* North Norwegians? Here is what Harjeet tells me: "They are some of the most genuine people I have met. What you see is what you get with them. I have never known pretense or sneakiness amongst them. They are warm and make you feel at home instantly. With Southerners, you often feel like you have to break a wall first to get to know them well. With the Northerners, there is none of that. They also have a very quirky sense of humor. Once, a man died on the island and one of his closest friends came here to have tea at the time of his funeral. I was puzzled and asked him why he wasn't attending the funeral. The friend replied, 'Why should I go? Will he be there for mine?' This was his way of coping with his friend's death, but it tells you how resilient they are in the face of life's adversities. The weather can sometimes be harsh on the island, and it is this sense of humor that carries them through such hiccups."

In the execution of her duties, Harjeet credits the other local politicians in Nordland who banded around her and made her feel confident. "They all knew it was my first time," she says. "There were many women politicians who took me under their wing. Each of them mentored me in their own way. I never felt discriminated against or unwelcome during any political event."

Harjeet is most proud of her work helping to prevent drug addiction. It's a common social problem in Norway, and even little Røst hasn't been spared. Given that her own children were of school age, this was a priority for her. She says, "We organized a lot of awareness activities in school. We wanted to catch them young. We made young students write a pledge in which they vowed to abstain from any kind of social vice that would lead to addiction."

I spent a whole day with Harjeet, Kulwant, their three children, and many assorted neighbors who dropped in for their fix of harmless gossip. One of the neighbors was just back from her annual vacation in France and came carrying gifts for all the children. This was an annual ritual for the Jassals and her. The children eagerly waited for their summer surprises and were delighted at what she showered on them. Harjeet mentions how the geography of the place creates a bond between the residents: "Today, I may be the one in need, but you know that tomorrow it could well be you. There is a lot of symbiosis and dependency between each one of us. This is truly my family."

I ask both Harjeet and Kulwant if they miss India. Harjeet confesses that idleness depresses her and makes her homesick, so she strives to keep constantly busy. Kulwant, though – the one who left, nay fled, India and the ties of home out of his own free will – is the one that makes me misty-eyed. He says: "Sometimes I shut my eyes and go wander in the bylanes of the street where I grew up. There is no one there anymore. The people I knew are long gone, the buildings where I played Hide-and-Seek have been razed. Newer ones stand in their stead today, unfamiliar and unlayered with no memories of my own. The place of my childhood exists only in my dreams, but I visit that place very often. India is hardwired into my heart. That disk will only be reformatted in my death. It is my destiny that I can't completely be at home either in India or in Norway. It is the fate of any immigrant. My only consolation is that I love this place and can't think of a better place to live."

Today Harjeet and Kulwant no longer live together. Differences between them have led to a separation, though they remain on cordial terms. Their children – two girls and one boy – range in age from 16 to 10. Harjeet says: "It is the strong social support that I have amongst the people of this island that I can continue doing my work. In India, single women and mothers have it very difficult, but here, Kulwant and I can both lead our own lives and yet be together for the important things. I have great friends and a great community, and I like my life here."

The story of Harjeet and Kulwant ends on the same note after all.

21 First female mayor strikes largest oil deal for dying Hammerfest

Caroline Sinclair, Bodø Graduate School of Business

Kristine Jørstad Bock
Photograph by Atle Espen Helgesen

Fishermen in the High North are a tough breed. They risk their lives to battle the frigid Arctic weather, using heavy, dangerous equipment in often raging seas. Consistently listed as one of the world's most dangerous jobs, deep-water fishing belongs to such men as these – strong, resilient, gruff, hard-working. Actually, this toughness and aptitude for survival runs deep in the bloodline of High North's women, too. That is why Kristine Jørstad Bock's appearance is deceptive. Her slight but athletic figure, smooth skin, forest-green eyes, and bright smile combine to make her a stunningly attractive young woman. But while her looks epitomize feminine kindness, behind those kind eyes she houses a fisherman's soul – the fight, the strength, the directness, the integrity. Her mother instilled these qualities in her from a young age. Proud of the unique heritage of the High

North, her mother had a passion for protecting nature's gifts of land and sea. She understood how vulnerable their people were on a small, yet strategically located, patch of Norway and she felt a deep obligation to protect the future of her countrymen.

Setting a strong example for her daughter, in the mid-'90s Eva Borkenhagen stepped up to become mayor of Kvænangen, the administrative center of Kristine's hometown of Burfjord. The population there, mostly of Sami origin, maintained the long-standing traditions of fishing, hunting, and agriculture. The Sami are an indigenous population who have populated the region for some 5,000 years and have a deep connection to nature. Many still work as fishermen or reindeer herders and continue to imbue the community with Sami values – a deep respect for nature, hard work, and fairness.

By the time Kristine left for college, her mother was one of only a handful of women in powerful positions of politics in the High North. It was no surprise, then, that Kristine went to Varehandelens Høgskole (now called The Norwegian Business School) with a focus on government and politics. Even as a young girl she showed aspirations for community leadership and exhibited no qualms about standing toe-to-toe with her male counterparts. At age 11, Kristine was the only girl to try out for an all-boys soccer team. When the coach told her she wasn't good enough to make the cut, she petitioned to start the first all-girls team in the region. That fight trained her for the battles she would negotiate twenty years later, for much higher stakes.

Around the same time Kristine graduated from college, the Norwegian government began to recognize that women were sorely underrepresented in politics. Norway, reputedly an egalitarian society, knew it could reap substantial benefits from a more diversified leadership team. As a means to achieve a more balanced boardroom, the government implemented a rule that required all boards to have a quota of female representatives. The effort effectively increased female board representation from 9 percent in 2003 to just more than 40 percent in 2009. The political climate was thus ripe for a talented, passionate woman like Kristine, yet she approached a career in politics with caution. While deeply admiring her mother, Kristine also knew what it was like to have a family in the political spotlight. She had married her high-school sweetheart, Ørjan Bock, after seven years of courtship and felt committed to make her family her top priority. She was careful to plan her next steps so that she could maintain a balance that would allow her to be foremost a mother and wife.

In 1995, pregnant with her first child, she moved with her husband to Hammerfest, a town just 250 km north of her hometown. Ørjan had accepted a position at the Rica Hotel where he eventually would be promoted to Director. Kristine became immediately active in the community and in 1999 was elected Deputy Mayor representing the Labor Party. In 2002, she gave birth to a second baby girl. As a new mother, she found that the dual effort of raising an infant while participating in politics proved taxing. Yet she felt secure in her purpose, confident that each component of her life complemented the other. The lessons of motherhood reinforced the compassion and sense of purpose she brought to her work. Through her work she was modeling for her children the importance of civic duty, as her own mother had done for her.

By 2006, Kristine held eleven directorships in local interests, making her a standout in the elite group of women who were now being dubbed the "golden skirts." These women, while granted leadership positions partly because of government mandate, had proven their worth. Reports indicated that the new gender-balanced executive boardrooms were more than 50 percent more profitable than the all-male boards of the past. One of the noticeable impacts was in improved education. Kristine made it a top priority as Deputy Mayor to help the troubled schools in her community recover from the recession which was then oppressing it. "Since I entered politics, I have fought for the armament [funding] of the schools. It is good to be involved in keeping the younger population nurtured," she said when discussing the new care plan and kindergarten level that would be adopted in 2007 with her support. The education issue aligned well with both her family's needs and those of her community. Kristine felt happy and in control. She had created her ideal life, feeling able to take care of her daughters and still contribute to the welfare of her neighbors and her country.

Then, one winter evening in 2006, came news that would change her forever.

Her mother, Eva, had just finished helping Kristine decorate her home with festive Christmas trimmings, including a pine tree decorated with white lights, tinsel, and Norwegian flags. Now they needed to venture out for a quick shopping trip. While waiting outside in the car for her daughter to join her, Eva absent-mindedly grazed a few radio stations. She stopped suddenly when she heard her daughter's name. Somebody was announcing that Kristine, till now the deputy mayor, would become the first female mayor of Hammerfest. Startled, Eva listened intently now as the reporter began filling in the details. Apparently the current mayor, Alf E. Jakobsen, had been called to duty in Oslo and would have to leave immediately to help with a national financial crisis.

Eva turned off the radio, grabbed the keys from the ignition, and headed back into the house only to find Kristine already on the phone with Mayor Jakobsen. But their conversation was over within minutes. Jakobsen had had all he could do to process the news himself. Kristine recalled the conversation: "I immediately called Alf E. Jakobsen. But that was a pretty short conversation, because our other phones began to ring about the same time. We agreed to talk later, but this was very fast."

Kristine felt panic rise in her chest. She had recently missed a briefing on the oil-and-gas situation. Now Jakobsen would be away and unable to instruct her next steps. She mentally steadied herself. She had to gear up quickly and suppress any insecure feelings. As she recalls now: "For three years I have followed Alf E. Jakobsen's tracks. There has been a steep learning curve, which I probably was surprised by the high level of activity that the office has. But his efforts have created wide and great respect for the role of politician, perhaps especially here in Hammerfest. That's my challenge ... to take this further. I'm definitely ready for this." The people of Hammerfest were in a precarious situation. The huge Snøhvit natural-gas field was to open within months in the Norwegian Sea, and the whole world would be looking for Hammerfest to set a good example for High North relations with mighty Statoil. The decisions that would be made in the coming days would prove historic for Norway and the entire High North.

Political interests in the dealings of Statoil and Hammerfest were highly contested and volatile. Kristine knew she had to fight for the region, having been present for all of the negotiations up to this point. She had been a proponent when the Norwegian government approved the efforts to extract oil and gas in Hammerfest, but Jakobsen had been the key decision-maker in those negotiations. This was a multi-billion-dollar international project. It would now fall to her to negotiate a fair deal for the people of Hammerfest. A daunting challenge indeed … She felt giddy and guilty. The thrill of the impending battle shot adrenaline through her body. She took a deep breath. The smell of the fresh pine tree in her living room filled her with the recognition that her family time was about to be severely compromised. She gripped the countertop, shut her eyes, and prayed.

Hammerfest

One of Norway's oldest cities, Hammerfest incorporated in 1789. But nomadic hunters and fishermen had already started inhabiting the area some 9,000 years earlier, a few thousand years after the ice had receded and made the area precariously fit for people and animals. The name "Hammerfest" originates from the Old Norse terms "Hamran," which refers to the many big rocks suitable for mooring boats, and "fest," which means "fastening" – here, for boats. A picturesque town with just 10,000 residents, it could easily be the setting of a fairytale, being carpeted much of the year in pristine powder snow. Arguably the world's most northern city, it's a place where migrating reindeer roam free, even in the downtown city streets, and where members of the local polar-bear club test their bravado in the frigid seas. Traditionally tourism, fishing, and livestock have been the economic mainstays.

The port has strategic importance because it services all points north, east, and west and remains ice-free year-round because of its proximity to the warming Gulf Stream. Much like the rest of Northern Norway, the terrain rises steeply from the coast, providing a stunning view with rich green forests and snow-covered mountains set off against the deep blue ocean. Its houses, many of them painted in cheery primary colors, stand in stark contrast to the wild lands surrounding them. On a trip through town you can find ancient rock carvings, a Sami church, a chapel built by the German friends of peace, one of Norway's longest suspension bridges, and the world's first tidal power station. The oldest still-standing building, a funeral chapel built in 1937, sits aside a small hillside graveyard. In 1890, a fire that began in a local bakery had destroyed more than half of the buildings in town. Many more were lost when Hammerfest, and the rest of Finnmark, was looted and burned by the Germans in 1945 as they retreated during World War II. This was a community accustomed to upheaval, rebuilding, and survival.

By the beginning of the twenty-first century, Hammerfest was again stressed, the economy dismal. The town had slowly declined after a peak in the fishing industry in the 1960s. By the 1990s, with the economy depressed and the town in decay, many young people abandoned hope and emigrated in search of a better life. By 2000, times were even worse. Crime was on the rise, there were fewer and fewer married couples, and the mortality rate outnumbered the birthrate, a stark emblem of the city's decline. With no young families to sustain them, schools were forced to scale down. Grades had to be combined and whole sections of buildings were closed off due to the decreased demand and the town's inability to hire qualified teachers. Those families that remained were there as unwilling hostages to the bottomed-out real-estate market, their homes now worth only half of what they had paid for them. Many businesses had closed, too, and those that remained had little capital left to survive much longer.

But what of the natural resources of oil and gas slumbering deep in the ocean's bed? Kristine felt strongly that Hammerfest's only hope for an economic turn-around was if the town could somehow entice oil-and-gas companies to come in and extract those resources.

Oil and gas

The extraction of oil and gas on the coast of Norway had already begun in the 1970s, triggering a surge in welfare, jobs, housing, transport, research, and education. By the time Kristine took office in 2006, Norway had become the world's tenth biggest oil producer and its third biggest oil exporter behind Saudi Arabia and Russia. About a quarter of the world's remaining undiscovered petroleum resources were said to lie in the Arctic. Global oil-and-gas demands were projected to jump 50 percent over the next 25 years, crystallizing the possibilities for wealth in Norway. Predictions indicated that the United States alone would need to import about 25 percent of its natural gas by 2030, six times its current import rate.

As the oil discoveries further south had started to dry up, gas companies began to seriously consider the High North, despite the huge investment needed to build infrastructure in such inhospitable terrain. Meanwhile, though, some Norwegians still protested the opening of the North to oil-and-gas exploitation. These ardent environmentalists argued that opening the Barents Sea to industry would diminish the environment and scare away the sea life. They feared that the increased CO_2 emissions from the extraction facilities would permanently damage the fragile ecosystem.

Kristine Bock, though sympathetic to environmental concerns and sensitive to the needs of the Sami, felt that the oil-and-gas industry offered her town the equivalent of divine intervention. The reality was, Hammerfest had nowhere else to turn. There were no back-up plans if the government said no to the exploration and extraction efforts of the oil-and-gas industry. She argued vehemently that "Norway should be a driver for the oil-and-gas industry worldwide. We are located in the front with stringent environmental requirements. The oil-and-gas industry provides opportunities for the development of other, renewable energy. We also set standards in the petroleum sector that we know are going on the Russian side of the border." At the same time, she knew that there had to be a good balance between the industry's interests and the financial interests of the people of Hammerfest and its surrounding municipalities. As Deputy Mayor, she had fully supported the initiative for Statoil to build an extraction facility off the coast of Hammerfest, but for a fair price. When the government and Statoil finally struck a deal, she knew that it marked a new beginning, a resurrection for the small fishing community.

Snøhvit

Statoil, the second-largest gas supplier in Europe and the sixth-largest in the world, had actually discovered natural gas just off the coast of Hammerfest way back in 1984. It had then tried to develop a project to access the resources there. It had failed, though. One problem was that the technology had not been suf-ficiently advanced to deal with the harsh Arctic conditions. Also, the market demand was not yet high enough to offset the understandably huge expense of development. But by the early-2000s, all that had changed. New advances in technology could allow for environmentally friendly, cost-effective extrac-tion even in the formidable High North. Demand in Europe had skyrocketed and was projected to grow steadily for the foreseeable future. Statoil was ready to stake a claim. In 2002, the Norwegian government gave it the green light to begin construction on a $10 billion project just 87 miles off the coast of Hammerfest.

The gas field would be named Snøhvit ("Snow White") after the mythical character from the Brothers Grimm fairytale. A technological marvel, it would be the first major development on the Norwegian continental shelf operating with absolutely no surface installations, fixed or floating. The field itself would be built some 250–345 meters below the surface, directly on the seabed, where it would be protected from the ferocious winter storms. The entire operation, consisting initially of nine wells, would be controlled remotely from land. And to appeal to the fishing industry, Statoil guaranteed to make the installations safely over-trawlable.

Statoil selected the nearby small island of Melkøya as the location for its central liquefaction plant. Statoil bought the 247-acre island from a private owner for roughly $1.5 million. It sits about two miles from Hammerfest and is accessible via an underwater tunnel. In this plant, the brew being piped under-water from the seabed field would be separated into components of natural gas, oil, water, and carbon dioxide. The natural gas could then be cooled to −260 °F (−162 °C), shrinking it 600 times and turning it into a liquid that could then be shipped in tankers. As a small concession to environmentalists, Snøhvit would install a special pipe that would capture the carbon dioxide separated from the well stream and send it back down underwater to be stored forever in a sandstone reservoir 8,000 feet below the water's surface.

Melkøya would be the first liquefied natural gas (LNG) facility in Europe and the northernmost one in the world. LNG has the advantage of burning more cleanly than oil, but in the past it had been far more expensive to process. This would be the first Arctic project to tap gas in water depths exceeding 1,000 feet. A gas pipeline would be installed to transport the gas brew from the nine subsea wells in three fields, which could eventually grow to twenty wells. At 143 km, the pipeline would be the longest of its kind in the world. Once operating, it would transfer 20.8 million scm (a meter cubed in standard conditions) of natural-gas liquids and condensate. Statoil would use antifreeze at the well heads and heat up the pipeline electrically to avoid problems that could arise from the high pressure and low temperatures at the seabed. Once the gas was processed, tankers such as *The Arctic Princess* could be loaded every five or six days to transport condensed gas to the U.S. (a twenty-day roundtrip) or Europe (a twelve-day roundtrip). Construction of Snøhvit and the Melkøya plant would take several years and involve more than 20,000 workers. It would be one of the largest industrial projects in all of Europe.

The new mayor in town

When Kristine took over the mayor's office, construction on both the field and processing plant was near completion, but the details of the money distribution were still being negotiated. She knew that the primary means for direct revenue for Hammerfest had to be through property taxes. But right there was the hitch – and it was a big one. For in order to collect property tax from an LNG plant, the municipality must first introduce property tax on *private* as well as commercial property. This meant that the oil company, the fishermen, and the residents alike would incur the tax. If it were too high, it could easily cripple an already struggling small business. A straightforward solution, it seemed, would be to funnel some of the collected tax revenue back to the community in direct and indirect ways.

Ah, but what about the needs of Hammerfest's neighbors?

Hammerfest resides in the state of Finnmark, and the neighboring towns were not about to stand idly by as Hammerfest drained all that liquid gold from the ocean floor. During her first week as mayor, Kristine received over a dozen calls from leaders of those towns, all demanding restitution. Word had spread that Hammerfest was anticipating an influx of 135 million NOK ($23.7 million) from the Statoil deal. It was not fair, they cried, that Hammerfest should reap all the benefits from a shared marine resource. Kristine agreed. Actually, she had never believed that Hammerfest alone should benefit from the business, but she also wasn't willing to give away shares unless there was a mutually beneficial arrangement.

The surrounding municipalities proposed that a fund be set up where all the oil money would be deposited and distributed evenly throughout the region.

On the surface, it sounded fair enough. But was it really? Dealing with that proposal was Kristine's first major challenge as the new mayor. She was the youngest leader in the region; also, the group's only female. She knew people expected her to be weak, to cave under the pressure. She knew, too, that this negotiation would set the tone for her term. And she was well aware of some of the pitfalls associated with such an effort. For example, in Canada, under similar circumstances, the local government was ill-prepared for the sudden deluge of money and jobs streaming into its economy. Lacking foresight, the community leaders allotted most of the money to build infrastructure to support the new workforce. Unfortunately, about the same time that the building of the plant was complete, jobs and consumers left town, leaving the local government in debt and with insufficient consumer demand to support the businesses that had been built.

Kristine knew that getting the first gas field for Hammerfest was only a Band-aid for the wounded economy. To have a sustained economic effect, government research indicated that the town would need to service at least *three* separate oil-and-gas fields. The deal she set up now would influence all future negotiations for the region. How could she spread both the burden and the wealth in a fair manner, but not scare away Statoil? If she came in at a low tax rate, it would benefit both the small business owner and Statoil, but it wouldn't maximize the profits for the region. Also, people would think she was pandering to the oil company's interests. Yet if the tax rate were set at the maximum rate, both Statoil and Hammerfest's citizens would suffer the burden of taxation while the rest of the region would win benefits cost-free. People would also think she was unable to stand up against the pressure from the other regional leaders.

By the end of her first week her head was spinning with all the different special interests involved. Yet she was confident in her position when she sat down and wrote her proposal. It would require Hammerfest to institute the highest possible property tax that the national government allowed. It would also establish a business fund that would hold the money, but the surrounding municipalities would be denied access to that fund unless they, too, raised their tax rate and contributed to the fund. A portion of the money would be earmarked for small businesses throughout the region who could apply for grants from the fund. Additional funds would be allocated to build roads, repair schools, build better nursing homes, and renovate public buildings. In addition, local residents would receive tax deductions on their homes.

It seemed to her a sound proposal, but she was still nervous about its acceptance. Within a week, though, she had received almost unanimous support from the other municipalities with little fanfare. One municipality had initially dissented, but quickly fell to peer pressure upon seeing all the others joining the coalition. Statoil also reluctantly agreed, putting up only mild arguments that Kristine quickly dismissed. She made it perfectly clear to Statoil that she would tolerate no bargaining.

Going home

In the winter of 2009, Alf Jakobsen finished his duties in Oslo and was headed back to town to once again provide mayoral leadership for Hammerfest. It would be like coming home to a new town. For after Kristine signed the deal with

Statoil, each year the business fund had received property-tax income of about 150 million NOK, 135 million of which came from Snøhvit. Since the success of Snøhvit, there were additional plans for two more installations: Snøhvit 2 (a second LNG field) and Goliat (the first oil field in the Barents Sea). Together, the three installations would support a financial ripple effect that could secure the foreseeable future for Hammerfest. The success in Hammerfest garnered global interest in the Barents Sea as a viable investment and natural-energy resource. Goliat alone was projected to bring another 500 jobs to the region and estimated revenues of $60 billion. Statoil had developed a research-and-development program to explore the entire Barents Sea beginning with a two-year drilling program in the Arctic to determine the size of available resources.

Since 2006, Hammerfest has seen a 2 percent annual growth in its population of 20- to 40-year-olds. Of the 25,000 people who worked on Snøhvit's construction, roughly two-thirds were Norwegians, 3,000 of whom were locals; the rest represented more than sixty other nations. The influx of workers had a noticeable impact on the community. Just a decade before, very few households had had any children. By 2009, most homes included two or more children. Kindergartens that had been nearly shuttered were now fully functioning again, and even a new one was being built. The ripple effects from Snøhvit were already quite apparent in Hammerfest. There were more pupils in the classrooms, merchants had more customers, real-estate agents were selling property again, and new building projects were sprouting up across town. Local industrial suppliers doubled and tripled their profits. The town had a heartbeat again and everyone was optimistic about the future.

Hammerfest had become the star of the North, garnering media attention not only in Norway but across Europe as well. Its business negotiations were considered a role model for relations with oil and gas. Citizens began to have pride again in their town. Volunteer rates for community events and political positions were at an all-time high. In addition, industry had attracted a highly educated workforce with a remarkable level of knowledge and competence. This new, educated population would be able to influence the town's future innovation and entrepreneurship. Hammerfest wasn't just surviving, it was thriving.

And the fishermen? Well, they were holding steady. With three trawlers and 120 workers on shore, their industry wasn't near the peak of 1,200 workers that it had employed in the 1970s. Still, no fish factory had ever gone bankrupt in Hammerfest. Also, promisingly, ENI, the Italian multinational oil-and-gas company that was part owner of the Goliat project, had begun to lay out a promising plan to develop a relationship with the local fishing fleet to improve maritime security.

Kristine was proud of the role she had played in the town's recovery. On her last day in office, she packed up her personal possessions and carefully put other things back in order for Jakobsen's return. It was bittersweet. She had learned so much from the challenges she'd faced, but she was also tired. She walked out to her car slowly, carefully. Her third baby was due in just three weeks, making her balance unsteady, and she also had to contend with the ice underfoot, for it was now the darkest part of the winter. The sun wouldn't shine again for another three weeks. A sudden loud boom startled her, punctuated with a huge burst of fire ripping through the black, otherwise silent night. It was hard to get used to, even though it was coming every few minutes these days. The 330-foot high-pressure flame from the processing plant burns off the excess carbon dioxide that builds in the pipelines. She'd heard people say it can be seen from 60 miles away. Only a few weeks ago she had conducted a town meeting after receiving over a hundred complaints about the soot that had coated nearby homes and cars. Since then, local health authorities and the Norwegian Institute for Air Research assessed the situation and concluded there was actually no reason for a health concern.

Even though the cold wind stung her exposed cheeks, Kristine paused before entering the car to gaze out at Statoil's processing plant two miles away. It always reminded her of a fire-breathing dragon with its long neck protruding into the night sky. And then her gaze shifted toward downtown Hammerfest, toward a brightly lit two-story building, the elegant new Arctic Culture Center. For her, it epitomized the rebirth of her community. She gently rested her hand on her pregnant belly and smiled. She had done the best that she could as mayor, in the time she had had and under the circumstances she was given, but now she was ready to go home.

22 The petroleum Renaissance in Alstahaug municipality

Krister Salamonsen, Bodø Graduate School of Business

Stig Sørra
Photograph by Jarle Vines

Sandnessjøen is a small, picturesque port town (pop. 7,361) now doubling as the administrative center of Alstahaug, an archipelago municipality in northern Norway. Though Sandnessjøen has had petroleum activities in its back-yard for decades, oil never had much of an impact there. Historically, its economy centered on fishing, shipping, and agriculture. But when the British oil giant BP announced, in 2007, that it would be developing the Skarv oil-and-gas field off the coast of nearby Helgeland,[1] the entire area began experiencing oil-and-gas fever. Local authorities, eager to participate in the coming boom, started positioning, preparing, and lobbying to ensure that their own municipalities would get their fair share.

That same year, Stig Sørra was elected the new Mayor in Alstahaug. With little experience in politics, and just returning from years of working in southern Norway, he soon realized he'd be steering his municipality into what could be a new era. He faced lots of questions. What are the costs and benefits of this change? What needs to be done? What will this mean for our community?

To learn how he tackled these questions, in early 2007 I made the 350 km journey by plane from my temporary student bachelor quarters in Bodø[2] to the coastal city of Sandnessjøen to interview him.

First encounter

On my way into town, I find myself blinking at a rather surreal sight. Dominating a harbor dotted with leisure boats and fishing vessels is a massive, front-heavy workhorse of a ship, nearly 100 meters long, its blunt bow rising almost vertically to a semi-circular, fully glazed bridge maybe five stories high. The ship's rear two-thirds, meanwhile, are almost comically chopped down closer to water-level and perfectly flat. Altogether, it looks like some marriage of a barge and a tub on steroids. Painted in dazzling emerald green and white, it's hardly shy. In fact, I expect it's visible from almost anywhere in the city. I can't tear my eyes off it. I later learn it's the top-of-the-line offshore supply ship *Bourbon Mistral*, in port waiting for supplies before leaving toward its destination.

But eventually I do and proceed through the quiet city center of Sandnessjøen, where I soon reach the Alstahaug city hall. It's a rather typical '80s-looking building, not really showing signs of hosting a municipality administration. Once inside, I instantly understand the importance of the municipality's coastal tradition. The walls are decorated, gallery-like, with large graphics that chronologically depict Sandnessjøen's evolution from a backwater fishing community to a bustling, diverse slice of modern Norway.

The receptionist gives me a warm greeting and offers me a brief history lesson of the municipality. After first emphasizing the traditional fisheries of which only remnants now remain, she proudly tells me about the development of its now-flourishing petroleum activities.

Minutes later, right on schedule, I'm greeted by the Mayor himself, a well-dressed, polite, and capable-seeming man in his early forties who possesses the charisma of a natural politician. "Welcome to beautiful Alstahaug!" he says, smiling, and conducts me into his office, which reflects a lot of very busy workdays. Documents of all kinds cover his desktop, though still managing to be almost fussily ordered. "Please, I apologize for the mess," he immediately tells me. Mirroring the historical embellishments of the city hall, his office is decorated with still more paintings and pictures of coastal themes. "It constitutes our livelihood, you know," he explains. "Now we hope that the petroleum developments will revitalize this tradition."

Back in the 1980s, he recalls, offshore developments had people thinking that Alstahaug was destined to be the next Norwegian oil hub. With a kind of Klondike mania, both the industry and the community itself basically placed all their bets on preparing for their own version of a gold rush. Yet, due to a lack of exploitable field discoveries, all of these developments came to naught, and the community was left even worse off than before. Its extensive investments, mainly in infrastructure and production facilities, suddenly served no purpose. But optimism in Alstahaug is once again palpable. The Mayor's cell phone rings. "I'm sorry about that," he says, blushing slightly. "The cell phone calling all day long is the reality these days."

National perspective and historic setting

The Mayor modestly tells me that the phone call will occupy him for about ten minutes, so while I'm waiting for him to finish his call, I meditate on what I've learned about the area prior to flying up here.

Until the mid-1960s, Norway was only a very minor player in the global economic landscape. Its economic activities were limited even at home and were mostly confined to domestic markets. Few people had any idea that some events that took place in the late 1960s were to forever change the nation and mark the onset of the Norwegian Oil Era.

On Christmas Eve, 1969, the Norwegian Government got an excited call from Ocean Viking, an exploration rig operated by Phillips Petroleum, announcing its discovery of "Ekofisk," the first exploitable oil-and-gas field on the Norwegian continental shelf. At the time, Norway had scant experience with this industry, but it quickly realized that it needed to establish office buildings, housing, and other infrastructure appropriate to a new European oil province. Stavanger, at the time a small coastal municipality in Rogaland County, was in dire need of new industrial activity and eager to step in. Its politicians and businessmen saw the opportunity to grow their little town, and soon cleared the way for infrastructure development. Success quickly followed. Since the late 1960s, Stavanger has burgeoned into the oil capital of Norway, representing the nation's highest petroleum-related employment density. Statoil, the mighty oil company, mostly government-owned, is headquartered there.

Actual production at Ekofisk got underway in 1971. Since then, oil valued at about NOK 9000 billion has been extracted from the Norwegian continental shelf (NCS). Thus, the shift in Norway's fortunes during the last five decades can largely be traced to its vast offshore natural resources. In 2010, some seventy fields on the NCS were busily producing 230.4 million scm of oil equivalents – including oil and natural gas – making Norway one of the largest producers and exporters in the world. That 2010 production accounted for more than 21 percent of the total national value creation, and represented a major contribution to the nation's direct and indirect employment (http://www.npd.no/Global/Norsk/3-Publikasjoner/Faktahefter/Fakta2012/Fakta_2012_web.pdf).

But Norway is now looking at diminishing resource bases. Both production and the pace of new discoveries in established fields in the North Sea have passed their peak, so the prospects for sustained offshore activities are now centered on petroleum developments still further north.

Regional setting

The evolution of Norwegian petroleum developments has led to a dramatic rise in the country's national welfare. But these activities have congregated around the North Sea in south and southwestern Norway. Meanwhile, petroleum activities off the coast of northern Norway have experienced rapid ups and downs. Extensive exploratory drilling there in the early 1980s resulted in a flourishing optimism in the Helgeland region, especially, but the optimism soon turned to dismay when drilling activities showed no sustainable results.

During the next decade, only limited exploration occurred, and any prospects of Helgeland becoming northern Norway's new "oil capital" seemed unlikely indeed. But in 1998, in what would ultimately prove one of history's great "Eureka!" moments, Amoco discovered an oil-and-gas field, called "Skarv," off the coast of Nordland County, which consisted of three individual blocks, and represented a potentially fabulous opportunity to extend the activities on the Norwegian continental shelf. Further investigations, though, were limited to exploratory drillings until 2002, and suspended post plug-and-abandon (P&A) procedures. The reasons the project was abandoned at the time are not clear.

In the following years, after the BP–Amoco merger in 1998, BP as operator mapped and analyzed every aspect related to the Skarv field development in the plan for development and operations (PDO).[3] This extensive process resulted in the Norwegian Parliament's approval of the PDO in late 2007. In addition to the Skarv field, Statoil had earlier initiated operations in the "Norne" field in 1997. For the past 14 years, petroleum resources have been extracted and produced on a floating production, storage, and offloading vessel, or "FPSO," located 200 km off the coast of Helgeland.

But, disappointingly, Statoil's operations never made much of an impact on the surrounding communities. The reasons for this have long been debated, especially in recent years. The most popular explanation is that Statoil made little effort to establish its onshore activities locally in Alstahaug. Also, contract structures were such that no firm in the region had an even chance to deliver its products or services. Those contracts were simply too extensive and demanding, so suppliers were selected among larger firms further south. This resulted in flows of material, both to and from the Norne FPSO, being transported hundreds and even thousands of kilometers either by sea, road, or air transport. This is not to say that Statoil's approach was unreasonable – it simply followed the best practice for profitable operations – but it certainly shows that something has changed during the last decade. After all, transporting truckloads of waste from Alstahaug to Stavanger by road (1,200 km) has quite a bad ring to it.

High North perspective

According to its High North strategy, created in 2006, the Norwegian Government promised that its greatest attention would now shift to northern parts of Norway. Central in that strategy was its desire to both maintain and expand the offshore oil-and-gas activities.

When BP Norway initiated its development activities on the Skarv field, certain guidelines were established concerning its contributions to surrounding communities – the so-called "ripple effects." Some of those guidelines were included in government documents prior to the start-up, while others were more or less hidden in an implicit grey zone with a mutual understanding for local contribution. The notion of ripple effects is currently a rather hot topic in the national debate, with northern Norwegian regions now pretty much demanding to benefit from petroleum activities. These demands are closely connected to the fact that smaller regions have been decimated by emigration and descending populations, potentially leading to communities being more or less abandoned. This has certainly been the case in several municipalities on Helgeland – and other smaller regions in Norway too, for that matter – where young people move out of smaller communities in search of better prospects.

Signs of change

The previous accounts of economic history, both national and local, constitute the very nucleus of mayors and other spokespersons fighting for regional development, especially when related to oil-and-gas activities. Since the oil-and-gas exploration and production launched in early 1970, numerous Norwegian regions have risen from small "backyard" communities to becoming some of the nation's most prosperous ones.

This idea – this unfortunate idea – that "now it's *our* time to rise" serves as a propellant for Alstahaug's mayor, especially when thinking back to the economic downturn following the failed local initiatives of the 1980s.

Back at the city hall, our discussion continues. The mayor is known for his inclusive and social public behavior, and he often blends with the local population. "I hear in people's voices, and see in people's faces, that the population is marked by what may potentially happen. People are very optimistic," he insists, and continues: "There is no doubt that the oil-and-gas activities affect the people in our community. No other external factors can compete, really." As in many small communities, he says, Alstahaug has suffered from declining population: "Unfortunately, young people moving away from small communities like Alstahaug are a trend we have seen for years, and actually I participated in those statistics. Now, however, we see the contours of youngsters actually looking at the possibility to move back to their childhood homes."

In his first year as mayor, he has faced great challenges as a result of BP's entry, especially when it comes to arranging port facilities and acres destined for industrial purposes. "Everything has to be financed," he says, "and that's a tough and risky move when the investments are based on vague hints and intuition. If we don't get the activity needed to justify the investments we have made, we will end up with a mess."

At the time of our conversation, BP had already announced that Sandnessjøen was to be the supply base for its Skarv field development. For the municipality administration, however, this complicated their investment decision since the supply base could be positioned at three locations there. Two of them were controlled by private actors, while the third and seemingly most appropriate was on municipal land.

"Even though I fully understand that BP needs to take all possibilities into consideration, I dare to criticize their timing," the mayor says. The oil-and-gas industry requires massive onshore support facilities, especially during the field development. In the municipality's long-term business strategy, the mayor has emphasized that current investments must also serve possible future field developments as well. "In the future we may even make more use of the acreage we have made for the new industry's disposal," he says. "We have to look in that direction and not act based on worst-case scenarios." Besides the BP Skarv field, at the time when I first spoke with the mayor, extensive exploration activities were underway off the coast of Helgeland. This resulted in the Norwegian National Petroleum Directorate announcing two commercially exploitable field discoveries in these waters in 2009. In line with the onshore development, the Mayor also has great expectations for still more offshore drilling, saying, "In order to sustain onshore activities and thereby facilitate the development of a dynamic and compound supply infrastructure, we depend on continued offshore activities."

Emerging ripple effects

It's now been a year since my first meeting with the charismatic mayor. Today, he glows with excitement as he tells me about all the developments that have occurred since we last chatted. The biggest one was BP's choice of locality for its onshore supply base. When I first met the mayor his optimism seemed edged with skepticism. The municipality had made heavy investments in supply-base infrastructure such as areas for industry and office buildings, and also port facilities, but would BP notice and reward those overtures? Well, much to the administration's relief, it did. May 27, 2009, stands as a memorable day for Alstahaug. BP proved its commitment to develop Alstahaug as a strong supply base for the waters off the coast of Helgeland. So the mayor is clearly a very happy man, and points out that this milestone has already facilitated even more development, "We see a rapid escalation in industrial activities at the new supply-base area where contractors set up extensive infrastructure," he says proudly.

On my way to the city hall this second time I had passed the new supply base, and found it teeming with workers in bright yellow workwear. As the mayor now looks back at 2008 and 2009, he reflects on the role of the local government administration. "We see the importance of keeping a dialogue with our stakeholders as a crucial task," he says. "We have emphasized that our role as administration is to facilitate development."

That strikes me as a particularly significant remark, for his administration had been subject to major critiques by various actors in the region. Many have claimed that it has been way too passively expectant and modest in how it handled the time following BP's announcement of Sandnessjøen as its future supply-base location. Some have even accused the administration of "wasting yet another opportunity" to facilitate entry into the oil-and-gas industry.

Despite such critics, the municipal administration seems to have made well-founded decisions. "We have received positive feedback from BP in the proactive way we have acted towards arranging areas destined for industrial purposes," the mayor assures me. No matter what the municipal administration has or has not done, it seems likely that any municipality would struggle in the face of sudden demands after years of declining activities.

The mayor now sees Alstahaug as thriving. "When talking about signs of ripple effects, you don't have to go further than talking to the local cab driver to realize the rise in activity," he says. "In percentage, our local airport has shown the highest rise in passenger traffic among the Helgeland region's airports, and we get worrying reports that the hotel capacity is completely bust at times. Clearly we are experiencing a positive development."

Also, he's happy to report a boom in the housing market. Housing prices have increased dramatically, and the municipal department for planning and infrastructure has seen a rapid growth in building applications, too. "In recent years, several apartment projects have been initiated in order to meet the increased demand for housing," he says. "In relation to land disposal, we are privileged. Historically, the problem has not been to find disposable areas for housing development; rather, the problem has been to find people wanting to settle down and build themselves a home."

Here, the mayor's cell phone once again buzzes. "I apologize, I have to answer this one," he explains, and takes the call outside. After a minute or so, he returns wearing a big smile. He tells me that he's just been informed that an airline company had decided to set up a direct flight between Alstahaug and Oslo.

The worry with all this good news is that not all ripple effects will prove positive ones, since rapid growth almost invariably brings fresh challenges to a small community. For example, economists have calculated that roughly 400 new jobs will be generated by the Skarv development. But given that the ratio of family to employment is typically two to one, that means the population in Alstahaug is apt to mushroom by about 1,200. Still, the mayor expressed confidence that his municipality is more than capable of providing the infrastructure, such as schools and municipal services, necessary to meet such an influx.

He also feels optimistic about the chances for harmonious inter-municipal cooperation in Nordland County with respect to facilitating BP's needs. "We have established a regional committee aiming for unified efforts in preparing for the new industry," he says. "The idea is quite simply that the surrounding municipalities have to cooperate rather than fighting for victory. We all depend on each other, and together we make up a strong unit."

BP itself certainly understands that need. Through the years, it has witnessed fierce rivalry among municipalities in the Helgeland region. Driving that rivalry may be an inferiority complex – or perhaps paranoia. Rana, the region's largest municipality in both population and industrial complexity, was met with dark mutters when the oil-and-gas industry signaled its move into the region. Smaller municipalities closest to these activities worried about the high-handed role that Rana might take, fearing a "stay away; it's all mine" mentality. Though this was, and to some extent still is, most prominent among businesses in the region, municipal interaction in the political sphere could be said to be equally rivalrous.

When I asked the mayor why the political committee was established, he explained it this way: "On the one hand, if we are to gain ripple effects from this opportunity, the four regional centers – Rana, Alstahaug, Vefsn, and Brønnøy – need to act jointly. The majority of potential suppliers are situated in Rana and in Vefsn, while Alstahaug and Brønnøy primarily hold the infrastructure needed to serve these activities [supply base and heliport, respectively]. Second, unifying the political milieu in the region is crucial when approaching the county municipality. Also, a unified political culture signals political stability for those looking at the possibility to establish on Helgeland."

The establishment of a regional committee for facilitating oil-and-gas-related development turned out to be a most welcome initiative for the county, especially with respect to helping develop the supply-base infrastructure. Here, the mayor says, the county's role proved decisive: "Even though we had hoped for more extensive funding, the county has actively supported us. This made it less of a risk for us to go through with the investments needed."

As in the political sphere, recent years' development has led to a similar move in the regional trade and industry. Helgeland has long traditions in the steel, mining, and mechanical industries, such as engineering and shipbuilding/maintenance. But only a handful of businesses have any experience in operating oil-and-gas projects. BP went through extensive rounds of information meetings with regional industry in the early stages of the Skarv development, and its main message to regional industry was that each firm by itself was simply too small. To compete for supply contracts, firms needed to join forces and present themselves as one compound unit. One of the main challenges that the regional industry has met has been to successfully respond to the contract structures set up by oil companies. Earlier I mentioned that Alstahaug has had oil-and-gas activities in its "backyard" for decades, first and foremost being an oil-and-gas field (Norne) operated by Statoil. Since field operations were initiated in the late 1990s, Statoil has based its maintenance and modification (M&M) activities on just a handful of extensive contracts, and this effectively shut out regional industries because of their liabilities of smaller size and capacity.

But BP came to appreciate the inequity of that, the mayor tells me: "BP soon signaled that they would facilitate their maintenance and modification activities using a different approach to contract structure." The main difference was simply that instead of organizing the M&M activities using only a few major contractors, this time BP sought to include regional industry by offering smaller contracts. These signals soon resulted in the establishment of various cooperative networks in the region, both municipal and inter-municipal, basically fostering a new way of doing business.

Only the future knows

In the years since my conversations with the mayor in Alstahaug, the municipalities in the small northern Norwegian region of Helgeland have experienced a satisfying sense of recovery. Population has increased, and, most interestingly, many hometowners aged 20–40 (commonly termed "northern Norway's biggest export commodity") are returning after years in the bigger cities down south. Trade and industry are generally prospering, and regularly success stories of firms entering the oil-and-gas industry are presented in local media. One feels a new sense of pride in the citizenry.

Alstahaug's mayor, having weathered the storms, is now unabashedly upbeat. "Currently, extensive exploration activities are taking place in the Norwegian Sea, thus we focus even more on what the future may bring," he says. "We now feel that the Skarv project has settled, so the challenge ahead now rests on making use of our experience and skills adapted from the BP Skarv project." He moves to the very tip of his chair and adds, "Only the future knows whether we really succeeded or not."

Notes

1 Helgeland, a region in northern Norway, consists of eighteen municipalities with a total population of about 77,500. The region has four city centers: Mo i Rana, Mosjøen, Sandnessjøen, and Brønnøysund.
2 Bodø is the County Capital in Nordland County (pop. 49,203) and home to the Nordland County Council.
3 The Plan for Development and Operations (PDO), a document required by the Norwegian Government, deals with all aspects crucial to an oil-and-gas field development.

Epilogue
Characters solve the complication writing about culture

Madeline Maxwell, University of Texas at Austin

I love this book. The stories succeed both on their own and as a collection, providing me a better sense of the High North, a region I've visited multiple times, though each time only briefly. It is both a gorgeous part of the world and a shining example of using natural resources to benefit the local population. So it is well worth understanding better who lives there and how they are responding to the challenges posed by the petroleum industry.

In this epilogue, I plan to offer a critique that I hope will prove useful especially to both teachers of ethnography and their students, for this is a book likely to become a major text for them. To that end, I will pose, and attempt to answer, three questions:

(1) How well does the book succeed as an ethnography of the High North? My comments will address not just the content of the book itself but also some of the broader issues it raises about contemporary ethnography.
(2) What was the experience of the authors, especially the less experienced ones, in writing ethnographic stories? My comments here will draw on my interviews with most of the authors about their experiences in Norway and later in "writing up" their stories as chapters for the volume.
(3) What value does the book demonstrate about this particular method of teaching ethnography? This may be where I am most excited, because I see this book as showing the world an innovative, and extremely powerful, method of introducing students to ethnographic fieldwork.

Does the book succeed as an ethnography of the High North?

In their Introduction, the editors characterize the book this way: "The present book is a collection of twenty-one ethnographic, real-life stories that help illuminate the social, economic, and cultural climate of Norway's High North in the first decade of the twenty-first century. They primarily focus on the problems and opportunities that exist there stemming from the oil-and-gas boom, now in its fifth decade. Our aim is to cast a human light on this time of change by telling stories of individuals who personify what is taking place in the region."

I would say the book meets these goals and is an engaging read.

What I want to raise here are some questions about just how "ethnographic" the effort actually is. Even though the book isn't aimed at an academic audience, it does call itself "ethnographic" and thereby invites being evaluated as such. Is it a problem that the mix of stories makes no attempt to be comprehensive or representative? I don't think so. Ethnographies are traditionally about local and particular knowledge, adopting the novelist/poet's conviction that there is universal (if not generalizable) knowledge in the particular. This book adopts that very assumption, presenting us with a set of snapshots of the changes and challenges of the High North. That is ethnographic and, indeed, is consistent with the modern trend of using teams of ethnographers (Moritz, 2013).

What makes me hesitate is that professional ethnographers, like myself, are used to expecting other methods and activities on the part of the author. Typically, or perhaps I should say traditionally, an ethnography is more than a story from some-one someplace. Instead, the ethnographer participates and/or observes exten-sively. An ethnographer studying, say, farming would usually spend a whole year farming, not just interview a farmer and visit their farm. One of the things that is truly amazing about this book is that most of the authors didn't spend anywhere near that much time with their subject, yet they still came up with stories that ring true for Norwegians and communicate to other readers some of the character of the region's people. Because the goal of telling stories from a region was more modest than the ethnographic understanding of a region, it succeeds.

So what sort of ethnographic study *is* the book? Obviously, it's not the old-fashioned kind of describing, in depth and breadth, the people of a place or their practices and beliefs. Nor is the book theoretical. While a few chapters – notably Professor McGlone's – demonstrate a fine grounding in academic literature via their questions and interpretations, most of these authors lack his old hand's command of theory and research. And it's not really a team ethnography, either, since, although the authors knew each other and met a few times, they never really worked together and made no attempt to interpret together. The authors worked solo.[1] Moreover, the chapters aren't based on participant observation, because the authors – including the Norwegian-based authors – never took up positions in the field and attempted to immerse themselves over time or deeply. Nobody worked in the oil fields or took up farming, for example, and nobody lived in the field site. The Norway-based authors worked and lived at the univer-sity, not with the subjects of their stories, while the Texas-based authors spent at most just a few months in Norway. Traditionally, ethnographers try to live among and participate in as much of a culture as they can. Traditionally, too, a year or more of fieldwork precedes interpretation and writing. These authors might have conducted only a single interview or visit. They were visitors and interviewers, not really participants.

Maybe it is the editors here who are the real ethnographers, using the materi-als generated by the chapter authors. Clearly, the vision about knowledge in the High North belonged to the editors more than to the individual authors of the chapters. But the editors did not conduct fieldwork or even see most of the field sites, so that is not satisfactory.

What is the basis, then, for calling the book an ethnography of the High North? I admit to qualms about using the term here, although admittedly ethnographers have always experimented a great deal with the form of presentation – everything from encyclopedia-style descriptions to novels and poems (but mostly descriptions).

Ethnography has actually become an extraordinarily multifaceted enterprise, with varied goals and practices. A notable writer on ethnographic methods, John Van Maanen, observes, "Ethnography occupies a borderland between the social sciences and the humanities, thus the virtues and felicities of stylistic writing and the narrative conventions and experiments that carry ethnography to readers are of more than passing concern" (Van Maanen, 2011). Some styles let the "natives" speak for themselves with very little reformulation, while others use styles more typical of social science. Clearly, the chapters in this book are closer to the end of the spectrum where the people's voices are only minimally edited. These chapters read like anecdotes of the High North. I go back to the metaphor of snapshots. None of the chapters stands alone, in my mind, as an ethnography, but together they provide snapshots of the inhabitants of the Oil North and some of the challenges to life there as things change. Each snapshot was chosen for its well-formedness – it makes a story – and it piqued the author's imagination because it "caught." As the author was looking around for something to write about, something about that person or that place or that practice "caught" the author's imagination. Michael Agar called such moments "rich points" – moments where native and non-native speakers alike are apt to trip themselves up or notice something striking (Agar, 1994).

Yet while the stories are toward the unprocessed, use-the-people's-own-voices end of the spectrum opposite the abstracted theoretical end, we are not really reading the voices of the people. Since people don't always supply the well-formed story or the concise and colorful quotation, the authors of these chapters, in the interest of readability, did that for them. So these are not unfiltered stories. They are non-fiction writing based on the stories of the people. Many of the authors supplied – filled in – missing parts of the stories. That is, the logic of the story supplanted the logic of research discovery. In writing the chapters, some authors said, the needs of artful presentation meant that some interpretations, normally identified as such in a research report, were incorporated directly into the story. So it's hard to be sure what the people offered directly and what the authors invented or added. Am I saying they falsified the stories? No. I'm saying the logic of the writing here is narrative logic rather than the logic of research. One of its advantages is that it eliminates much of the awkwardness of the research report that appears when the researcher has to argue that the interpretation is sound even in the absence of a clear statement from the people, so it makes for a more effective story *as a story*. The danger is that it makes it hard, if not impossible, for us to evaluate the author's interpretations because we can't separate them from the story; they're embedded in it. The story thus seems more "true" and less "interpreted" – more transparent and less argued. Better stories do not necessarily make for better knowledge, but they make for better reading. Of course, we can reverse the emphasis, too: Better stories make for better reading, but they don't necessarily make for better knowledge.

From the point of view of ethnographic understanding – finding culture – another danger in proceeding this way is that it's easy to assume that what emerges from such a set of stories is dispositive about reasons for the way things are. Writing about culture, or assuming that writing is revealing of culture in some direct way, is dangerous. It's easy to over-interpret – for example, to believe that things are the way they are because of some historical or cultural determinative. The editors write in the introduction that Norwegian culture is revealed through the stories. Obviously, this is true in the sense that any experience or story makes culture available to the reader, but one can overstate that and end up reinforcing easy stereotypes. The introduction traces the success of Norway's "petroleum evolution" to Norway's lack of aristocracy, its status until the twentieth century as a territory of either Denmark or Sweden (and thus the domination of Norway by Swedish and Danish aristocracies), and the rural character of the sparsely populated High North, with its dependence on fishing and farming. The people worked hard to subsist in a harsh but beautiful environment. But how does this history explain why the Norwegians responded to their newfound oil wealth the way they did?

There are other possible reasons that are not considered if we take the history we know best as determinative. Norway is outstanding, even unique, for avoiding the destructive pattern of states that discover huge reserves of non-renewable natural resources (Ross, 2012). Maybe it has done so well because it never had an aristocracy. But is that choice or circumstance? Some analyses of a weak nobility in Norway attribute it to the soils being not rich enough to support large estates – or to the fact that the upper classes were almost completely wiped out by the Black Plague in the fourteenth century – or to the strength of the kings who wanted no rivals – or to the strength of the Danish and Swedish aristocracies who wanted to interfere in Norway. Or maybe the discovery of oil and natural gas so recently meant the country could learn from countless negative models around the world. But wait! The comparisons are to the U.S. a century ago or to modern nonindustrial states with weak institutions, countries that already had huge economic and social disparities.

Another view is offered by stories about Farouk al Kasim, who was a young executive who had grown up in Iraq and watched one of the bad examples, where the benefits of oil eluded the people of the country. As Lisa Margonelli wrote in the January 2014 issue of *Pacific Standard: The Science of Society*: "Norway's anti-resource curse is often attributed to exceptionalism: Viking genes or the like. But one secret of its success – maybe the secret – is not Norwegian at all, but a twinkly 77-year-old Iraqi-born oil geologist named Farouk al Kasim" (Margonelli, 2014). With a Norwegian wife and an education from Imperial College London, al Kasim and his wife wanted better care for a child with cerebral palsy, so they relocated from Iraq to Norway. In this tale, a year or so after the discovery of the Ekofisk oil field, al Kasim and a colleague wrote a white paper designing Norway's oil development structure to avoid the exploitation he had seen growing up in the Middle East: "Statoil [the state company] would develop local expertise and provide jobs for Norwegians. The Petroleum Directorate, then, would be a sort of referee, making sure that the oil projects served Norway's interests by minimizing environmental impacts while maximizing jobs and profits for Norway."

The point is not to argue for or against a historical rationale or the good luck of an enlightened executive but to caution us about easy explanations. In a full-scale, truly searching ethnography, the ethnographer is responsible not only for the stories that reinforce stereotypes or match a popular national narrative but for applying methods that challenge those stereotypes and assumptions. In a collection of stories, there is a danger that they will reinforce stereotypes and assumptions that will be allowed to stand in the absence of methods that test them. Fortunately, the editors were well aware of the danger of trying to create a linear representation of the whole of the High North, and so warned us. As their Introduction says, "telling another twenty-one stories could have easily showcased different people and professions," and "Our stories are a collection of individual representations; they are scattered rather than unitary."

The stories behind the authors' stories

For this section, I interviewed most of the Texas-based authors and had copies of interviews that Jan-Oddvar conducted with the Norway-based authors. We asked the authors about their experiences in finding and writing their stories, as well as their previous experiences traveling in general and conducting fieldwork in particular. They came from two academic institutions in two locations, Norway and Texas, and from several countries of origin. Some of the interesting findings from these interviews focused on the challenge of writing something very different and the delight of the experiences the Texas-based authors had in Norway.

Remarkably, most of the Texas-based authors had not previously traveled outside the U.S. and were in Norway but a short time. A few from both countries had traveled extensively, but most had not. The air of this travel was more summer vacation than the rigors of serious fieldwork. The Qualitative Camp was on a gorgeous island, and the visit to Norway was in the summer. Thus, the harsh cold of the far northern climate was something they heard about but did not experience. Their time in Norway was astonishingly beautiful – and a respite from the summer heat of Texas, too. Their lodging was arranged by the university in Bodø, and students from the Norwegian school helped them find their way around, shop, and so forth. Most of the Texas-based authors had minimal experience with Norwegian-style outdoor recreation – few hikers, no birdwatchers, no boaters – and the opportunity to walk around gazing at the scenery was for them part-and-parcel of "Norway." The local hosts arranged things, found people to interview, and suggested issues and places. Yes, there were friendly, curious, open people for them to talk to (in English, no less), but it's also true that they were spared tackling anything that posed difficult access. Given their limited time and untested fieldwork skills (for most of the authors) on the one hand, and the lack of previous literature about the area on the other, there were new stories everywhere.

I don't mean to diminish the accomplishments of the authors but merely to point out the air of excitement and delight and ease that infused their experiences. This was a wonderful experience both intellectually and recreationally.

A second remarkable fact concerned the academic backgrounds, in either Business or Communication, of almost all the authors, whether based in Norway or the U.S. Most of their academic training had been in quantitative social science or business analysis. Few had much education in literature, the humanities, or qualitative research methods before the week-long Qualitative Camp in Norway. As such, they didn't consider themselves story writers – or, indeed, any kind of "real" writers. The methods of research and writing they brought with them, for the most part, involved abstract research. In most of the academy these days, there is a strong preference for abstract theory – distilling even qualitative research into abstractions and theories that lead to predictions about what people will do. Not surprisingly, some of the early approaches to this book included attempts to distill such theoretical abstractions from the slices of the research they'd conducted. But, as they found, the fieldwork of a month or two, an interview or six, and nothing that could really be called immersion or participant observation could probably not support many big abstract theoretical insights.

The decision to use the story framework, then, was a brilliant work-around. The authors were encouraged to look for a story instead of looking for themes and theories. Ah, *this* they could do. Writing a story was a new sort of challenge, yes, but the framework the editors provided gave them an approach to the task that told them, above all, to be *interesting*. The challenge to be interesting (instead of deep, or brilliant, or seminal, or any of the other qualities graduate students usually use to evaluate their research) was apparently very freeing for many of the authors. The editors gave them Jon Franklin's *Writing for Story* (1986), and, as expressed in their own Introduction here, "Following Franklin's strategy, we challenged our writers to draw the reader into a compelling story instead of showing off their expertise on the subject with a slew of scholarly references." Franklin's template focuses on finding an interesting character with an interesting problem. As presented to the authors, Franklin's scheme has three parts: (1) identify a significant problem or difficulty the protagonist is facing, (2) explain why that problem is momentous, and (3) convey why the reader would be interested in it. This character-in-action formula is written into these ethnographies of the High North of Norway to give a sense of the environment and the time in which these stories take place."

In my interviews with the authors it was clear that most did not really follow this exacting template once they identified their story. Where it seems to have been most influential was in their search for a story. It gave them an idea of what they were looking for and seems to have helped them recognize the opportunity that caught their imagination. Most of the authors focused on finding an interesting character. They chose people who were important or just personally interesting. One author chose someone because "The character is one of the most influential persons developing business cooperation between Norwegian and Russian companies." Another said, "I was having a drink [in a bar] and telling this guy sitting next to me what I was doing and he started talking about himself and I realized he could be my character." Yet another identified with someone: "I realized this woman was unique and that her story would have to be interesting. Plus, her [ethnic] background was the same as me." A few of the Norway-based authors realized that they already were acquainted with appropriate "characters" for their stories. As one said, "My choice of topic came from my character. At first I went through a long process of identifying an interesting character for my story; however, he appeared closer than I thought. Actually, he was a colleague. We had met many times, and he always amazed me with unique stories and experiences .... Mostly these [stories] were told over a beer at a local pub and there was always some new story to be told."

Most of the authors, once they picked a character, sat down and talked with them many times, looking for a story angle. Some recorded the interviews, and others went home and wrote drafts from memory. Others identified a problem first and then looked for a character for their chapter. For example, Ashley Barrett and Hin Hoarau-Heemstra identified their topic (the difficulties for tourism in the High North) and interviewed three people who were very informative, but they decided they still needed drama – the drama that only a focus character might provide. Thus, Hin explained, "[we chose the character that] was the most dramatic, turbulent and lively. He has strong character and was perfect for framing the paradox of the co-existence of tourism and petroleum. He seemed to personalize duality between pulling and pushing."

Ethnographers are always looking for the great informant, the telling quotation, or the revealing event, so in many ways this is the normal search for a vehicle to convey meaning to a reader. But it does have the potential for distortion. The fieldworker usually tries to follow a strategy of looking and listening until it seems that nothing new is left to discover. The ethnographer might even avoid spending much time on someone who seems too unusual or too much of an oddball. If dramatic value is prioritized over descriptive insight, there may be a tendency to focus on the most unusual or colorful person instead of more typical people. That is, indeed, one of the reasons the stories in this volume are so good as stories. The authors went for the dramatic, so the reader is the beneficiary of that drama. As an ethnography, though, the drama may not be as informative about culture as more mundane folks.

The authors I interviewed talked about their fear of failure – but it was a fear of not finding a story or of not writing an interesting story, instead of a fear of not being smart enough to produce credible research. It was an uplifting challenge that they wanted to live up to rather than one arousing a fear of not measuring up to their graduate-school standards. Almost everyone talked about the difficulty of supplanting their customary social-scientific format with the narrative format requested, but most had high praise for Franklin's book and its step-by-step formula. A few complained, though, that once they had a narrative drafted, they had to abandon what one called "the narrow strictures of the Franklin framework" and invent a different narrative. As the authors got into their work, many stories diverged from the model. In reading the chapters, sometimes I can see the Franklin framework as an obvious organizer and sometimes not. Whether the chapter looks like a "Franklin narrative" does not seem to have much to do with how the author thought about his or her narrative. That is, some who talked about conscientiously following Franklin produced narratives that don't look to me like they follow the template, while some who claimed that they abandoned the template seem to me to have produced narratives that exemplify it. In the end, of course, one does not value the product by whether it follows Franklin. The Franklin template was a tool for authors to learn to do something very new for most of them, and it worked. Franklin proved a good heuristic, but the success of the final stories doesn't necessarily reflect Franklin's influence.

All writing is rewriting, of course, and that is something that everyone talked about. Even though they felt that they were using a template, they recognized that they did not really know their stories until they'd finished them. Several people contrasted the stories they were writing with the kind of writing they were used to – namely, social-scientific research writing, characterized as a record of what they had done and found, with some small argumentation about what it means. The search for a dramatic character-in-action led them to keep discovering the "actual" story they were writing, with a reader's response in mind. Their stories developed in the rewriting process as they strove to be more effective in their presentation. Several people said they felt that the process would make them better writers in the future. That improvement would come because, as one author said, "[I see now] how deeper the writing and thinking can be and should be." Another said, "[W]riting this story has to some extent broadened my view towards my own research .... I have realized the importance of personality and how this reflects on how we do our job." Several authors thought the drama and vitality they had learned to appreciate in the process of producing their stories would help them make all their writing more effective. Others said the effect would extend to their interpretation of data. As one author said, "In a way, even more traditional formats need a good story. I learned a lot about developing the plot and the characters and this is very useful for interpreting my data and writing about my findings." None of the authors expected to keep publishing in the narrative format, though, as none thought the journals they esteemed would publish what most called "pure" narratives. Some expressed relief that they had "lived through" the process and did not expect to attempt a narrative again. Yet all thought the learning process would serve them well in their expected careers.

The book as pedagogy

A very exciting element of the book is found in its value for pedagogy. The editors' goal was to produce what they call "knowledge of the High North." It did that, yes, but the book also has value as a demonstration of effective teaching. Let me talk a little bit about that angle.

I have taught ethnography for thirty years, and this book made me think a lot about what has worked and what has been difficult for students (and for me). Unlike some other research approaches, there is an open-endedness to ethnography. Students usually want to know, What recipe should we follow? How many people should we interview? How many hours do we need to spend in the field? What theory should we use? What methods of analysis should we use? The vague, but honest, answer is always something like, "It depends; you have to let your data drive the structure of the final product." That can make them feel as if they're taking an unacceptable risk. What, they wonder, if they spend all that time doing fieldwork and taking notes and they don't come up with anything? That would be worse than a failed experiment – not least because ethnographers usually spend so much time in the field – and could even be the death knell for an academic career. You can give examples and talk about traps to avoid and rules of thumb to follow, but the exercises you can have students perform never seem to provide them with much useful experience for doing the real work of ethnography. They often look to the materials they have collected – their inter-view transcripts and observation notes – like so many items to be tossed up and sorted, as if that would produce insights in some mechanical way. A bad attempt at ethnography can seem devoid of thought, even while it offers copious material.

There are textbooks about ethnographies, of course – books on taking field notes, books on conducting interviews, books on various permutations and styles of ethnography. There are arguments between scholars about the values of various practices in ethnography. Many of these have been helpful for students, but most of my students are like most of the authors in this volume. They have more (or only) experience with social science, with surveys, and with experiments. They have learned to do their own research by extending some previous researcher's study to a new context or new method. They have learned that their job is to do a study to test some aspect of a theory, so they start their papers with the history of that idea in the journals. That is, they quote all the people who have previously worked on that theory and tell the reader what they will do differently. They find topics by looking into the published literature. They probably came to graduate school because they had a question about how things work in the world, but their education tells them to look at the literature instead of the real world. One thing I love about the injunction the editors gave these authors is the direction to the real world: "Go find someone interesting dealing with some problem and write a story about it." It strikes me as a method for getting students to test whether the literature is dealing with the problems they think are important; that is, it might be a way to get students to look for important problems to study.

Social-science writing is largely a matter of reporting what happened in the study – the previous research, the research question, the techniques of getting the data and analyzing it and testing the findings against the hypotheses. The thinking mostly takes place in the design of the project, and the writing describes it. Ethnographic writing is different. Yes, you have read the literature and picked a likely topic and site and so forth, but the ethnographer does not try to narrow and control the project as much as try to find order in the chaos of what happens. Too much control will make it likely that the ethnographer misses the most important stuff; not enough will leave the ethnographer drowning in too much information. I have long struggled with how to get a student to plunge into the writing, because the writing is the thinking and analysis, and it prompts ideas and insights. You can't just assemble an ethnography; you have to produce it through some kind of transformative writing. Well, just reading what I have written probably frustrates you readers. I will stop trying to describe the frustration of getting people to deal with their materials and try to explain why these stories strike me as a useful teaching method. As I have said, although ethnographers need to have some ideas before they start, and they should have read about the people or issues they will study, they ultimately need to let their experiences lead them to the interesting, important stuff. It may turn out to be very different from what they imagined beforehand.

Here's where the search for a story offers an intriguing approach. That search gave these authors a sense of purpose almost right away. Instead of worrying about what shape the final product would take (as it grew organically from the materials they collected), they knew their goal was simply to produce an interesting story involving the High North. They didn't have to worry about representing or investigating "the High North" because it was okay just to be there and find the story there. They were not trying to produce a linear or comprehensive report that they could not be sure they would find. In a way, and even though they were nervous, most of the authors thought, "Anybody can do *that*." They didn't have to evaluate themselves as ethnographers or create an analysis; they just had to find a story. The presupposition was that the story was out there to be found – not invented or discovered through painstaking analysis, but *found*. So that is the first wonderful thing about these chapters. The budding ethnographers were relieved of grandly analyzing culture and experience to get it right and simply dispatched to find a compelling story. As their comments to me made clear, actually writing it well was not easy, but that difficulty was discovered organically as they tried to create drama for the reader. Instead of asking if an idea was important enough or theoretical enough to write, they asked if it was dramatic and interesting enough. *Important* and *theoretical* are academic terms in this context, requiring expertise; *dramatic* and *interesting* are everyday terms that anyone can judge. I am not saying that it is easy to write non-fiction, and neither were the authors. What they described, though, was a challenge that felt far less daunting and did not challenge their egos as graduate students in their fields. That seems quite useful as a task.

Second, most of the authors seemed to realize, as they followed the Franklin recipe, that they needed to write early and often. Instead of collecting forever and then sitting down at the end to try to organize and write, they wrote drafts as soon as they could. Thus the process accomplished the goal of getting them to write by writing, to think by writing, and to keep judging and rewriting their work. It made them aware of the writing process in a way many had perhaps never experienced. Writing these stories also offers another benefit, and that is that the author can judge the success of the writing. It's normally hard for ethnographers to develop judgment about how clear, how insightful, how organized, and so forth their writing is. They look to teachers and editors to provide that feedback. The authors of these chapters also depended on feedback, of course, from various editors, but they also had a template in their own heads already of what made an interesting story and could use that, plus the Franklin template, to help guide their rewriting. The template is simple, if not easy, and therefore accessible to self-evaluation in a way that professional writing may not be.

The third wonderful thing about these chapters is that they did not have to be developed together as a collaborative process but yet they still inform each other in the aggregate. As with a book of short stories about the same characters or in the same town, these chapters feel more like parts of a whole than discrete forays. Yet the authors had to write on their own. This seems to me like the best of both worlds. Real teams of collaborating ethnographers learning the process may suffer from varied levels of skill and commitment and run the risk of groupthink. Independent ethnographers working in the same geographic or organizational world – like the High North or the university, or the music scene, or some other locus – grow by association while they need to work independently. I have led classes of independent ethnographer students working in the local music scene or deaf community and other contexts and found that the students' works gain stature and heft by association with the others. I have never been satisfied, though, when we tried to collaborate in a single product. I think the editors made a wise choice to avoid collaboration.[2] Once they had the stories, the editors identified themes to organize them, but these were developed after the fact. In a way, the editors came along as meta-ethnographers to take the set of stories and arrange it into an ethnography of the High North. The chapter authors did not have to take on that responsibility.

These three values – the search for a story embodied in a character-in-action, the ongoing writing and rewriting as a thinking tool, and the independence but association of authors working in the same scene – are great learning tools. What are we trying to teach ethnographers? We are trying to teach them to see rich points – those paradoxes that lead to a sorting out of how things work and how people do things. We are trying to teach them to analyze deeply instead of just describing, and we are trying to get them to analyze from near and far. One of the precepts for ethnographic understanding is viewing cultures and practices both from a distance and from the intimacy of participation. A common metaphor is for the ethnographer to stand simultaneously in the stream and on the bank, for such a dual perspective leads to insights.

In the proposal for this volume, the editors cited Malinowski's classic Trobriand Island studies as the lead example. Malinowski left England in 1914 to spend four years in New Guinea as the classic outsider who immerses himself in a strange culture. The editors wrote: "Rather than being limited by his lack of cultural familiarity, strangeness for Malinowski was seen as an asset in that taken-for-granted presumptions were reduced and even the smallest functions were novel material for interpretation. That stance – the outsider may have something unusual to say – has been prominent since Malinowski completed his analyses (Clifford, 1988)." The editors used this history of ethnography to give credence to the Texas-based authors in Norway. The Texas authors, however, did not live with the Norwegians for four years, so I will come back to that in a moment. One of the key purposes of Clifford's 1988 book was to explain the problems with the stream metaphor I used just above, the idea that an ethnographer can combine the insider's empathetic position in experiences and gestures with the outsider-scientist's objective point of view, which aims to situate them more broadly or in contrast to other events or groups. Clifford (and others) have exposed problems with the paradox. Perhaps it is not so much a paradox as an impossibility.

Yet there are other dialectic hermeneutics that do not send scholars into fits of resistance. Clifford shows us that we cannot even come close to a fair job if we do not recognize the power of language to shape the personal experience of both those being studied and those reading about them. We need to deal with the language of experience, participation, interpretation and reading; deal, too, with the multiplicity of voices in the collaboration of doing, studying, and reading across languages and cultures.

Do the story chapters take this dialectic into account? I am not sure they do. The creation of a story, a character-in-action dealing with a problem, requires an author's voice. In ethnographies the issue has always been largely one of authority – how could a researcher speak for a culture or even another person without falling into a distortion? Just as Western powers colonized parts of the world and distorted their history and practices as seen through the political, historical, social, and religious lenses of the viewer, so the U.S. government once made treaties with Native American Indians like Southwestern Apaches as if they were nation states, when in fact they were bands with changing leadership. The U.S. government and the people who supported it couldn't understand how differently the Apache people organized themselves, and lacking an awareness of the potential differences didn't even try to understand them. A narrative is a cultural product. European and American narratives are more similar to each other than to Japanese or Kenyan tales, so there is no reason to think the shape of the narratives is a problem for the collaboration of the people who contributed to the project.

Yet a narrative imposes a structure that does not exist in nature. In what ways does the imposition of the dramatic narrative structure, with its character, its problem, and its resolution, distort the experience the story recounts? The authors in this collection picked characters because they were colorful, dramatic, or important instead of trying to present the experiences of the many. Since that strategy is what makes the book so interesting to read, it is hard to reject it, but it does present us with something to think about. When bird experts choose illustrations for a birding guide, they pick the pictures that best display the identifying characteristics of the birds, especially those that help us distinguish one bird from a similar bird. But when we then take their book into the field to help us identify birds, many of them will not match the ideal picture in the book. We will not be sure of our identification because the cardinal in our backyard is more pink or rose-colored than the red bird in the book. In the same way, stories – especially dramatic ones – can create a heightened reality that is more interesting to read but potentially distorting.

So I am saying two things at once. I am saying the story challenge seems to me like an excellent and powerful teaching technique. It teaches a useful process, and the products produced have great value, especially as part of an organized collection. It is the collected nature of the set that makes the book so powerful for enhancing our knowledge of the High North.

Splendid as it is, though, it's not sufficient for teaching new ethnographers. I myself still have to figure out how to train students to be their own devil's advocates (as I have tried to be here), using the well-established usual methods of the ethnographer to challenge stereotypes and assumptions, such as the idea that the egalitarian Norwegians are culturally prepared to avoid elite exploitation of their oil-and-gas riches when in fact their good luck may be owing to some wise choices by a few leaders who could avoid exploitative structures because as a small European state they had strong institutions. That is the weakness of using this method alone for an ethnography. But the second thing I'm saying is that I have never seen a better method of getting students of ethnography to confront the challenge of finding meaning in the events and words of people they encounter. I'll definitely be using the technique of sending students to find a story and recognizing (shaping) that story by looking at it through Franklin's eyes. The results here are inspiring.

Notes

1 Three of our ethnographers used second authors on their chapters.
2 Three of our ethnographers used second authors on their chapters.

References

Agar, M. H. (1994). *Language shock: understanding the culture of conversation.* New York: William Morrow & Co.

Clifford, J. (1988). *The predicament of culture.* Cambridge, MA: Harvard University Press.

Franklin, J. (1986). *Writing for story: craft secrets of dramatic nonfiction by a two-time Pulitzer prize winner.* New York: Atheneum.

Margonelli, L. (2014). How Farouk al Kasim saved Norway from its oil. *Pacific Standard: the science of society.* Available from: http://www.psmag.com/navigation/nature-and-technology/iraqi-vikings-farouk-al-kasim-norway-oil-72715/

Moritz, M. (2013). Teaching ethnographic research through a collaborative project. *Anthropology News, 54,* 11–12.

Ross, M. L. (2012). *The oil curse: how petroleum wealth shapes the development of nations.* Princeton, NJ: Princeton University Press.

Van Maanen, J. (2011). Ethnography as work: some rules of engagement. *Journal of Management Studies, 48,* 218–234. p. 224.

Index

For Product Safety Concerns and Information please contact our
EU representative GPSR@taylorandfrancis.com Taylor & Francis
Verlag GmbH, Kaufingerstraße 24, 80331 München, Germany